OUT IN THE OPEN
People talking about being gay or bisexual

Stephanie Norris and
Emma Read

A Pan Original
Pan Books London and Sydney

First published 1985 by Pan Books Ltd,
Cavaye Place, London SW10 9PG
9 8 7 6 5 4 3 2 1
© Stephanie Norris and Emma Read 1985
ISBN 0 330 280919
Photoset by Parker Typesetting Service, Leicester
Printed and bound in Great Britain by
Cox & Wyman Ltd, Reading

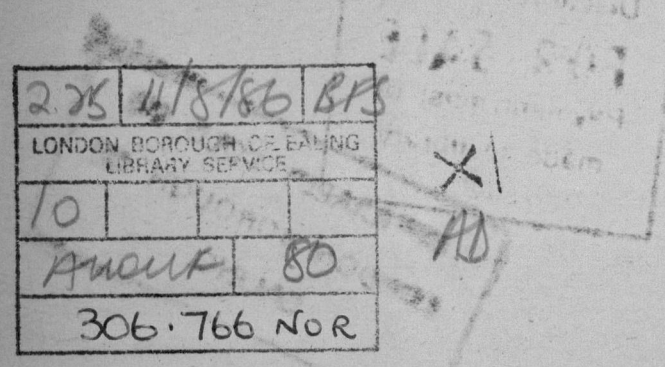

To all the gay and bisexual
women and men who talked to us.

Contents

Acknowledgements

We would like to express our thanks and appreciation to all those who, in addition to giving us an interview, voluntarily assisted in the research for this book. In particular, we would like to thank Vicki, Jenny and Jeanette, all of whom helped us along the way; Ted, for his generous help and advice; Mike, for consistently making himself available and providing many valuable insights; and last, but certainly not least, Heather, our fast, efficient and supportive transcriber.

The legal position for gays today

In Britain gay men and women, especially men, are not equal with heterosexuals before the law. In brief, gay men cannot lawfully have sex with each other before the age of 21 (compared with 16 for heterosexuals); soliciting or importuning of one gay man by another – in practice, any sexual interest shown in public, from an invitation to come back home to a goodbye kiss – is a criminal offence; homosexual activity between men and women is prohibited in the armed forces and, for men, also in the merchant navy; there is no legal protection for gay men and women against discrimination on the grounds of sexual orientation in such areas as employment and housing; and homosexual relationships and households are not recognized in law as equal with heterosexual relationships and households in the area of custody rights and rights arising from the death of a partner.

Australia is divided into two territories and six states, each of which has its own laws on age of consent in regard to homosexuality. In A.C.T. and New South Wales it is legal at 18, in South Australia 17, in Victoria 16, but in Queensland, Western Australia, Northern Territory and Tasmania, it is illegal.

In **Canada**, as in the UK, the age of consent for homosexual activity is 21, but prosecutions for acts between men over 18 are rare.

In **South Africa** homosexuality is illegal, but in practice prosecutions are restricted to men over 19 who commit homosexual acts in public.

Preface

Emma Read

The material for this book derives from the gay and bisexual people from all over the UK with whom I have worked for the past ten years.

As well as my extensive counselling work, I founded and helped to manage Gayway, the first dating service in this country for gay and bisexual men and women. But Gayway was more than a dating service; it was a much-needed means simply for gay people to meet one another. Unless they are living or working in specifically gay or gay-oriented environments, gay people do not enjoy the same day-to-day interaction with each other as do heterosexuals; in the mid-seventies, when there were far fewer social outlets for gays, this was even more so.

Thus gay men and women joined Gayway to enlarge their circle of gay friends, to get to know one another away from what some of them saw as the pressurized atmosphere of gay pubs and clubs, and to break out of their isolation, whether personal, social or geographical. But one of the most important functions that Gayway fulfilled was to help gay people of both sexes, all ages and diverse backgrounds, to come to terms with their homosexuality, and the personal letter that Gayway required all its members to write was an important part of that process. These letters, in which Gayway members (many for the first time) articulated their thoughts and feelings about all aspects of being gay, provided a revealing and fascinating insight into the lives of gay people at a particularly active and expansive time in gay history; and my friend Stephanie Norris, a journalist then working in television, suggested writing a book drawing on the organization's unique and extensive files. I had always felt strongly that while it had been my privilege to come into such close contact with so many gays and bisexuals, many thousands of others could benefit from the wealth of material I had accumulated over the years.

In 1982 I parted from Gayway to concentrate full time on psychotherapy; Stephanie will take up the story, but for my part I would particularly like to say a very big thank you to all of my clients, past and present, who have been so forthcoming and supportive, and last, but not least, to Stephanie, who believed in this book and gave up so much of her professional and working life, in order to bridge the gap between gays, bisexuals and heterosexuals.

Emma Read,
London, August 1984.

Stephanie Norris

After many weeks of research and discussion, Emma and I drew up a list of interviewees whose experiences we thought particularly representative of gay and bisexual people in general, such as being young and gay, or married and gay, or not coming to terms with their sexuality until relatively late in life. Then in June 1982 I left my job in television and worked on the project for the next couple of years, sustained in no small part by Emma's moral support, for which I am very grateful.

The result is this book in which gay men and women, from those with largely heterosexual backgrounds to those with exclusively homosexual backgrounds and all the ones in between, speak for themselves about what it means to them to be gay in all areas of their lives. We have changed their names and personal details in order to protect their identity.

We make no attempt to explain or analyze homosexuality, believing it more useful to present gay men and woman as they are, in the hope that gay readers will be reassured and uplifted by this pooling of gay experience, and that heterosexual readers will gain a greater understanding of their gay sons and daughters, sisters and brothers, friends, neighbours and colleagues, and come to realize (if they do not already) that they have far more in common with them as human beings than not.

And if the end result is a greater tolerance and acceptance by society of gay people, and perhaps even, who knows, a more equal treatment of them before the law, then this book will have been well worth the toil that has gone into it on the part of all those involved.

Stephanie Norris,
London, August 1984.

1 The young gay

♂ 'I've got no hang-ups about being gay; it's nothing new, it's been going on for thousands of years and I see myself as a totally normal person. If I go off and have sex with guys, It's a natural thing – it's not evil, it's not dirty, it's not disgusting. I feel being gay is quite a fantastic thing, because you're free to live your life as you want to.'

♀ 'I think it's important to be confident about being a lesbian and not feel it's something to be ashamed of; I don't think you should ever think twice about mentioning it to people. You should expect people to accept it, because it's your right to be like that. It's your right to love women and to live with a woman.'

Young gay people today are much less prepared than the older generation of gays to hide their sexuality, much less disposed to look upon it as a problem. While they may still suffer discrimination at work, abuse or ridicule at school and rejection by their families, there is a growing tendency among them to regard prejudice against gays in all its forms as the problem of those who exhibit it rather than those at whom it is directed.

♀ 'I'm still Trish – gay, straight, pink, polka dot, black, white, indifferent – who gives a shit? People say, "You're not gay, you can't possibly be" – so what? What does it matter? I am me and I'm very happy the way I am, and as I see it if you can't handle that, that's your problem.'

♀ 'The lesbians I know don't see any problems about being gay; I think they would prefer it, the same as I would, if there was more acceptance, if it wasn't treated as something peculiar or interesting, but as an everyday thing. But I don't know anybody who is not glad to be gay, who wishes they were straight.'

And while the liberalism that has percolated down from the sexual reforms of the late sixties may be thought to have benefited young gays in particular, they want more – the same rights and freedoms as heterosexuals, acceptance, not just tolerance.

♀ 'On the whole people think, oh well, it's a bit odd, but it's OK so long as they stay away from me. They're not prepared to question their beliefs and their ideas, they're not prepared in any way to make life easier for the gay person. However OK they are about it to your face, they go away and think it's a bit strange.'

♂ 'I think society's attitude to gays is pretty rotten . . . It's improving, but you think, why the hell can't I talk as freely as I like, why can't I go along the street holding my boyfriend's hand – the sort of things that straight people take for granted? Things like that piss me off.'

The most glaring and unjust inequality of all is embodied in the law on the age of consent, whereby the sexuality of young male gays is not recognised until five years after that of young male heterosexuals. While young female gays are not subject to this law – more an act of omission than benevolence – they face the problem of getting their homosexuality taken seriously in a society which, until very recently, was generally dismissive of the whole idea of assertive female sexuality.

Fourteen years ago, the particular problems of young gays inspired Mrs Rose Robertson, 67 and a former social worker, to set up Parents Enquiry, an organization that mainly counsels young gays between the ages of 14 and 17 and their parents.

'It started accidentally; my whole involvement with the gay movement started by accident. What happened was that my husband and I let the top half of our house to two young men, one about 18, the other about 23. they were a couple, an affair, which broke up after a few months – the older one left and the younger one stayed on. And it was because of him really that I became involved, because there was this young man, very talented, very nice, looking just like everybody else, and yet in law he didn't exist. Now that seemed to me to be an obscenity almost, that you could have people like him walking around, both boys and girls who in law weren't recognized, who could be discriminated against, who really only lived when they went to some gay club or pub, where they could then be completely natural.'

Not surprisingly, Rose does not mince her words where the law is concerned. 'The danger in having this arbitrary age of consent law is that even in a very valid, good and loving relationship between somebody who is, say, 16 or 17 and somebody who is over 21, the older person may be charged with corruption – in extreme cases, may go to prison – and the younger one put under the care and control of the local council, on the grounds that he's in moral danger. No account is taken of what either of them say, even if the younger one tells the police or whoever is dealing with the case that they are a couple, they are in love and that it wasn't corruption, he went willingly. That is, to a large extent, discounted totally in cases that come to court.'

Life for the gay teenager, then, is not easy; not only is his sexuality denied by the law, but also his access to information still tends to be of the most random and inadequate kind and he is unlikely to turn to an adult, especially a parent, for fear of rejection.

The gay teenager

The gay child is likely to experience from a very early age a feeling of being different or alienated from other boys and girls, and may already be aware of the special attraction the same sex holds for him or her. As Rose Robertson points out, 'What comes through consistently with young gay people, both girls and boys, who come to see me, is that they have felt from a very early age – from about 5 or 6 – uneasy when they were with their peer group, without knowing why; some of them will say, "I always knew I was gay." And in many cases they are quite unable to come to terms with the fact that their fantasies during masturbation, their wet dreams, are not of girls or boys, whichever it may be, but of their own sex.'

Later, when the gay girl or boy reaches puberty, her or his sexual experiments with the same sex mean much more than just the physical act.

♀ 'My father used to get *Playboy* and *Penthouse*, and I remember cutting out these pictures of lovely women and pasting them on my wall of favourite things . . . I shared a room with my stepsister and when we were about 12 or 13, we often sort of explored each other's bodies; I remember our lying on top of each other, not quite sure what we were doing, but knowing that it felt really good.'

♂ 'When I was 12, I schemed to get this boy into the shed down the end of his garden. He was a bit worried about his mother finding him, so we locked the door from inside and barricaded it up with boxes and I started making advances to him. At that age you couldn't really come, so we just sort of played around with each other's penis and sat on each other, just cuddling. I felt as if I'd discovered something special.'

But feelings such as these are all too often dismissed as merely a phase the child is going through, the so-called 'homosexual phase', a misleading and misused phrase because it makes no distinction between the gay child and the heterosexual child. Rose Robertson elaborates on this.

'What people really mean by that is a mechanical exploration of sex by two people of the same sex, without any emotional over-tones. It's a purely physical reaction to stimulation by each other, and that's got nothing whatsoever to do with true homosexuality, which is a gradually developing awareness in young people that their deepest feelings, their feelings of love and of wanting to be close to another person, are centred round their own sex.'

The gay boy or girl invariably receives little or no help in coming to terms with these feelings, all the more powerful for being experienced for the first time. In Britain homosexuality does not feature in the school curriculum, and least of all where it might be thought to belong, in sex education classes. Rose Robertson is characteristically forthright on the subject.

'Sex education isn't education at all, it's a lesson in procreation which bears no relation to the way boys and girls feel about the things their bodies are doing. There's an enormous lack of any real education in schools about being a human being – it just does not exist. Homosexuality should be incorporated into one whole sub-ject on sexuality and the human being, sexuality and human emotions, sexuality and the art of living.'

In the absence of any ready source of information and uncertain of whom to turn to for reassurance, many young gays, particularly in small or isolated communities, become introverted.

⚣ 'I spent a lot of time alone, wondering why I didn't have girlfriends. I used to go walking through Whitby harbour and admire the fishermen – big, burly guys – and think, that's what I like – why don't I like women? Why hasn't it turned out the way people said it would? My dad wanted me to grow up like him – any question of being different was unacceptable. So inevitably I withdrew and read a lot; it was a very lonely period and for the first time in my life, I started feeling depressed.'

With only heterosexual models to emulate and sensitive to playground or classroom talk of 'poofs' or 'lezzies', it is not surprising that many young gays yield to peer-group pressure – particularly acute in the teens – and appear to conform.

⚢ 'I always had lots of boyfriends, but it was just the right thing to do . . . I never really felt love for them; they were friends. That's what I wanted, and it was their problem that they had to be jumping in and out of bed. It was so boring; I used to think, "If this is all there is to it, what's going on?" So I was never really happy.'

But the gay teenager who, despite the odds, has already begun to express and explore his sexuality soon finds that there are problems associated with that too.

Spencer is 16 and in the fifth year at school. He has CSEs in biology, economics, computer studies and music and wants to be an actor. He lives with his brother and sister, mother and father on a suburban housing estate. Since he was 8, Spencer has had a close relationship with another boy, Adam; they used to see each other every day until Spencer's family moved about a year ago. 'When we moved, I felt I'd lost the only person that I knew was like me and I wouldn't find anyone else.'

Spencer has known for several years that he wasn't like other boys, but he was 14 before he made the connection between himself and the word 'gay'. 'I heard other people saying the word and talking about what it meant. And I just said to myself, "Well that's me – I'm like that." ' But Spencer keeps the information to himself; at his all-boys' school, the word 'poof' is used snidely and indiscriminately. 'They call everyone "poof" – I just say back to them, "*You* must be", or something like that. There's this one boy I know, who sort of says, "He-ll-o, *Spencer*," and I just do it back to him. I go along with what they say, so they don't suspect – because if they did, I wouldn't go back to school.'

As it is, there are areas of school life that Spencer finds a strain; for example, he avoids sports altogether. 'I go in late on Monday morning and miss PE, and then on Friday I just go somewhere till the games lesson is over. I just hate it; I don't like going in the changing rooms – seeing the other boys in the shower just embarrasses me.'

Spencer is very conscious of a need to keep up a pretence. 'I go along with my friends to fairs or discos. Some of them get off with girls – it looks a bit funny if they do and you don't, so I just dance with a girl. Then it isn't suspicious.' He has even tried sex with a girl. 'Everyone at school was saying how good it was, so I just decided to find out. It was all right, but girls just don't turn me on; I just like to be friends with them.'

At home by himself, he spends a lot of time in his room, playing the records of his favourite pop star, Boy George, and even dressing up like him. 'Ever since he came on to the pop scene, he just sort of appealed to me, with his make-up and the weird way he dresses, so I just decided to dress up like him. I use bed sheets and pyjamas for the clothes, and the make-up is my mum and sister's.' In an effort to attract his mother's attention, he recently presented himself to her thus attired. 'I said, "I'm a bit funny," and she said, "No, don't be stupid, you're not." I said, "I am – look, I've got make-up on." She said, "No, you're not." She doesn't want to think that I'm gay, so she just forgets it, she doesn't take it seriously. That's the only time I've sort of tried to tell her.'

Spencer has no intention of telling his father, who is a builder. 'When I'm in the car with him, he says things like, "Look at that girl's big arse", and I just have a quick look. If I see a boy, I sort of look out of the corner of my eye so that Dad doesn't see me.'

Spencer's isolation within his family is increased by the fact that his older sister opens all his letters. 'I open hers, to get my own back, but she just takes no notice. She does it all the time, poking her nose into my business; it makes me angry.'

The only person Spencer has told he is gay is a girlfriend his own age. 'I was up her house and she was looking for a dictionary and I really felt like telling somebody, so I turned to the page where it said "gay"; I said, "Look on that page and see if you can find a word, and that's what I am." She didn't react as I thought she would – I thought she'd say, "Get out of here, don't come back", but she just came and sat next to me and said, "Don't worry about it; there are other people in the world like you, you're not the only one." I'm glad I told her.'

There are times when Spencer feels very lonely. 'I lock myself in my room – I just say I'm going up for a lie-down. I just lie on the bed, crying, and I drop off. Then I wake up and go downstairs.' He says he is getting sick of waiting for the 'right boy' to come along; at night he dreams of him. 'He's a bit older, about 18 or 19, blond, with blue eyes. I think to myself that he might take me home with him . . . I'd just be so really happy if I met someone who cares for me and me for them. And I'd just like the relationship to go on and not end.'

Family

Rose Robertson gets most of her referrals from family GPs, social workers, agony aunts and organizations like the Mothers' Union. In spite of the greater availability of information about homosexuality today, she estimates from the number of letters and phone calls that Parents Enquiry gets every day that many gays are still spending two or three years in complete isolation, unable to talk to anyone about being gay. The problem is compounded by the fact that they are almost invariably growing up in a heterosexual invironment, where their heterosexuality is taken for granted. As Rose puts it, 'The last thing parents think of is that any child of theirs could be gay. They know homosexuality exists, but it's in some other family, in some other street, in some other city – certainly not in theirs. This is particularly true in small communities – say a mining village – where the macho image is so strong that the thought that any of their sons or anybody they know could possibly be homosexual is just not on.'

In Rose Robertson's experience, the reaction of most parents when confronted with the knowledge that a child of theirs is gay is still largely one of shock, horror and guilt.

'The attitude generally is, "What have we done? Where did we go wrong? Is it likely that he or she will grow out of it if we don't allow them to meet anybody else who's gay? Will they be cured?" – "Cured" is not the word they use, but that is really what they mean.'

Christine is now 25 and living with another woman, a situation her large South London family has reluctantly come to accept, though not without difficulty. She remembers vividly the day some years ago when her father, a lorry driver, found out that she was gay.

Christine has always been attracted to women. 'Even when I was less than 10 years old, I admired and felt closer to women.' Throughout her teens Christine followed a pattern of deep and close friendships with girls, and occasional sexual relationships with boys. Then at 18, Christine developed a crush on a straight girlfriend. 'I was very close to her; it was the first time I had ever converted my feelings for women into sexual terms. I thought about having sex with her, literally. I wanted to tell her, but didn't.' Instead, Christine decided to confide in her older brother. 'I had always told him everything; we had always shared secrets. We used to write to one another a lot, so one day I wrote and said, "I have something to tell you: I'm 'queer'." I got a letter back from him immediately, saying, "If you don't write back and tell me this is a sick joke, I'll send your letter to Dad." I wrote back, saying "Fuck off", so he sent my letter to my dad.'

Christine recalls the day it arrived. 'The rest of the family, my other brother and two sisters, knew that I was gay, although that was a word I had never used to describe myself. I had never made a point of telling them, but I had always talked about my girlfriends – only not to my dad. He got home from work, opened my brother's letter and passed it on to my other brother, who didn't say anything. Dad then asked me if I wanted to be cured. He was very upset. I was upset that he felt like that, and that my brother had been so stupid as to tell him that way. I'd have told Dad anyway.'

Christine's dad now 'sort of accepts' the situation. 'He has to,' says Christine simply. 'Even though I don't live at home any more, I always take my girlfriends back home to meet the family.'

In Rose Robertson's experience, telling parents is still the biggest ordeal that young gays have to face; the situation will only change when the attitude of parents to homosexuality in the family changes. 'If a dozen parents in this country would stand up and say, "Yes, I have a gay son/daughter; yes I'm proud of him/her; yes I'll fight for him/her", then you would have a change of attitude. In America, we're affiliated to Parents and Friends of Gays, who march in Gay Pride Week with banners saying they're proud of their gay children. And that's something we desperately need here.'

Becoming aware

What holds many young gays back from coming to terms with their homosexuality sooner is the lack of any positive public model with which to identify; all too often the images presented of gay men and women are crude and negative stereotypes, to which young gays have as much difficulty relating as they do the heterosexual models constantly upheld to them.

♂ 'I was aware of homosexuality, because I read papers like the *News of the World* and that sort of crap. But that's why I never realized that I was gay, 'cos I never associated myself with those sort of weird people – perverts and all that. I never dreamed that I was one of *them* – heavens above – it just didn't click.'

♀ 'I had always imagined that lesbians were what I had heard at school – big, fat, ugly dykes – and I certainly did not feel like one of them. I had never thought about what the word really meant, because it was a put-down. But when I did discover that gay people weren't just certain types, but all sorts of people, it became different.'

Not only is it invariably incumbent upon young gays to find this out for themselves, it may also fall to them to disabuse their heterosexual friends and colleagues of the illusion that gay men and women are the caricatures so often depicted.

Tom is 25 and still speaks with his native West Yorkshire accent. He is unemployed, but spent a year in the Army where he was out to his fellow soldiers, before he was discharged for homosexuality.

Tom recalls being attracted to men from well under the age of 10. 'I used to look at men and I was fascinated by the male side of my family. Cousin Jack was a miner, who'd lost some of his fingers; I had a bearded uncle whose knee I loved to sit on; and my dad had a motorbike and would always wear leather pants and jackets.'

In his early teens Tom indulged in 'the usual messing about' with other boys, and also had girlfriends: 'Because everyone else did, I took it as part of what senior school was all about. I never really got anywhere though.' At the time it didn't bother Tom; he thought he'd 'grow into it'.

But by the time he'd left school, Tom had become increasingly aware that he was not sexually attracted to girls. 'I spent a lot of time in my room, wondering what it was about me. I thought, I don't enjoy going out with my mates any more, because they've got girlfriends and I haven't.' Eventually Tom became 'very depressed' and turned to his elder sister, to whom he was very close. 'We went down the pub and after a few drinks, I said, "There's something different about me" – I was crying by now – "I don't like girls, I like men." She said, "Look love, what's wrong with that? There's nothing terrible about it; it's how you are." She was very understanding; she said, "Take it in your stride; don't feel that you're a freak, because you're not. Don't worry about it." '

To Tom it was the best thing that could have happened. But he was still very upset: 'Not because I was homosexual, but because I couldn't identify with anyone. I almost thought I was the only person in the world who felt like that.'

Not long afterwards, Tom left home and went to live in a bedsit; it was there, at the age of 18, that he had his first sexual experience with another man. 'I remember feeling drained but wonderfully exhilarated, and thinking that if that was what it was all about, that was *exactly* what I wanted.' But Tom had also fallen in love. 'I found it difficult to cope with my feelings; I couldn't handle the emotional problems, knowing I wanted to be with him day and night, but knowing that although he liked me, he didn't feel the same way. So I thought I'd go in the Army, to get away.'

Tom duly joined up as a vehicle specialist. 'I hadn't intended to tell anyone that I was gay, but I was sharing a dorm with ten other guys and it didn't take them long to cotton on to the fact that I wasn't quite like them. I remember this young guy coming up to me and saying, "You're queer, aren't you?" I said, "If you mean am I homosexual, then yes." And that was it; from then on they accepted me, which was very surprising.'

But then Tom was out to prove he was as good as they were. 'Of course they were a bit wary of me in the beginning, but I became close friends with three of them and it was fine. There were the odd remarks like "Put a zip on your arse tonight", and "Don't go in that corner over there or he'll have you", but I was able to protect myself verbally. And when they realized that I could run as fast as they could, shoot as well, and go over the assault course and help the fatties, it seemed to make it all right. I'd proved myself in a masculine sense: I wasn't a queen who was going to prance around.'

Although Tom had gained the respect of his fellow soldiers, they didn't let down their guard completely. 'Often we'd go down the NAAFI for a drink and I'd try to tell them what being a homosexual was. I was received cautiously, but not with animosity. Admittedly, I refused to be bullied and if I did get snide remarks, I'd give as good as I got – and therefore I was as good as they were. I opened a lot of people's eyes; the guys all wondered if I really was gay, because I was just like them, and not like the camp guys – they got shit, because they couldn't stand up to us.'

Tom had his own eyes opened when he started going up to London regularly at weekends. He bought the now defunct *Gay News*, and contacted the gay organization, Icebreakers; soon he was going to gay discos and parties. 'It was a whole new world to me. Going back to the Army after that was really difficult. I knew I *had* to get out. I went and told the padre I was homosexual, and he told the other officers; they couldn't believe it. But I was given sick leave for homosexuality.'

It took two months for Tom's discharge to come through; when it did, he bought a flat with another gay man and they have been living together ever since. But Tom's experience in the Army has stood him in good stead. 'We share the flat with two other gay guys. The whole street must know we're gay; we say, "Good morning" and all that to our neighbours and they don't seem to be hostile.'

Carol is 23, a computer operator who has come to terms with her homosexuality only in the last year. As a teenager, Carol didn't want to go out with boys; instead, she had 'special friendships' with other girls. She recalls one in particular: 'It lasted a very long time and I'm still friends with her. I wanted very much to be close to her; I wanted to sidle up to her and cuddle her. At the time I thought it was only happening to me; I felt a little bit sorry for everybody else, talking about boys, because I had something that they were missing out on.'

But it never occurred to Carol that she was gay. 'I didn't really know what lesbians were; I probably thought they were older women and they were completely different from me. But I used to get worried, because you know what school kids are like – if you got too near to someone, they'd jump a mile across the classroom – "Oh lesbian, les, go away." I would think perhaps I shouldn't feel the way I do.'

Carol reassured herself with the thought that her feelings 'wouldn't last for ever' and eventually she'd 'just melt into everybody else's way of life'; as she puts it, 'Nobody ever gave me any alternatives.' So she thought she was simply on course when she left school and started going out with a young man she'd got to know. 'He was just like a brother to me, but closer; I could discuss things with him which I can't with my brother. It was never all that sexual – he was never dragging me off by the hair to bed.'

But then Carol fell in love with a girl at work. 'I'd never actually fallen in love before and it was just a really exciting feeling, I couldn't get it out of my head.' Carol and her colleague became lovers. 'The whole thing was such a relief, to be with a woman, to be able to express myself and feel completely good about it.'

But another, older, colleague of Carol's had found out what had happened. 'She's 60; I hadn't actually spoken to her about my situation, but she knew I'd broken up with my boyfriend and she'd obviously picked up from somebody else that it was because I was a lesbian. And one day while I was talking to one of the managers in the office about my work, she decided to say, "I don't think it's fair that we should be expected to work side by side with these gay people." She said that they had a hormone imbalance and that really it was very unfortunate, but that they should keep that side of their life completely separate. I said I couldn't believe she thought like that; perhaps she didn't come across gay people, but by speaking out like that, she could be treading on people's toes.'

The incident drove Carol to seek support; as a first step, she bought *Spare Rib*. 'I read one or two things about lesbians and I decided to send off for a *Spare Rib* diary; in the back it has places to join and I phoned Lesbian Line to ask if there was anywhere I could go along to. The girl I spoke to suggested a consciousness-raising group, because I wanted to meet other women who would help me.' Carol duly went along to the group. 'There was only one other lesbian woman there; the others were all feminists, but they were all independent, they weren't married and they were completely different from anyone I'd ever known. I was able to talk to them really unselfconsciously about everything and they understood; it made me feel good – I could carry on and do what *I* wanted; I didn't need to do things that were against the way I felt just to please everyone else and fit in.'

Carol made friends with some of the women in the group and went with them to a gay club for the first time. 'I was very apprehensive; I thought, gosh, what if there's anybody there who tries to accost me – I won't know how to deal with it.' But Carol was 'pleasantly surprised': 'It was like an ordinary disco without the men. I was in no way self-conscious and it was just so nice to see all these women dancing together. There were one or two women that were wearing suits and ties and dancing with girls who were obviously very feminine, but on the whole they were just women like myself – just ordinary.'

But Carol now also thinks of herself as gay. 'I'm always aware of being a lesbian, in every situation I come across. I just notice how very much it's a straight world, how all the radio and TV programmes, the advertising, etc. are geared to men and women couples, and I suppose I get a bit uptight about it; I don't think it's fair that one section of society has a complete run of the whole world and everyone else is just expected to fit in.'

First gay love

One of the things that worries Rose Robertson is that when she asks young gays, 'Who are you? How do you see your life?' she is nearly always met with a blank stare. 'They simply don't know.

'Heterosexual kids can go to discos, for instance, from probably the age of about 10. And even at that age they're very much aware that they may or may not be attractive to boys or girls; subconsciously, they're absorbing knowledge of the sort of people that they like and don't like, the sort of relationships that they may like to have later on in life. But the homosexual child doesn't have that at all. He has no models about which he can say, "Well, these two seem to have a fairly good life, and that is the sort of relationship I would like to have." '

And yet, despite the lack of guidance, despite the difficulty in meeting each other and so forming an idea of who they are attracted to and how they might relate to their own sex, the ways in which young gays conduct their relationships, their ideals and expectations of love, are not so fundamentally different from those of young heterosexuals.

Mark is a member of the Gay Youth Movement and describes himself as 'basically quite a sort of slow conservative little person that plods along'. When he was 21 he had his first serious relationship with another man he met at the gay youth camp which he recalls in the following terms: 'There must be about fifty or sixty people, basically men, from different youth groups; it's all under canvas and it's an absolute riot. You get to know people from all over the country.'

One of the people Mark got to know was Eddie, from Newcastle. 'He's not my type at all really; he's a bit punkish, completely different to me, but we got on very well.' After the camp, Mark and Eddie wrote to each other and took it in turns to visit each other at weekends. 'We had quite a good relationship; in one sense it didn't feel very different from a heterosexual love affair really – the niceties of it all – "I love you", and all this. It was very nice.'

But Mark never made what he calls 'a full commitment' to Eddie. 'I was never 100 per cent sure if I loved him or not, and I tend to be quite traditional in that sort of thing; if I'm going to say something like that, I have to really mean it. I'm not the sort of person to go into a relationship quickly. Eddie pushed me into it more than I really wanted to go. And so we ran aground really this year, because I was used to a free sort of life and I didn't want to be tied down.'

But by then Eddie had moved down to London. 'I told him, "If you're coming down to London, it's not because I'm here, it's for your own reasons." I made that very clear to him. So for a couple of months we didn't see much of each other at all really.' Recently, however, Mark and Eddie have begun to see each other again. 'We've steadied our relationship into a good friendship now; we don't have a sexual relationship any more, we're just emotionally very close to each other. I find that very satisfying and I think he does too.'

Patti is 26 and has been living with Judy for over a year. 'Without Judy I think I'd just die. It sounds really sloppy and mushy, but that's how it is. She's my best friend, we're lovers and we have a great life.'

Before she met Judy, Patti, who is a rock-and-roll singer, was 'in a bad way': 'I was going through boyfriend after boyfriend, drinking too much, taking too many drugs – because I was so unhappy. I was writing things but they weren't making sense, maybe because I didn't know what I was really feeling; I'd just sit there and think that something was missing. And then when I met Judy, I realized I was holding everything back – it was like a release tap.'

Patti remembers the night they met. 'We didn't like each other at first, because we were both arrogant and very strong. Then I realized I must like her, because I gave her my phone number five times – she's still got the pieces of paper. But I was the one that did the chasing, because I didn't want to lose her. I just felt that this was it, this was right for me. I phoned her up and we started going out and it was great.'

With Judy, Patti felt able to be herself. 'She taught me how to let go and just be me. When we go to bed; it's wonderful. Before, I'd just go through the motions and now there's no acting; it's warm and it's honest, and I think, oh wonderful, this is great, I'm just so free.'

Patti and Judy are 'very much in love and very secure': 'We go out and party and I'm sure we could both run off with a million people. But what a waste of time that one fling would be – look what I'd have blown by doing that. Before I'd have blown anything, because I didn't care, but I could never find another relationship like the one I've got with Judy; I'd be an idiot to do it and so would she. We don't even discuss it, we just laugh about it sometimes. She loves it when people find me attractive and I'm flattered when people find her attractive – as long as they don't get too clever.'

As far as Patti and Judy are concerned, they are as good as married; they even wear 'wedding' rings. 'At Christmas we were laughing and rolling about on the floor, and I said to Judy, "Will you marry me?" And she said, "Yeah." So I said, "OK, I think we should get some rings." And we went out and got these rings. I'm more married to Judy than I'll ever be to anyone.'

Profiles

Martin ♂

'If I'd had some positive information and guidance at an earlier age, I wouldn't have gone through that bloody awful autumn; if ever I was going to have a nervous breakdown, it was then – I was really on the edge of going over. And those wasted years from 16 onwards, when I was just doing nothing . . . I'd have come out a lot earlier had I known where to go: had I had Gay Switchboard's number when I was 17, I'd have phoned them then. It's totally your own work, your own motivation; I've had to go through all this aggro to find my niche in society. And that's annoying; it makes me quite bitter, in fact, to think about it.'

Martin is a well-built, ruddy-cheeked young man, brought up in the country, who speaks slowly and carefully. He has just turned 22 and has been out for three years. The realization that he was gay was for him, as for so many others, a 'gradual process': 'It's not as though you wake up one day and say "I'm gay", and that's it; it wasn't like that at all. It was as if it was there all the time and it was just a process of becoming aware about yourself.'

From about 10 or 11, Martin was physically attracted to his own sex. 'I used to fantasize about people I knew, boys in my class, that sort of thing . . . The changing room was always good fun; nothing ever happened, but it was enjoyable – all the men walking around with nothing on. That was quite a turn-on.' But at the same time Martin had quite a lot to do with girls. 'I had one particular girlfriend and I got on with her very well – nothing sexual, we were just great friends. But when I went to comprehensive school, the friendship broke down, because to have a friendship with a girl then would have been taken as a sexual sort of thing.'

Throughout secondary school, Martin was firm friends with another boy. 'But it wasn't anything sexual; we just played in the playground together and sat next to each other in class. I didn't have the chance to experiment with other lads at all; that was quite a disappointment really.' By the time he left school at 16, Martin was aware of a growing attraction to men. 'Obviously my sexual feelings were getting stronger and stronger, and I noticed men more – I looked at people at work and thought, they're nice – that sort of thing.'

Martin responded by throwing himself into his work and, at 18, went to college. One year later and still without sexual experience of any kind, he decided he had to do something. 'I realized I couldn't just carry on pretending and doing nothing; I was entitled to a sex life like everybody else. And I was reading the *Sun*, believe it or not, and it had a letter from a bloke who was gay; he had a girlfriend, but he just wasn't getting anywhere, and they gave him Gay Switchboard's number. I made a note of it, thought – yeah, I'll give them a ring.'

But it took Martin some time to summon up the courage to do so. 'It wasn't easy. I'd ring the number and then I'd put the phone down, and if it was engaged, I'd think, oh good. Then suddenly it rang; it was answered quickly and I just sort of froze for a second. Then I just talked, business-like, very sort of matter of fact: I referred to the letter I'd read in the *Sun* and said, "I think I'm in a similar sort of situation." It was just a way of saying, "I think I'm gay." ' To Martin, the voice at the other end was the best voice he'd ever heard. 'It was so relaxed and reassuring . . . He was very understanding . . . asked me what I fantasized about and that sort of thing. He gave me a few numbers of organizations that could be helpful, and said, "In these places, you'll get to know people." '

The call put Martin on an 'emotional high': 'I really felt good about it; I felt I'd done something constructive.' But he waited until he'd settled into a new job and lodgings before he contacted a teenage group whose name he'd been given. 'I wanted to meet somebody my own age, because you read things in the *News of the World* about older men and everything . . . So I gave them a ring and they sounded like ordinary sort of people; I felt quite reassured about that.'

Nevertheless Martin was 'extremely nervous' when he went along for the first time. 'I was absolutely petrified; I just didn't know what to expect. I felt it was the biggest thing I'd ever done. I walked in and there were two rooms; the first room had a pool table and music playing, like a youth club. I suppose there must have been about ten or fifteen punky-looking people in there, just playing pool and chatting. They just looked up as I came in and looked away again. I wasn't sort of mobbed or anything.' The second room was quieter, with people sitting down. 'I introduced myself, they introduced themselves. And really I was just sort of standing there and taking things in, just looking at people and thinking, he looks ordinary. I suppose I stayed there for about an hour or so; I didn't really want to go, but I felt that was enough.'

Martin got into the habit of going to the teenage group twice a week. 'I made the effort to get to know some of them and I started slowly to build up some friends.' And so he began to get out and about; one night he went to a gay pub with a drag act. 'I found that really exciting; I'd never seen that before and I couldn't quite believe it. I felt very good after that.' Then he went to his first gay disco. 'I went with this guy and I fancied him a lot; I don't think he was really interested in me. But I was gradually learning how to go about trying to pick someone up, observing, listening. It wasn't something that instantly clicked, it had to be learnt; it still has to be learnt.'

But Martin had still not had sex with a man. 'I thought, how the hell do I go about it? It was such a mystery to me. One minute you read in the *News of the World* they're always doing it and there's me thinking, well where? It was quite frustrating.'

In general, Martin felt under increasing pressure. 'I was still 19; this had all been packed into a few months. In some ways I was feeling very bad: living away from home, in a strange place anyway, coming out, pressure at work – all these things were building up. I really felt as if I was going off my rocker at times; I'd never been under such stress.' Martin's mother sensed something was up. 'I didn't see her that often, but we spoke on the phone. I was giving out vibes not that something was wrong, but different, and she picked these up. She came up one day and I wasn't myself; I think I was trying to tell her, but she didn't push me at all.'

Then Martin got picked up one night in a gay club by a man about the same age as himself. 'I was nervous about the whole idea; I was torn – one half of me was saying, no, no, you can't do this, and the other half was saying, yes, go ahead and enjoy yourself. Anyway I said yes and we went back to his place.'

It was Martin's first experience of gay sex. 'There was a lot of heavy petting and kissing, and that I really enjoyed; I felt really close. But I was also very green; it sounds a joke now, but I wasn't really that sure what was going to happen. So obviously he had to lead. We got into bed and when he fucked me, I just wondered what was going on. I wasn't prepared for it really; it hurt quite a bit. Then I fucked him; I enjoyed that. And when I left next morning, I felt good – I'd had sex and I felt like I'd come of age.'

The fact that technically he was still under age didn't bother Martin at all. 'I knew it was illegal, but I just thought, what the fuck, it's my life, I can do what I like. I just didn't consider the law, because I thought it was so unjust; it was just daft.'

About a month later Martin had his second sexual experience, with a man he met at his group. 'We didn't have penetration, it was just caressing, gentle sex. It was very nice.' In the morning Martin went off to work; at the time he was working in a building gang. 'I turned up and someone said, "What the hell were *you* doing last night?" I thought, my God! How do you know! I said "What do you mean?" He said, "Well look at that on your neck." I hadn't realized, but I had a whacking great love bite. I thought, oh my God, how am I going to explain *this* away?'

All of a sudden Martin found himself having to account for the love bite to five intensely curious heterosexual workmates. 'They came and looked at it and said, "Cor – you must have had some fun and games last night – how did you get it?" And I just said I'd met a girl, simple as that. I just didn't have the bottle in that situation to say I'd picked up a man; it just wasn't conceivable at that time. So I had to make this story up; it sounded very dodgy, I'm sure, but there was no evidence to prove otherwise, so they had to buy it. I hated doing it, I really did, but it was that or sink really.'

This wasn't the only bit of bother to arise from Martin's second sexual encounter. 'I'd contracted NSU, which was a bit annoying; it was my first dose of something and I thought, oh my God. So it was a trip down to the old clap clinic, a rather nerve-wracking experience.' It was the first time Martin had been to such a clinic. 'It was a male doctor; I told him what the problem was and then I just said, "I am gay" – simple as that. And he just took a test from my backside and said it was nothing to worry about, I was to take some pills and come back in a couple of weeks' time. I felt quite good, because I'd said I was gay. Every time you say that out loud positively, it gives you a bit of a kick.'

But Martin had still to come out to his family, in particular his mother, who was divorced from his father. The opportunity arose at Christmas, when he spent Boxing Day with her. 'I had a couple of drinks, which helped to loosen me up. It was very emotional for me; I felt this was it, I was going to tell me mum. And she did too, it was obvious. We talked for several hours without actually mentioning the fact that I was gay, going round and round, getting nearer and nearer; she didn't want to guess wrong, you see. And in the end she said, "So what, it doesn't matter if you're gay – I still love you." She was very supportive; it was really nice. I really appreciated having a parent like that.'

Martin felt as if a great weight had been taken off him: 'It was a super feeling; that was one whacking great hurdle over. She said she'd realized a few weeks before, because she'd discussed it with my brother; they'd gone through everything – like drugs, being arrested – and being gay was the only thing that could be left. And things I'd said matched in with it.'

Martin then told his brother that his mother had something to tell him. 'By the time I saw him again, he knew. I think he was a bit shocked, a bit perplexed; he wasn't quite as close, he didn't quite know how to tackle me. But he came to terms with it. He still thinks it's a bit odd, he's got a bit of a loony brother, but now we have a fabulous relationship, we really get on very well.'

The one member of his family Martin has not told is his father. 'I didn't *have* to tell Dad, because I've always been closer to me mum and brother – that's the difference. He must realize I'm gay, because of the kind of life I lead, but we still get on OK. There's no barrier between us or anything like that.'

Martin began to enjoy life. 'I'd really got on my feet; I was going out a lot; I had a lot of close and good friends, whom I still have today.' It was therefore with some reluctance that he went back to college for a year, to finish his course. 'When I first went to college, I hadn't come out, I was very much pro-work and study. But I'd since found out what made me tick, so the idea of being stuck in a straight society pissed me off quite a lot. But I think the fact I was aware of who I was, in some ways gave me the strength to carry on.'

At the end of the year, Martin got another job and then started looking for somewhere to live. 'The first thing I did was ring Gay Switchboard, because I knew they had a good accommodation service, and I wasn't prepared to live with a straight family again. That was a decision that was very strong. I wanted my freedom, I wanted to be myself; when I came in from work, I didn't want to have to pretend.' Martin accordingly took lodgings with another gay man. 'It's completely different. You can come home and you don't have to be careful about what you say; we can have a good scream, a good camp-up, it's super. You can be yourself entirely, live how you want to live and that means a lot.'

As far as relationships are concerned, Martin 'falls in and out of love all the time': 'I have very intense feelings for other men; I think, oh yes, this is Mr Right. But I don't know if I'm looking for a Mr Right to be with for the rest of my life . . . It's a nice little fantasy to have, but when it comes down to it, you don't really want to know, because life is fun regardless. I think really I'm looking for a good emotional relationship with someone, with sex.'

Louise ♀

'The first time I saw Gail, it just hit me like a bolt of lightning; suddenly from that moment I felt absolutely convinced that I was in the wrong role as a wife, even as a girlfriend and I've never questioned it since. I was gay from the moment I fell in love with her and I'm so sure about it and I'm so glad.'

Louise is 23, an office worker with fashionably short spiky hair, who describes herself as 'the girl-next-door type, who just happens to go for women rather than men.'

Throughout her teens, Louise recalls never feeling at ease with men. 'So I didn't go down the disco, I didn't have boyfriends that I went to the pictures with; I read a lot and wrote diaries and I had special girlfriends I used to go on walks with and that was much more important. I suppose I also had a feeling that I wanted to keep my friends to myself; the more time I spent with them, the less time they'd have for boys too. A few times I imagined what it would be like to go to bed with them, but that wasn't really on my mind: I was content with very close friendships.'

Then Louise met Nick; she was 18 and had just started work as a bank clerk. 'I met him at a railway station. I'd lost my ticket and was in floods of tears and he was really kind; he came over and said he would buy me a ticket. He had very kind eyes, very big cow's eyes and I felt unafraid of him; he didn't come on to me in a threatening way.'

Louise arranged to meet Nick to pay him back; then he invited her out and so they began seeing each other regularly. 'He was a cuddly person, a warm person, and I never felt, oh if I sit close to him, he'll think it's going to lead to something. That never seemed to be on his mind. I got the feeling that I was being nice to him, that he couldn't talk to anybody else and it was nice for him to be able to talk to me.'

At the same time Louise found herself attracted to a girl at work. 'I don't think she ever really thought about relationships with women; she just liked to have a good time. She was a very strong person with a fierce temper; I suppose I admired her in a way. I used to go and stay with her; we'd sleep together and it would be nice to be near her.' But it still didn't dawn on Louise that she was gay. 'I thought I might be, but I never thought it would be possible to live my life as a gay person, as part of a gay couple. I thought in order to get along and keep on good terms with my family I would just have to do what everybody else did.'

And so, without too much thought, Louise married Nick. 'Quite a large part of it was me wanting to pay him back for being a nice friend and sort of protecting me from marauding males; quite a lot of it was that I didn't want to hurt his feelings because he obviously wanted to marry me. I suppose I thought that since I would have to be married anyway, it would be nice to be married to somebody who could just be like a friend and not a husband that I would have to perform with.'

The feeling of unreality stayed with Louise for eighteen months. 'We lived in a small bedsitter; it was a fun place to be. All the time we were there I could still play at being carefree and uncommitted and irresponsible. I suppose I thought I had the best of both worlds: I had a good friend who was never going to leave me because we had this commitment of a marriage, but he wasn't going to be forcing me into things which I didn't really like.'

Louise and Nick had sex, but not often. 'Sometimes I got edgy and towards the end definitely more and more aware that sex upset me; I felt used; it intruded upon me when Nick wanted to have sex, because it wasn't nice for me. He accepted that I didn't really like it; I think he knew anyway about me. He knew that I liked to look at women on the telly and things like that and he sort of joked about it. If a man came on the telly, he'd say, "Oh, I suppose you're going to make the tea now – I'll tell you when the dancing girls come on."'

Then Louise went to work for the local council; the very first day in her new job, she fell 'head over heels' in love with a girl called Gail who worked in the same office. 'She was very strong and seemed very positive; she was in jeans and black boots and she had dark hair and a very strong face. And I just lurched – my stomach turned over, I just really fancied her. I hadn't felt like that before about anybody.'

The two young women began going for lunch together. 'I'd just use any opportunity to be with her; I'd wait after work perhaps to talk to her for a while. Then she said she would like to go out for a drink with me. So we went and she told me about herself. And it came out that she had fallen in love with me.'

Louise and Gail did not start a sexual relationship straightaway. 'We would just hold hands and hug each other when we said goodbye – and kiss, more than just a normal kiss.' But Louise realized she could not carry on with Nick. 'What with not being able to express my feelings for Gail, and getting more and more disgruntled with the prospect of moving into this house Nick and I had decided to buy, which signified I'd have to be a real wife, it all just fell apart. I decided to leave Nick and spoke to him about being in love with Gail, and he was really very understanding; I thought it was all too good to be true.'

And so it was. Nick told his parents what had happened; the

first Louise knew of it was when he brought them round to confront her parents. 'Nick's mother came storming in and said, "There are a few home truths I want to tell you about your daughter; there are one or two things you ought to know. Your daughter is a lesbian, she is one of the lowest people in society; she has used and abused my son, just to cover up how she really is. She's deceiving everybody, she's caused untold heartbreak and how do you feel about that, eh?" She said to my dad, "You're the father of a freak; you must be some kind of freak too, it must be something to do with you that she's turned out like this. Look at her – how do you feel about being a father to *that*?"

Nick and his parents eventually left, leaving Louise alone with her parents. 'I was really bewildered; all I could think about was my parents' reaction. My mum was absolutely furious and my dad stood up and banged his head against the wall and said, "You're my daughter and I love you, but I won't accept that you're one of those people. Do you know what they're like, have you got any idea what they're like – they are vile." I said, "Well I don't understand, because that's me you're talking about. I can't believe that the feelings I've got for Gail are vile; I can't believe that you want me to stay with Nick, knowing that there's something better for me, something that is going to make me happy. Gail is a very special person, she's not a vile person at all. I'd like you to meet her and then you can understand that it's a good thing."'

But Louise's father would have none of it. 'He got upset and began to sob and rock backwards and forwards in his chair and then he dashed out and was really sick in the kitchen – threw up really violently. It was just horrible. And my mum began to rant and rave and say, "Look what you've done to your father; you've always had to be different, haven't you, but this really takes the biscuit. Your dad's ill – for goodness' sake, say something to him that will make him feel better."'

But Louise stood her ground. 'I said, "Well I can't – I mean, I don't know what you expect me to say; I can't suddenly say it's all a big mistake, I don't feel like this. It's really special and important; it's something that's come from very deep inside and it's a relief to be able to identify it, to be able to see Gail and understand how I feel about her and also for me to be able to tell you. I can see that you're panicking – well there's nothing to be afraid of."'

By this time Louise's father had rallied sufficiently to return to the attack. 'He said, "I was in the Navy and I've seen all these men at the docks and they're all perverted. I don't want you thought of as some awful woman that's going to go round dragging young girls off the streets. I don't know what's got you into this; you've obviously been lured into it." And I said, "No – you're wrong; I made all the running with Gail. If only you can think of lesbianism in terms of me, your daughter Louise." It was like a dream really – I was so frustrated that I couldn't get my point across; I couldn't make him understand it wasn't horrible. I couldn't believe that something I was feeling was making him so disgusted. I didn't understand why it was such a big deal.'

Louise turned to her younger brother, with whom she'd always been very close, in the hope that he would understand. 'I tried to pave the way by talking about gay people and he said, "If you're going to tell me anything to do with yourself, I really can't handle you sleeping with birds; I don't want to know, because my sister isn't like that.' Louise was very disappointed: 'I honestly did think that he cared enough about me to accept the way I was; it's no skin off his nose after all. Whoever I choose to be with or sleep with, it's nothing to do with him; I accept him, with all his faults, and make allowances for him and if he can't do the same for me, then it just leaves a great big gaping hole in our relationship.'

Her family's hostility has, if anything, made Louise more resolute than ever in her sexuality. 'I just want a loving relationship with somebody that I can love, who will love me and not worry about what other people think. I want to live with a woman and I want it to be open. I don't want to pretend in any way at all.'

2 The late starter

♀ 'I think that what made me realize I was gay was not the fact that I could not have a relationship with a man – although I must admit that became more difficult as time went on – but experiencing a real relationship, a physical relationship with a woman. The intensity of the response was so different to what I had accepted as being the normal sexual experience.'

♂ 'Certainly, had I been brought up these days, I'd have come out as being gay very early – meaning that in my late teens and early twenties, I hardly knew anything about being gay, I didn't know anybody gay. In a way I'm angry, because I feel I've missed a ten-year experience if you like. In the time that could have been my heyday, I could have been meeting interesting people, having interesting experiences and all that is gone.'

There are many gay men and women whose homosexuality did not begin to dawn on them until their late twenties, thirties or even older. There are many reasons for this: some had very strict upbringings, others lived in isolated or conservative parts of the country, yet others were by nature more conformist, more anxious to make their way in the heterosexual world, and fearful that their homosexuality would impede that ambition. But they all, in days when there was far less information about homosexuality than exists today, shared a common ignorance or naivety about it, or believed that in some way it was wrong or bad, and therefore to be shunned.

The moral climate

The phenomenon of late starters is in large part to be explained by the repressive moral climate in which they grew up, and although this gave way to the permissive sixties, it was not until the end of that decade and the beginning of the next that the women's liberation movement and the Gay Liberation Front (GLF) came into being and challenged conventional ideas of sex roles, sexuality and personal identity.

The passing of the 1967 Sexual Offences Act, which decriminalized adult male homosexual acts in private, and the GLF's proud and defiant assertion of homosexuality, blazed the trail for an explosion of gay activity throughout the seventies, from the setting up of most of the well-known support organizations like Friend, Icebreakers and Gay Switchboard, and the emergence of a gay national newspaper, Gay News, to the opening of the big commercial gay clubs and the provision of services exclusively for gays, such as *Gayway*, the gay dating service.

Gay men and women were now struggling to cast off falsely assumed heterosexual identities and to come to terms with their true homosexuality.

⚣ 'I remember vividly going on holiday with my parents in the summer of 1975 and looking at a man on the beach and thinking, why should I feel ashamed of looking at him? I don't know why this happened, I mean there wasn't any intellectual input into this from anywhere: I think it was a reaction, perhaps left over from the sixties, in the sense that people were now ready to look at themselves.'

Many late starters were brought up in an atmosphere of stifling decency and convention, and were exhorted to live their lives according to a strict moral code, which set perimeters for their sexual behaviour and the way in which they should relate to one another. Thus they grew up to lead ostensibly heterosexual lives, even to the extent of getting married and having children. The expectations of society, parents and others were drilled into them from a very young age.

⚢ 'My life felt very free up until about the age of 12 or 13, and then the one difficulty I found was the things you were expected to do, like being fancied by boys or fancying boys; that seemed to be some sort of club in which there were very clear rules, but I didn't know what they were, and I never liked playing them. Now, it feels dreadfully repressive, but I didn't know then that I was being oppressed in any way. I can remember doing the obligatory things like realizing I was very clever, but you hadn't to be clever with boys, and getting into trouble for it.'

In no area was the moral repression characteristic of the post-war years more apparent than in the sphere of sex, which was barely talked about in the family or at school and even then, only in the most clinical or biological of terms. As for homosexuality, if it was talked about at all it was in a whisper. Thus the odds at that time were against young men and women coming to terms with their homosexuality.

'I had heard about homosexuality; I'd heard that an older girl at school and her very close friend had been caught kissing in a darkened room and everybody thought it was dreadful. There were occasional instances of that, and everybody knew it was a bad thing. I don't know why – it just was. And therefore *I* knew it was a bad thing.'

'I had no exposure to gay things at all, really. In my twenties I became aware of the existence of *Gay News*, but I'd never seen a copy and I didn't know how to buy one. I couldn't understand how you ever met anyone gay; I didn't realize there were gay pubs and clubs and things. I knew there were drinking clubs in the old days where people would go, and I though these were places that got raided by the police and everybody got carted off, and this sort of nonsense. I thought, how do you meet anyone? If you see someone you like, you can't go up to them and talk to them – you have no idea whether they're going to be gay and you're going to end up getting punched on the nose. I couldn't imagine how anybody gay ever connected with anybody else gay.'

One of the worst aspects of the prevailing climate was the attitude of the medical and psychiatric professions, which endured well into the sixties, that homosexuality was some kind of particularly nasty and virulent illness which called for a dramatic cure; some homosexuals were even subjected to aversion therapy, in the misguided hope that it would turn them into heterosexuals.

Alan is 47, a big man with an academic air and a quiet, ironic manner. He knew he was gay when he got married in the early sixties at the age of 29. 'But I hadn't had any real sexual experience; I had avoided it. I felt no sexual attraction to women at all, and my gay life was equally sexually inactive, although I was very aware of men. If the opportunity for a gay relationship had arisen, I'd have taken it. But in those days there was no such outlet. I remember while a student at Cambridge feeling rather desperate, but I never came across any man that I could tell was gay. This was in the fifties and there was no GaySoc or anything; it was just unheard of.'

Alan went out with his wife for about a year before they got married. 'We both lived in Sheffield and we met through our parents. For the first eighteen months of our marriage, it wasn't too bad. I found that by getting fairly sloshed and by using my fertile imagination, I was able to get through reasonably well. In fact my wife actually got pregnant, believe it or not, which I regarded as an enormous achievement at the time, but she had a miscarriage and that was the end of that. It was really after that that the rot set in; what happened was that she got incredibly desperate to have another child, so that at the right time every month, she would get very demanding. And of course, the more demanding she got, the more inhibited I became.'

The situation rapidly deteriorated. 'She got more and more frustrated and I got more and more guilty. Day-to-day living varied according to her moods and my moods. After a time we sort of drifted apart and led our own lives. There were terrible flaming rows from time to time, which were always, always rooted in this frustration. Looking back, if she'd known about the fact that I was gay, it would probably have been better. She just thought I was completely uninterested in her sexually and she was hurt and she'd get bitchy; it's understandable really. Then I would get defensive and indignant and so there would be this awful spiral.'

In 1970, when he was 35 and had been married for six years, Alan had a nervous breakdown. 'I was set upon by a psychiatrist and I spent seven weeks in a clinic. They managed to drag out of me that I was gay, but their first concern was to get me over my depression and then they'd talk about "the other thing".'

Alan was eventually offered 'treatment' for his homosexuality. 'I said, "OK, why not?" So they sent me to a psychiatric hospital, where I got involved with a doctor who believed that my basic problem was fear of women, and that his job was to get me over this fear.'

For this, the presence of Alan's wife was necessary. 'She and I would sit together and he would start by relaxing us both with a yoga-type exercise. When we were in a total state of relaxation, he would make me close my eyes and present various images to me; if I found an image frightening, I was supposed to raise my finger. So he would say, "You're entering a room; in this room there is a beautiful girl, wearing a scarf, hat, overcoat, thick stockings and gumboots. Now she takes off her coat", and so it would go on until she was down to her underpants. I didn't find any of this in the least bit frightening; it didn't do anything to me at all. But I thought, I suppose it's time I *was* frightened, so when we got to the underpants, I raised my finger! But it really was ludicrous, and in the end I said, "I really don't think this is the basic problem."'

Alan was then handed over to someone else, who tried aversion therapy. 'This time I was presented with pictorial images of men, mixed up with people being chucked in gas chambers, and every time they were nice – naked men or something like that – they'd send this dirty great electric shock through my arm. I said to this bloke after I'd had the shocks for several weeks, "They're not enough," and he said, "Well I can't make them any stronger."'

When Alan was threatened with hormone treatment, he decided it was time to withdraw. 'I felt deep down that it wasn't on, that it wouldn't work and I was what I was. I knew by this time that I had to accept that I was gay and do something about it, instead of sublimating it.'

Sublimation and conformity

Gay men and women who knew that they were gay, but didn't know what to do about it, or whose homosexuality was so deeply suppressed they were not even aware of it, invariably chose one of two ways to deal with it. Either they sublimated their sexuality into work or career, sport or leisure activities, and thus kept themselves so busy they literally had no time for a sex or social life; or they bowed to the pressure to conform and unwittingly fell into the role of girlfriend or boyfriend, wife or husband, until forced to look at themselves by, for example, falling in love with a member of their own sex or, in the case of women, becoming involved in the women's movement.

♂ 'In the sixties I was playing in bands – you didn't have the disco scene then – so when the Beatles came along, we were going out playing replicas of the stuff that was in the charts, and working very hard, learning two or three new songs a week. It was a very busy time in the youth clubs and dance halls; so you see I had no time to think about whether I should be getting a girlfriend. That went on until I was about 20, when I started being a DJ and found myself even more busy; I was working in clubs and doing three or four nights a week. Girls would come up and talk to me because I was "the DJ", but everybody knew I was busy so it was a marvellous cover – how can Mike have a girlfriend, he's out working all the time.'

♀ 'I'm sure that feminism has enabled me to feel comfortable in my lesbianism and probably, in fact, to realize it. I can say that all the way through school, university, whatever, I always had fantasies about women and I always had crushes on them. I went through the rituals of going out with men, but there was always something wrong with these relationships. Until feminism, I was totally isolated from other lesbians; feminism did provide a whole community, I think, of women-identified women, of which lesbianism was part and parcel.'

Lindsay is a lesbian feminist playwright. 'I describe myself in different ways, depending on who's asking – you know, I call myself Lindsay and yes I write, but "feminist" is a label I accept with pride, "lesbian" is a label I accept with pride.'

Lindsay was nearly 30 before she began to come to terms with her homosexuality through her involvement in the women's movement; by the time she'd completed the process, she'd been married for ten years.

Lindsay's upbringing was fairly typically middle class. 'I'm one of four children. My father was head of a training college and my mother was "a mother", and we had a very happy childhood, which was not rich except in experience. We were all bright and did well at school as we were expected to, and that's about it, I think.'

As a child, Lindsay was already aware of an attraction to women. 'Certainly I liked them and certainly I did the usual things like practising kissing and playing intensely passionate games. But it never occurred to me that it was sexual, because really very little occurred to me as sexual; I didn't know what that was until one of the older girls at school told us how babies were produced and that you went out with boys.'

Until the age of 13 or 14, Lindsay was much more interested in girls than in boys. 'Then I think we all realized it was incumbent upon us to start liking boys, and it was quite difficult to do, because they were just not attractive. But we knew we had to be attracted to them.'

Lindsay duly started going out with boys and at the age of 21, got married. 'I don't know why, except that it was 1969, and I was very aware that it was about the last moment that people like me did get married – perfectly intelligent girls who went to college and had a good education and didn't think they'd get married – and yet did, mindlessly. That's what I did – I got married without stopping to think. There is no reason why I got married, except something – I presume it was conditioning – must have led me to suppose that that was what one did next.'

For several years, the marriage was a very happy one. 'We got on terribly well; I think because in a lot of ways my husband was how I wanted him to be – he accommodated me because he loved me very much. So for a long time it worked very well, sexually and in terms of the the things that we did.'

Then in her late twenties, Lindsay took a career turn and began to change. 'I'd been a teacher and then I started writing and realized that in a way I'd discovered the love of my life, but in order for me to write about people, I had to understand myself and the world much better than I had before. And I started being more and more interested in how women behaved, and in writing women's parts and things from a woman's point of view.'

This brought Lindsay into contact with women in the theatre and in the women's movement. 'They interested me – at first not sexually, at first simply in the way that they thought and practised their lives. Gradually they opened up my mind; I think the biggest change was realizing how much I and other women accepted what men told us we were. It seems such an obvious thing now, but then it was a truly remarkable discovery – and it wasn't a sudden discovery, it was a gradual unfolding of the layers and layers of behaving how you didn't want to behave. I became aware that anything was possible; I think I learnt what lesbians were.'

Up until then, Lindsay had thought of them as a 'very, very small proportion' of people. 'I didn't know that lesbians existed, except as a total aberration, and something that had nothing to do with me. I mean, I didn't realize I could be a lesbian, because nobody told me. I'd met two who were friends of my sister's and I remember being quite gobsmacked, and not understanding why they were, although they were.'

A gap began to open up in Lindsay's marriage. 'The writing and the different lifestyle gradually separated me and my husband. Our minds started inching, and then really drifting apart. And so I felt like I couldn't really have a sensible conversation with him, because there was just too much open ground between us to cover, before we could even start.'

At the same time Lindsay found herself fancying women. 'I think, you become very interested in women physically, and then I slept with a woman. At the time it was like going back to the beginning again – you know, I suddenly felt very like a novice and I thought, oh it's quite similar, and yet it's quite different, and then of course I worked out that actually it's still the same thing – it's about two people making love.'

Delayed adolescence

Late starters tend to feel as vulnerable and clumsy as adolescents as they begin to come to terms with their homosexuality and grapple with the strange new emotions aroused in their first sexual encounters and relationships with their own sex – emotions all the more overwhelming for being experienced late in the day.

Gay men and women who have pointed themselves in a heterosexual direction for a good part of their adult lives may have come to accept low-key sexual and emotional responses as the norm in their relationships, and thus many of them find themselves unprepared for what amounts to falling in love for the first time. They may also find themselves having to unlearn heterosexual roles into which they have been deeply conditioned, and relearn how to relate to their own sex in new and more open ways, particularly when it comes to lovemaking.

⚢ 'I didn't feel like I was being manipulated or playing the little woman role; it wasn't a case of, "Lie there, darling, open your legs," or whatever. I felt good because I was doing exactly what I wanted to do, and I knew I was making this particular girl feel good too. It was give and take, in equal amounts.'

⚣ 'To put it in a nutshell, I was 100 per cent active in my first relationships with men – not passive at all. I was essentially ignorant; it was only when I realized that the other guy seemed to be having more fun than I was, that I thought, well maybe there is something to this after all. I was a bit scared – just a fairly rational physiological kind of fear, not a psychological fear. It took quite a long time to overcome that, but when I did, I really changed – I'm now about eighty per cent passive. That doesn't mean I'm incapable of being active, it's just that I don't tend to be, out of preference.'

Generally late starters experience a sense of ease at no longer having to fit into roles in which they may never have felt comfortable.

⚢ 'Why my primary relationships are with women these days is that it's much, much easier to eyeball a woman and say "Yes, we're different, we disagree, but we're equal", than it ever is with a man. He might be light years behind you intellectually, but he'll still think he's better.'

⚣ 'You do want that ability sometimes not to be making all the decisions, not to be having to make *your* mind up all the time. I found the biggest frustration in relationships with straight women was finding out what they wanted, because they always look to you to make the decisions – it seemed to be expected. And I didn't want to make the decisions all the time – why should I always be the one who knows what to do – I don't.'

Most late starters go through a period of considerable self-adjustment before they complete the coming-out process and find their footing in the gay world; for a while they may wonder if they are bisexual, in an attempt to rationalize a heterosexual past with the gay feelings that are just beginning to surface. Like adolescence it is a time of confusion and excitement, a roller-coaster ride of emotional highs and lows.

Chris is a 33-year-old businessman, sharp and energetic, from what he calls 'an essentially lower-middle-class background': 'My parents were not particularly wealthy, but comfortable. My father worked hard, I saw very little of him – my mother brought myself and my brother up really.'

From the age of 13, Chris was aware that he was more interested in boys than in girls and at 18 he still hadn't got a girlfriend. 'By then it was beginning to be noticeable, in that all my friends had girlfriends. Eventually I went out with a girl, but that was absolutely hopeless; we went out for three or four months, but it never got anywhere. She was a bit worried, because nothing ever happened, and in the end she broke it off. Then at 19, I started going out with my wife; in a way I didn't understand enough about being gay to appreciate it could be a fulfilling existence for me.'

So Chris 'drifted' into marriage. 'We hadn't had any real sex, but we put that down to not having had the right opportunity and not living with each other. When we got married, we got into what I suppose would be reasonable, but not very frequent, sex.'

For several years, Chris kept up a heterosexual front. 'I had a stereotype image of the gay limpwristed queen and I thought, I don't want to be like *that*. So I consciously avoided everything gay; I thought that if I kept involving myself in heterosexual society, I might find that I wasn't gay.'

But Chris eventually gave up the pretence. 'I realized I was gay, there was nothing I could about it, and it was a little bit silly to suppress it, because I was just getting frustrated. I thought it was about time I started exploring things a little bit, just in case I woke up at the age of 50 and realized I'd thrown my life down the drain.'

Chris accordingly wrote off to Gayway, for which he'd seen an advertisement in a newspaper, and was introduced to a man who told him where to go to meet other gay people. 'The first time that I went to a gay club I was very frightened. I stood on the other side of the road and watched the people going in. I was amazed. I stood there, almost open-mouthed, watching these perfectly normal young lads going in, who you'd pass in the street and wouldn't know were gay. And this was a tremendous eye-opener.'

Not long after, Chris had his first sexual contact with another man. 'The first time I kissed him it felt . . . right. I immediately realized that the heterosexual experiences which I'd had, not only in my marriage, but the limited experiences before, were wrong. I imagine by comparison they felt just as having to kiss a gay guy, say, would feel to a heterosexual guy – uncomfortable, you don't want to be any part of it. This felt completely right; if you like it was a confirmation of all the doubts and feelings I'd had.'

Chris was elated. 'I wondered where I'd go from there; I felt very happy. So much so that my wife noticed and said, "What's the matter? You've been so withdrawn and moody of late and all of a sudden you're really happy." I wasn't aware that it showed that much, but it obviously did – I was bouncing about.'

For the next eighteen months, Chris did the rounds of the clubs. 'I got myself involved with a couple of guys in fairly one-sided relationships – I got infatuated or really keen on them and they were so-so. I got a little bit disillusioned with that and ended up placing an ad in a magazine, trying to find somebody who wasn't particularly involved in the scene – because if you meet somebody in a club, they've possibly got a boyfriend already or they just want a bit of fun; whereas if you meet somebody through one of those columns, which are normally pooh-poohed by lots of people, you share the fact that you're both lonely and you're looking for somebody, which is a very good starting point.'

Through the advertisement Chris met a man with whom he has now had a relationship for six months; since then he has also separated from his wife. 'I think I'm a much more relaxed, happy person now than I was two years ago.'

Gay men and women who have come late to their homosexuality frequently find that their first full relationships with their own sex are a deeply transforming experience; it is not uncommon for them to speak of being born again.

Profiles

Born again: Gloria ♀

'Looking back on my relationships with men, my gayness has certainly given me a concrete reason for having failed in them; it now makes sense. I certainly now feel at ease with myself and belong far more to myself than I ever did before, when I related to men. I enjoy men's company, but I have no wish to sleep with a man again.'

Gloria is a tall, strong woman of 40, who lives alone with her two young children. She left her second husband when she was 31, and two years later fell in love for the first time with another woman.

'The feeling was totally unexpected, terrifying, because of the *force* of what I felt. I hadn't experienced anything like it before; it was mind-blowing.'

Gloria was an only child, whose parents were in private service: her father was a butler, her mother a cook, and the family moved round southern England from one domestic post to another. Gloria recalls that sexually, she was very unaware. 'When I was a kid, the bedroom door was always closed, so you never saw anything.'

As a child, Gloria was an out-and-out tomboy. Girls were sissies, boys 'great fun'. An ardent movie-goer, Gloria's favourites were Edgar Wallace and Hopalong Cassidy – 'Because I was into guns and climbing trees. Because I spent so much time with boys and I was a girl, I had to do it better than them. So if there was anything dangerous, I'd do it, even if I was terrified, because of the praise I'd get from the guys. I always liked praise and to be admired.' So Gloria enjoyed being followed around by smaller girls, who admired her prowess at tennis and netball.

At about 13 or 14, Gloria remembers 'having conversations' and 'making love' to her pillow, 'which was always female'. And at 16, she had a girlfriend with whom she used to go dancing. 'One Saturday evening I stayed over at her house. We had to sleep in her single bed and it was so cramped that we were hunched up talking nose-to-nose. Eventually she turned over and I snuggled up into her back and put my arm around her. I remember thinking that it felt good, it felt warm.'

At 18 Gloria left home to become a policewoman in the Forces. 'I landed up with 500 or so girls, several of whom developed crushes on me. I was bossy and arrogant and I suppose I attracted a certain type of girl who goes into the Forces looking for just that kind of woman. But it never dawned on me that I too might be gay. I was now actually physically aware of men, although I had never slept with one. I was aware that I was made to be made love to by a man – women for men, men for women. I had no doubt that I would marry eventually and have children, although I wasn't maternal.'

Then Gloria was posted to the Far East. 'As there were 8000 men and only 100 women, there was a lot of scope. I had several boyfriends, but I never slept with any of them. Then I met Brian, my first husband. He was certainly the best I'd been out with; he was kind and gentle and I believed I loved him. He was decent, and that was important to me. We went out for about a year, although for six months of that, he was in the jungle.'

When he came back, they decided to get married. It was a marriage of convenience: 'I was due to return home, unless I signed on again, which I didn't want to. So getting married to Brian was a way of remaining out there.' Accordingly plans were made for the wedding. 'It was the works – a white wedding with 200 people, a really big do. It wasn't really what I wanted; it was for the folks back home, because they couldn't be there. So it was taped and filmed, the lot.'

At this time, aged 21, Gloria was still a virgin. 'Brian and I had petted, but I wouldn't allow full intercourse until we were married – for all the reasons my mother had instilled into me: you don't keep a man by sleeping with him too soon, you might get pregnant, he might lose respect for you – all the usual mumbo-jumbo. Anyway I didn't, and like a good girl, went on the pill. We were both emotionally and physically exhausted on our wedding night and decided not to do anything; the next day my period started and that was that!'

Gloria and Brian only had three weeks together before he had to return to the jungle. 'During that time we never had proper intercourse, because it always went wrong, for one reason or another. When he came back the situation didn't change; it really was awful. I thought it was me: being sexually inexperienced, I didn't know what to do and I felt very guilty.'

The marriage broke up when they returned to England. A few

months later Gloria met another man. 'After a couple of months we made love and it was fine. Whether or not this was partly due to my own need for wanting to be made love to properly by a man, I don't know – but I was bloody grateful to him!' But eventually this relationship too broke up. 'He was exceptionally macho and I didn't want to live in anyone's shadow. I knew it wouldn't work, so we parted.'

Then Gloria decided to go back in the Forces; while waiting to be interviewed and for her divorce to come through, she started going out with a soldier called Dick. 'On my birthday we went out and I got very tiddly; I had already come off the pill because I had no intention of sleeping with anyone – my mind was firmly fixed on divorce, freedom, the Forces. But that night Dick made love to me in the back of his car and I got pregnant. He wanted to get married and I agreed; I convinced myself that I must love him because I was having his child.'

The marriage, like Gloria's first, was 'disastrous'. 'It was dreadful; I hated being a mother. I was totally disoriented; I had gone from being a totally independent woman who knew exactly what she wanted and where she was going, to a situation where I felt I must be someone else, it was such a contrast. I was trapped and had to depend on someone else financially, and Dick was a selfish man, who hated the responsibility of a family.'

With the arrival of another unplanned child, the marriage became a 'travesty'. 'I was so physically worn out by the kids' demands that when Dick wanted me sexually, I couldn't reciprocate and I didn't want to; I'd lost all physical desire. We were both suffering, but he thought that the kids would hold me there and that his wife belonged to him and he could do what he liked. I tried to persuade him to move back into barracks while I stayed at home, in order to save the marriage, but he blatantly refused, saying that it was his home and I could leave.'

Things came to a head when Dick warned Gloria against taking the children with her. 'I warned him in turn against trying to stop me. The week before I left, he came towards me in the kitchen; I knew he was a man who could be violent and I had a knife. I said, "Dick, if you come near me, I'll gut you." I would have done – I'd come to the end. From that day to this, he has never sent us a penny.'

For the next couple of years Gloria struggled to keep herself and the children; with social security she could just about manage. 'I had my freedom to work, which was very important to me and, of course, to the children, because I was happier. I was on my own and making it in my own way.'

The turning point for Gloria came when she started taking the children to school and meeting other mothers. 'One of them was Australian, in her late twenties, with three young kids of her own – very, very attractive and totally heterosexual. I loved her accent, the way she handled her kids; we used to talk a lot, mainly about the kids, and I liked her. Anyway, for some unknown reason I used to think an awful lot about her. I began to look forward to going to pick up the kids and I used to go early to make sure I'd see her. I'd never been to women's coffee mornings before, but because of her I began to go; I couldn't see anything but her, and it was *agony*.'

Gloria couldn't make sense of what was happening to her. 'I thought, what on earth is wrong? I go to bed, I dream about her, I can't wait for school in the afternoon – if her husband came to pick up the kids, I'd be so disappointed. After about three months of this I thought, this is absolute madness; I'm not going to see her, I'm going to deny it exists. And I became so miserable – but I was afraid that if I carried on, I'd blow the gaff and put my arms round her or something.'

Gloria decided to contact the Campaign for Homosexual Equality (CHE), which advertised in her local paper. 'I wrote to them and received a reply from a woman who was supportive and said that if I wanted to, she and her girlfriend would come and talk to me. So they came over, I talked about myself for a while and then they went, with the idea that I would meet them at a CHE disco.'

It was with 'great trepidation' that Gloria took up the invitation. 'I met them there and sat at a table with them; I was all agog – I'd never seen anything like this in my entire life, women kissing and feeling each other – God, was this new! But I felt unsure of myself; I knew how to behave in heterosexual society, but in this I was a novice, and an old novice at that, who suddenly did not know what to do.'

Then Gloria was asked if she'd like to dance. 'We did a fast number which I enjoyed, and then a slow number and God, it felt good. It felt strange and exciting and *right* to be holding a woman. I thought, this is what I want, this is what I need.'

The two women arranged to meet again. 'We had a good evening; I knew what I wanted to do, we were talking silly nonsense by this time, but I was afraid to do anything. The long and the short of it was that I kissed her, because I knew the vibes were there, and wowee! It was new, something I'd never done before, exciting, a totally new experience. I touched her, it felt good, but I thought back to my upbringing again – "You've got to know someone before you do anything." I thought, Christ, you never did it straight out with men, don't start doing it with women. So I went off, but not long after, circumstances brought us together again, and it was then that I made love to her a naturally as if I'd been making love to women all my life, and she made love to me.'

The encounter turned out to be a one-night stand, but Gloria had no regrets. 'I knew that emotionally, she wasn't right for me. But I realized I was pointing in a gay direction; I wanted to do it again, but this time with a woman I could really get involved with.'

Three weeks later, Gloria fell in love with a woman she met at another gay disco. 'I have never known anything like I experienced in the first six months of that relationship; I have never felt so lost, so happy, so excited – everything I had ever wanted was wrapped up in this one woman. No man had ever ruled me and yet she was doing just this. I didn't know any better; I was so infatuated with her that I would have done anything for her, bar murder! We couldn't live together: she was divorced with three kids, and I had two. But she wanted me all to herself, and I had enough sense to know that we both had our responsibilities. She began to possess me, to own me, and in the long term, this was totally destructive, so I had to break it off.'

Although the relationship lasted two years in all, Gloria admits, with hindsight, that she 'made many mistakes': 'But it's difficult to judge the responses of a woman when one is only experienced in the ways of men. Yet I feel that I have learned a great deal about myself, and know now how very important my own sexuality is to me. Certainly had I not changed course sexually, I would not feel emotionally enriched as I do now. Knowing who I am, and finding a relationship that is right for me, is what I'm after now.'

Born again: Andrew ♂

'1981 was, I think, probably the most glorious year of my life – the most exciting, memorable, important year. I began not only to accept being gay, but to take pleasure in it; I began to explore what gay life was about; I began to develop a kind of gay social and political philosophy; I began to start coming out to close friends – that was all in 1981.'

Andrew is 35, an intelligent, articulate man in a well-paid professional job. Like many late starters, he took a couple of years to come out fully as a gay man; by then he was 32. Looking back, Andrew can see that he dismissed early homosexual feelings. 'When I was in the fourth form at boarding school, there were still kids in the dormitory who'd wank each other off and that was not regarded as homosexual behaviour as such; homosexuals were regarded in a disparaging fashion, they were a joke. So I didn't see that the feelings I had were particularly abnormal, and I had every reason to believe that I would fancy girls the same as anyone else.'

At 17 Andrew even had a girlfriend. 'I thought I ought to. I didn't have a great deal of enthusiasm for the project; we didn't actually make love – it was more snogging in bus shelters along the seafront. I just thought I wasn't very good with girls, I was a bit shy and all that. I can remember being distinctly attracted to some of the younger boys at that stage; I took the attitude that these feelings were inappropriate, wrong and that I was just frustrated – I wasn't making it with girls and that must be the reason. Basically I was a conformist little prick at the time and only too happy to be so.'

At university Andrew's sex life was 'a complete zero' as far as girls were concerned. 'I can remember being attracted to girls physically – obviously not that much, otherwise I might have been a bit more successful. I think I formed a view of myself that I wasn't attractive to women, I don't know why; I think I had a very poor body image at the time. In some ways I'd become sexually repressed; I was sublimating most of my activities into studying.'

But at 20 Andrew had a homosexual encounter while on a fell-walking trip in the Lake District organised by his old schoolmaster; the party included an 'old boy' in his late thirties. 'The first night we all got pretty pissed in the bar of the hotel where we were staying, and when we went to our rooms, this guy said,

"Come and have a chat", and before I knew where I was, he was all over me. I didn't resist, I was totally pissed. Nothing particularly came of it; he was obviously attracted to me and I was very disturbed by the fact that I hadn't resisted at all. He tried it again the next day: I said, "No, I haven't given women a proper chance – I don't know I'm that way."'

Andrew was 27 before he had a sexual relationship with a woman. 'She had a slightly boyish appearance: short hair, nothing up top, cheeky personality, very clear complexion. I was very strongly physically attracted to her and eventually we did go to bed together. I could almost stand apart from myself and see myself screwing her and thinking, this really does look ridiculous. It was altogether not a terribly satisfactory experience. I remember thinking at the time, it's not all it's cracked up to be; if that's what it is, what have I been missing? – not a lot.'

Nevertheless Andrew asked her to marry him and was distraught when he was turned down. 'I'd actually got myself up into thinking that I loved her – I desperately *wanted* to be in love with her, it was important to me; I was beginning to feel I'd been left out, something was wrong with me.'

But at the same time, Andrew found himself attracted to a young, good looking man in his office. 'That may have been why, when my girlfriend and I packed it in, I started mulling things over; I thought maybe now's the time to give the other a chance. Somehow I plucked up the courage to buy a copy of *Gay News*.'

Andrew then went to a gay pub. 'I took one look and I thought, what have I got in common with these people – they're much handsomer than me, they're all tall and slim and I'm none of those things; I've made a mistake, I'm just reacting to a bad relationship – I'm not really homosexual.'

The next year he spent in long hours at his job; when he found he needed an attractive female escort for formal occasions, he got himself another girlfriend. 'But we didn't go to bed once, although we slept in the same room. I often wondered whether it was because I had a low sex drive or because I was a misogynist. When she and I split up, I thought, this is the second time I've screwed up – why?'

On a business trip to Berlin, Andrew went with two prostitutes in one night. 'I thought, it's not physical, it's not the mechanics, it's not because I'm not actually sexually capable; I can make it with prostitutes, why can't I make it with women I like? I remember thinking, well maybe I'm bisexual, behaviourally. I didn't *know* that I was gay; all that I knew was that I'd fancied other guys, I'd been with another guy, I'd been with women. I thought, let's try with a man and see what happens.'

At about this time Andrew, now 30, saw the play *Bent.* 'It really impressed me, moved me; it was like the drawing back of a veil. I kept buying *Gay News*, and at some stage I made a decision to go along to a CHE meeting, because I wasn't meeting anyone, I wasn't talking to anyone.'

At the meeting Andrew found people very helpful. 'I went on a day trip with them, they held a disco in the evening and things like that; it was helping me to come out in the way that CHE has done for so many people. At one stage I chatted to an older guy about everything, and he said, "I don't think you've got a problem; all you've got to do is get out there and get stuck in."'

So Andrew kept going to CHE meetings. 'I was trying to get laid, basically, to find out whether I was bi or gay or not, but I was scared; I was inexperienced, I didn't know all the little signs, little looks, little gestures – I didn't have the language. I was conscious of all these things that I was trying to learn very fast and nothing was happening. I didn't quite know how to put into practice this new way of thinking, this new way of life that I seemed to be getting into.'

In 1980 Andrew marched in Gay Pride Week. 'But I still had no proof that I was gay and that was a source of frustration. I was buying gay porn magazines and finding that I could be attracted to what was in those, if I thought hard enough about it. I didn't know enough about gay sex, so I got a copy of *The Joy of Gay Sex*, which was a great help; I bought a lot of gay books and read an awful lot. I put ads in various magazines and answered ads and met a few people, but nothing really happened.'

Then Andrew joined Gayway; his first date was a teacher called Bob, who rang him up and arranged to meet him. 'It was a Saturday night and we went down to the local wine bar. I was obviously very nervous and I had quite a bit to drink. Then we went back to my place. We were listening to some music, it was Vaughan Williams, and I was flitting around making drinks and being a bit silly, really; I didn't quite know what to do next. I was attracted to him; he was not unlike me, well-built, not exactly a gay man's dream – just a nice chap. And I was just walking past him and he just said "Come here", and took my hand and pulled me towards him and kissed me. It makes me emotional to think about it; it was like panes of glass shattering. And I knew with every ounce of my being that I was right; it was like some kind of chemical reaction, it was like my body said to my brain, at bloody last! It's about time you got it sorted out. And we went to bed together; it wasn't particularly exciting sex, it was a typical first-night fumble.'

But from then on, Andrew didn't look back. 'I started to meet other guys and have sexual relationships with them; I didn't at that time have any particular desire to have an ongoing relationship, I wanted to try different things out. I was on a learning curve, I was learning about my responses – what I liked and didn't like. All of a sudden I'm having an active, exciting, interesting sex life with people I like, going out to discos – I'm having a wonderful time, the best time of my bloody life.'

After a series of casual pick-ups, Andrew has come to the conclusion that he is monogamous, but more importantly, he finally knows for sure that he is gay. 'What I experience day after day is the sheer joy and pleasure of it; I am *glad* to be gay. I'm glad to have discovered it, I'm glad my head and body are now together.'

3 The married gay

♂ 'I went out with my new boyfriend for about two weeks before I told him that I was married. This is my policy with new people; I prove to them that I have complete freedom socially, just by virtue of the fact that I see a lot of them, then I tell them about the rest of my life. I explain that I'm married, I have two children, I have a house where they live and I spend some time at the house, and that it is a situation which I'm happy to have continuing.'

♀ 'I felt very much that the family should come first – probably because my lesbian feelings were so strong. I decided that since I had three children and my husband wanted us to have another go at making the marriage work, that it just wasn't on, my doing my own thing. Apart from that, I'd have had to have the time, the energy and the know-how to do something about it, none of which I had. I was, I suppose, making the best of a bad job.'

It may be a source of amazement that people can be married and yet gay, but as we saw in the last chapter, it can take years, for many extenuating reasons, for some gay men and women to discover or come to terms with their true sexuality.

And the pull of marriage is particularly strong; in a heterosexual society it is the ultimate act of conformity, conferring legal and social recognition upon those who enter into it, a place in the world, a sense of belonging. Thus some gay men and women have opted to conceal, or even hoped to bury, their doubts and fears about their sexuality behind the facade of marriage.

♂ 'I got married because I didn't really want to be gay. I saw marriage as something very positive against something which wasn't very positive at all – I hadn't had a real gay relationship, I really didn't know how to get into one and everybody would have frowned on it anyway. I much preferred just to get married and be perfectly normal.'

Many gays resorted to marriage out of just this confused and mistaken belief that it would somehow contain their gay feelings.

♂ 'I'd been having homosexual experiences on and off, and then I had a spot of bother – I appeared before a magistrate on one of these bloody bye-laws – and I made a frantic effort to do something about it. I thought that if only I could meet a girl and marry her, everything would slot into place; regular experiences of sex with her would drive away "the other". I was completely ambivalent and naive at the time; I joined a marriage bureau and met my wife through that.'

♀♀ 'I was still living at home with my parents when I started going out and about on the gay scene; they weren't at all pleased or happy with me, and I thought that perhaps by getting married and living to all intents and purposes a conventional life, I'd satisfy everybody and shut them up. So after a while I married a friend of mine whom I got on with very well; I thought, all right I'm gay, but there's no reason why I shouldn't live with him and have children.'

Some gays get married, conversely, out of a positive desire to have children.

♂ 'I never thought that by marrying my gay feelings would disappear, but I wanted a family: although I'm gay, I do like the idea of family. And it was the children that kept the whole thing going; as far as they were concerned, my wife and I saw eye to eye on everything, so that did have a tremendous uniting effect. We did everything as a family; to all outward appearance we were a happily married couple with kids.'

For older gays in particular, who had to observe far more rigid social mores than is the case today, there may simply have seemed no alternative to marriage.

♂ 'I was living in a society – remember this was some years ago – in which one played tennis, one went to dances, one mixed with people and one got married – it was just a way of life. I was fairly old – nearly 30 – when I did anyway; I remember people saying, "Aren't you married yet?" I met my wife through her brother, who went to school with me; we just drifted together. It was one of those things.'

The pressure to get married and have children has been even greater for women than for men; until relatively recently, women were considered to have no other worthwhile future. They were expected to be economically dependent on men; as for sex, it was something more to be endured than enjoyed for its own sake.

Many married gays complain that their heterosexual partner is too highly sexed for them, and sex usually takes place out of habit, or basic physical need, or simply the intimacy of years of living together and bringing up children.

⚲ 'Sex with my husband worked OK, it was all right; I was never deeply emotionally involved. It was like doing a job; I read up about it and I just got on with it. It was part of the deal, and I went along with it most of the time, but occasionally I had terrible "headaches".'

⚢ 'I wouldn't say sex with my wife is not enjoyable – it's obviously a physical and emotional release – but the fact that I cannot possibly envisage having sex with any other woman obviously qualifies it. A lot of it is the fact that we are very fond of each other and have built up a tremendous bond with each other. I enjoy sex with Jill because she is Jill, not because she is a woman. But I don't mean that it necessarily satisfies me as much as a gay sexual experience.'

Thus sex for married gays with their heterosexual partner is usually a low-key affair, lacking the sexual and emotional fulfilment of sex with a homosexual partner.

⚢ 'In the beginning the sexual side of my marriage was not too bad. I quite enjoyed some of it – it was just the frequency I found too much. And always the initiative came from her, very rarely from me. From time to time I would have the odd homosexual experience and when I got home, I wouldn't feel like doing anything. I found sex with her increasingly less exciting than sex with a man.'

Frequently married gays use homosexual fantasy in order to pass muster with their heterosexual partner in bed.

⚲ 'My husband is very masculine-looking; he's very big and very hairy and very broad. I just found him sometimes to be physically too macho. I felt there was something missing; I just wasn't getting something that I wanted, and that was the warmth and affection from another woman. So I would fantasize about being with a beautiful woman.'

It is common for married gays to find that they have a close friendship, rather than a love relationship, with their heterosexual partner; and so, in some cases, fearful of upsetting the equilibrium of their marriages, they frequently relegate their homosexual desires to the level of the purely physical, so that they do not get out of hand.

♂ 'I put my gay needs on a physical level, maybe because I don't want to accept it any other way; I really don't know. So it's a physical thing, but out of that I want to be able to talk about it, I want companionship; I don't want it to be something that merely happens in the bushes. I don't want to sit and talk to my wife about my gay relationships – I think that would be intolerable and why should she want to know? But one does need someone to talk to.'

Gays who stay married may do so because they consider they have too much to lose, not only materially, but in terms of standing within their families and communities; or they may simply be reluctant to embrace the gay life as a viable and positive alternative.

♀ 'It's the sexual thing that's really attracted me; I haven't thought about any emotional involvement. I think two women sleeping together and having sex and making wonderful love is great, and that's as far as I have gone. But when it comes to the commitment of the emotional thing, there's something that tells me, "This isn't right; what would people say? How would they look at me if I lived with a woman?" It confuses me, because I know it's much deeper than that; there's much more to it than sex.'

♂ 'I wouldn't want to leave my wife in any circumstances; we have a vast number of mutual friends, family, everything like that, and our life together is based on companionship and support. We share a number of interests, but I have a particular interest in classical music, so she is quite happy for me to go to concerts with my gay friends and is quite aware

that something else will go on afterwards. She probably has
the bad end of the stick; I do try and make it up to her, but
then that's a rather cowardly way out really, isn't it?'

In the next section of this chapter we look at several gay men and
women who are, or have been married, and how they have dealt
with their homosexuality in the context of marriage.

Profiles

The family man: Frank ♂

'I don't want to upset things at home; we're a very close family, it's
a happy atmosphere – I don't want to spoil that. But I don't think
I'd marry if I were a young homosexual now. I still resent – this is
awful to say – I still resent my situation, I still resent my wife, I
still resent my family, although I love them all.'

Frank is a young-looking 50, small and dapper; he occupies a
senior local government post and lives with his wife, Doris and two
of their four grown-up children.

Frank and Doris have not had sex for twelve years. Frank had
his first homosexual experience in his teens with a man he met in
the gallery of Sadler's Wells: 'But I couldn't identify it as such,
because thirty-odd years ago, you didn't really think of it in those
terms.' He got married at 21, and a few years ago he and Doris
celebrated their silver wedding anniversary.

Frank was the youngest of seven children; his father worked for
London Transport and the family lived in a two-up, two-down
cottage with an outside toilet. He has known Doris since he was a
child; they were part of the same crowd of young people whose
activities revolved around church and youth club, and who eventually paired off together – although not without misgivings on
Frank's side. 'I remember when I was 17 feeling Doris and I were
not right together, and saying to her, "Something's wrong here,
we've got to finish it." And in fact we did; she'd asked me to a
dance and I said no, I didn't want to be involved any more.'

Frank thought no more about it until he went on holiday with a
couple of friends. 'They were talking about their girlfriends and I

thought, what *is* the matter with me? Why isn't it happening to me? I thought, well, there's Doris. So I phoned her up and said, "Look – is it OK for me to come to the dance after all?" and she said yes. I went to the dance and we were friends again.'

Then Frank did his national service, where he again felt pressure to have a girlfriend. 'Also there were lots of "queer" jokes. By the time I was demobbed, I was engaged to Doris and a few months later, we were married. I was still very much aware of my homosexuality, but I just thought, I'm going to have to hide it.'

A year later, their first child was born. 'From then on I was doing things like buying health and strength magazines and hiding them under the mattress; I also joined a gym – Doris had no idea it was a sexual thing.'

Two more children followed in the next five years, and the last arrived five years later. 'But we never had a very active sexual relationship; I don't think either of us ever had any real big sexual drive. So when we stopped having sex altogether I didn't feel guilty about depriving Doris of any great thing.'

It wasn't until the end of the sixties, when the gay liberation movement was just getting off the ground, and Frank was nearly 40, that he began to feel a 'strong homosexual urge'. 'It was a time when people were talking about their homosexuality, and I began to think I'm not the only one, there are others; I really felt I wanted to meet other homosexuals. I became very depressed both at work and at home, and went to see a private psychiatrist, who referred me back to my own GP.'

Unknown to Frank, Doris had also been to their GP. 'She asked him what was the matter with me, and he said, "Frank thinks he's becoming a homosexual," and she shouldn't encourage me. It was crazy, the expression "becoming" a homosexual – I always had been. But that's how Doris found out.'

The marriage hit a bad patch. 'I was exploring myself and all sorts of things. I was going out on my own, I was going to gay pubs and I even replied to one of the personal advertisements in *International Times*. Through that I met a guy, but I lied to him: I didn't tell him that I was married, I gave him a different name and I knocked a few years off my age. He was really very nice, but because I was dishonest with him, I couldn't keep it going; we had a sexual relationship for a few weeks, that was all.'

Then Frank joined the Campaign for Homosexual Equality. 'I told Doris and she asked me why I'd done it. I said it was what I was, it was what I needed. I got quite involved; it was great, it was marvellous. I actually went out and met other gay people; I got involved in gay politics. It was like life beginning all over again.'

Doris accepted Frank's gay activity up to a point. 'We just didn't talk about it at all; that's how we both coped at home. There were times when it got a bit unpleasant, when she resented me going out. She said she became jealous of me, jealous of my friends. She would never meet my friends and still won't. There were opportunities for her to do so – when I joined a married gay group, for example – but she was adamant that she didn't want to.'

The high point of Frank's gay life occurred in 1974, when he met and fell in love with a gay New Zealander called John. 'It was the happiest year of my life. I think it was the first time that I'd ever been in love; I really felt all the things one feels when one says one's in love. That was the nearest we got to ending our marriage – I got very close indeed. Doris realized that something was happening, because I was getting home terribly late, in the early hours of the morning. The pressure came from both sides, because John couldn't cope with me getting up in the middle of the night and going home; he said I had to make a choice, and in fact I chose my family. John wouldn't accept this, he still wanted to carry on the relationship; I didn't want to end it, but I felt I ought to. We still didn't end it there, but in any case he was going back to New Zealand.'

Some years ago, Frank wrote *Gay News* a letter about being married and gay, in which he said that he got 'sick and tired of reading about married homosexual men who forsake wife and children because of their own gayness.' The letter went on: 'The decision to get married at all was theirs, even though they knew they were gay, and if the result of that decision was the birth of children, then surely this is enough in itself for them to act responsibly towards them.' Frank ended by making his own position clear: 'I still say that the happiness of children should come before my own happiness.'

Frank's gay life now consists of the odd foray for 'sexual gratification' and the occasional visit to a gay club 'to be among gay people': 'You can also be anonymous; nobody really cares about some old queen walking around on his own – I feel quite comfortable.'

Meanwhile Doris has made herself very busy with her teaching and church activities and never asks where Frank's going: 'Usually it's to some gay function, which I'd love to discuss at home.'

But Frank's homosexuality is a family secret. 'I remember my eldest daughter, when she was about 15, saying to Doris, "You know what the trouble with this house is, don't you? This big secret about Daddy being a homosexual!" I overheard this and I tackled her about it later on; we talked about it very sensibly. She said she'd known for some time and that it didn't make any difference really. But she must have written to one of her friends about it, because I happened to come across a letter which said, "How awful to find your dad's a repressed adolescent!"'

Frank's 'big worry' is his sons. 'I've never really discussed it with my eldest son. I once said to him, "Does it worry you? Do you want to talk about it?" and he said no. That was that. My youngest son, Edward, and I have talked about it. He took a telephone call a few months ago from somebody who said they were from CHE and he asked what it meant. And I explained that I'd been a member for a number of years and that I was homosexual. He said, "I've known that for years, Dad." But although we had that conversation, we still don't talk about it.'

Frank is constantly reminded of his uneasy situation. 'A rather sad thing happened to me a few weeks ago. When I go to CHE meetings I usually wear a pink triangle, but I never wear it at home; I came back this time to a house full of Edward and his friends, still wearing this badge, and I noticed that Edward, who's usually very close to me, was suddenly very cold. I said, "Ed, what's the matter?" He said, "Oh nothing." Then, "Will you take that badge off?" And I got all flummoxed and I said, "Oh I'm sorry Ed, I didn't mean to keep it on." And I took the badge off and I suddenly thought, this is wrong – I shouldn't have to take my badge off in my house, and I want some support from my children. I was *so* upset. I could have walked out of the house then and there. And I wanted to have a row with Doris. This is it; I can campaign for gay rights outside my family, but where I *ought* to be discussing it . . .'

As far as Frank and Doris's friends are concerned, they are 'a very happy, normal married couple': 'We've always got on extremely well; even now we're very good – silly to say it – friends, I suppose. We go out an awful lot together – to the theatre, round to people we know. Quite a nice thing happened recently; it was Edward's birthday and we went out as a family – we had one of these theatre-dinner tickets – and it was lovely, because we just sat at this table, my wife and I and the children. I felt really good.'

But Frank worries about the future alone with Doris. 'I still have this fantasy about finding a gay lover. I think I'm too old now. But I'm not looking forward to the two of us being on our own, I'm not looking forward to it at all. I just wonder what it's going to be like when the children really are off our hands, when we really are on our own.'

Mid-life crisis: Valerie ♀

'I met a divorced woman with a child through a contact ad, and even though it was a short-lived affair, it made me realize that I didn't want to continue with my marriage; I'd rather be on my own.'

Valerie is a 41-year-old teacher who now lives alone with her three teenage children since separating from her husband of 19 years. She was one of four children who were brought up in an isolated part of Norfolk, and led a 'very cloistered' life until she went to college. 'Then I went to dances, and when boys used to clutch me close at the last dance I could feel myself freezing and I'd disappear as fast as I could. I had close friendships with women throughout college, but at that point I found the thought of homosexuality utterly revolting; I'd cut that part out of me. I decided that men weren't really for me, but never identified that this might be due to my homosexuality. I was a pretty dreamy type of person, who went cycling round the countryside.'

Valerie's first real boyfriend was a photographer called Les whom she met at her village amateur dramatics society when she was 21, and married a year later. 'As far as I was concerned at the time, I loved him; whether I was conditioned by women's magazines and romantic novels, I don't know. He is the gentlest man I have ever met; he's become more assertive with age, but he's certainly not aggressive. He is still a great friend – kind, considerate, loving and sensitive.'

To begin with, Valerie and Les just enjoyed 'doing things together': 'We lived in a bedsit and did daft things like spending all our money on records. We'd had sex prior to our marriage and it was reasonably satisfying. I didn't want children, but Les did.'

Their first child, born a couple of years later, was 'a mistake'; Valerie gave up her job when he was born and 'just drifted' into having the other two. 'We still did an awful lot of things within our marriage. Les got very interested in trade unionism and wanted to take O-level Economics, so I took that with him for company. And we were busy with the children; I never seemed to be without anything to do.'

When her youngest child was 3 years old, Valerie went back to teaching. 'A few months later I thought, something's wrong. I saw two people in the street who were so obviously in love and I thought, I used to have this lovely romantic feeling about doing things together and I don't have it any more. It made me stop; it was 1973 and we'd been married nine years. I realize now that Les and I didn't have an intense emotional relationship, we had had a closeness that had completely gone.'

Then Les admitted he was having an affair with another woman. 'I was hurt and angry and threw a pewter mug at the wall and stood there wanting to scream my head off. I had this feeling that I'd like to walk into the sea holding all the children and drown the four of us. It took me about six weeks to get over it. What amazes me even now is that I could still feel so intensely about it without there being an intense sexual involvement. I think it was just rejection and pure egotism. Then I thought, what the hell – it's not going to work between us; I've got to make my own life.'

Valerie and Les continued to have sex. 'I suppose this is the area in which we came to grief. Had he been a normally sexed man, I could have accepted a twice-a-week relationship, within this very deep friendship. But no way could I take the sexual involvement that Les really needed. I can't say that I ever closed my eyes and thought of England, but I used fantasy to be able to cope.'

At this point Valerie had a brief affair with another man. 'I felt unattractive and asexual, and I thought, hell, I don't care! But it was such a non-event that I thought I needn't bother, it didn't help my ego.'

Then one day a girl that Les had met came to stay. 'She was very interesting and I enjoyed being with her. Then one night I got thoroughly drunk and she kissed me. I thought, wow! This is what kissing's all about! Where have I been all my life? I'd always had this feeling that something was wrong with sex, but after this experience I thought, there's not – it's absolutely fantastic.'

The girl went, leaving Valerie even more disillusioned with her marriage to Les. 'Even though I'd hardly known her, it had meant much, much more than my sexual relationship with Les. Gradually I cut off from him more and more, though I carried on having sex with him. But he knew he couldn't really turn me on in any way.'

Eventually both Valerie and Les agreed that the marriage wasn't working. 'He said we ought to do something about it: I'd told him about what had happened, and what he meant was that since lesbianism turned him on, he wanted to enter the swinging scene – threesomes; me, him and another woman. After so many years of marriage, he still meant a lot to me and interested me as a person, so I tried to convince myself that I was bisexual, and that he and I still had a good thing going for us.'

So Valerie and Les had 'threesome' sex a couple of times. 'It was disastrous. But it taught me what I wouldn't do just to save a marriage, and it made me realize, looking back, that in anything other than a one-to-one gay relationship, I'm just quite cold.'

Valerie then answered an ad from a woman in a contact magazine. 'What got me about her ad was that she said she was lonely, and I thought, well I'm lonely as well. We got together and things clicked; I was very much in love with her and probably still am.'

Shortly afterwards Les moved out on amicable terms, but the children had difficulty accepting the situation. 'One of the reasons they can't understand why Les and I can't live together, is that we're friends and don't have rows. Kay – the woman whose ad I answered – talked to my son about our relationship, because she thought it should be in the open; I wouldn't have done that – I'm very reserved. He was OK about it, but what he didn't like was that she dressed in a very mannish way and he found this embarrassing when he brought his friends round. And my youngest daughter got antagonistic because she's always had more of my attention than anyone else. The final crunch came when Kay gave up smoking and became abusive and aggressive; immediately my kids lined up behind me.'

In all, the relationship lasted about a year. 'It was very satisfying, both emotionally and sexually. I did see it as a lasting relationship, but there were so many imponderables that came between us. I know I want and need a relationship with another woman, but I have to support myself and am therefore very aware of my job; I teach near where I live, and I feel I have to be careful about what I am, even to my children's friends. I can't *really* be me.'

In the closet: Jim ♂

'I'm always terrified I'm going to be caught by the police – God, would that blow my cover. I'd have a lot of answering to do, and that would probably drive me to suicide. I've got too much to lose – my job, my wife, my kids – just for a 20-minute sexual fling. It just isn't worth it. But in my situation, being married, it just builds up to a point where you've got to get relieved by a man. You've *got* to have that involvement.'

Jim is a good-looking, fast-talking Cockney in his forties; He lives with his wife, Shirley and their three grown-up children, none of whom have any idea of the clandestine gay life he has been leading since the age of 19. 'Even though Shirley is very broadminded, there is no way I can tell her what I am. She wouldn't share me with another woman, never mind a man, so I feel it's best all round to keep the whole thing quiet and as it is.'

Jim was 18 and had been in the Royal Navy two years when he met and married Shirley. 'She was working in a shop at weekends in my home town, and I fancied her. I used to stand for hours watching her and buy things I didn't bloody need, just to have a conversation with her. She hit me, just like that. I went out with her for three months, in which time she got pregnant, so we ended up getting married before I went away to sea.'

Jim was away for thirteen months on a voyage to Australia. 'But I'm not making the lack of sex with Shirley an excuse for what happened. After all, we stopped in places like Lisbon, which has one of the most fantastic brothels in the world, and straightaway I was in there. My first homosexual experience was in Australia; God, I can remember it as clearly as if it were yesterday.'

Jim had been out for the night and was thumbing a lift back to his ship. 'A guy stopped and took me to the wrong ship. I said, "Oh, I'm ten miles further on." I think he knew it was the wrong ship, he knew what he was doing all the time. He was chatting me up and I was feeling elated. He was talking to me about being horny, and turning me on. Anyway, he parked the car and started mucking about with me. I was like a board, totally unresponsive, but I thoroughly enjoyed it.'

But when Jim got out of the car, he was very upset. 'I thought, Christ, what have I done? I'm bloody queer. And this really shook me; I didn't do anything else for six months as a result. I can remember getting worried about it, and the feeling stayed with me for many years. The fact that I did it because I wanted to and because I was excited, made me look into myself and think, I might be homosexual.'

Back home on leave Jim, now a father, had his second gay experience. 'I had been out with a gang of the lads and ended up in this bar where you could get alcohol after hours. I was in uniform and I was standing there drinking. This guy got chatting to me; he asked me if I had to go home to my wife. Then he asked me if I'd like to go on with him to another club for a drink. Right at the start I thought, come on Jim, he's queer – catch the last train home and blow out. But there was this excitement building up in me, he wanted me, I had this power over him; I felt elated, the same feeling that I'd had before, that I'd been fighting against. I thought, he doesn't know me; it's a sexual experience, something different to Shirley.'

Jim missed his train and ended up going home with the man he'd met. 'When we got to his place, he said, "Look, rather than make up the spare bed, I've got a double bed – do you mind?" I said, "No, but I'll be honest with you – I'm not experienced in any of this." 'That's all right, don't worry; I'll give you a few bob in the morning." So we ended up doing nothing heavy, but because he gave me ten quid in the morning, which in those days was a bloody lot of money, I thought, Christ – that's not bad, just for doing that. And, of course, I'd enjoyed it – but I wasn't going to admit that: if anyone had asked me, I'd have said, "Ah no, I only did it for the money; I hated doing it really."''

Again, Jim was worried. 'I thought, God, when I go back on the ship, I might start fancying blokes.' Accordingly, throughout his twenties in the Navy, Jim set out to prove with a vengeance that he was one of the lads. 'There were three main things: going for a tattoo, which I wasn't into, on to the nearest bar to get pissed out of your mind and then, if you could make it, on to a brothel. My thing was to have a quick drink, rush to the brothels and stagger back for another drink. Now I look back on it, I can see that I definitely overdid it to prove to myself I wasn't gay. I got to a point where I could go for about six weeks without thinking about men. But I knew that with a click of the fingers, I could get any fella I wanted; I could go to a gay bar and, in uniform, I was away.'

When Jim left the Navy at about 30, he initially found his gay life curtailed by life on shore. 'It wasn't easy for me to just go out and get men: I now had a proper home life, with a wife and three kids. We moved into a council house and I just didn't have the opportunity to get out for gay sex. It must have been nine months before I got into it all again. I met someone in connection with my job who openly admitted that he was gay, and who said, "Wish you were, Jim, 'cos I'd fancy you." I said, "You shouldn't jump to conclusions, just 'cos I'm married." So he invited me back for a drink and all that sort of thing.'

But Jim still felt guilty afterwards. 'There was Shirley and our life at home with the kids, and then I had this shadow, where I would go out and do my gay thing. I used to get bottled up and do all sorts of things to have gay sex. But I used to hate thinking I was gay. I didn't exactly resent the person I'd been with, but I just did not want to know them; I couldn't get out of the place quick enough.'

Nevertheless, when Jim was about 35, he found that his need for gay sex had become paramount. 'It almost took me over. By this time I had a few gay friends I could ring up. Eventually I found that I couldn't get an erection with any woman except Shirley – you see, I always kept my hand in with other women as well, to keep trying to prove to myself that I wasn't totally gay. To begin with, I thought it was because I had a guilt complex about going with other women, but then with a fella, I used to get an erection just like that. That's when I realized that I was definitely gay. Even with Shirley, I began to waver; that went on for about a year, when I couldn't do it properly. I still like to think I'm bisexual, because I sleep with Shirley, but really I know I'm not.'

Jim's reluctance to face up to his homosexuality has forced him on to the 'swinging scene'. It all began two or three years ago when he and Shirley went out for a drink with Jim's friend, Mal. 'He's married, and doesn't know a thing about my other side. He's a good-looking sod in his thirties, the butch married-looker that a lot of gay men fancy – muscular, does a lot of time under a sun lamp. Mal's a bit of a lad and can pull birds very easily. Anyway, this particular night we all got pissed, went back to his place, his wife was asleep and one thing led to another. I ended up making love to Shirley on the floor with him watching, and then he made love to her. It was only then, sitting back on the sofa watching, that I got excited; it was like watching something in 3-D. In the beginning I thought I was excited watching Shirley, but since it's happened again and again, I've thought about it a helluva lot and I've realized it's *him* I like watching. It got to the point where I wanted to join in and do things to him, but of course I couldn't, because they both think I'm straight.'

Then Jim got to know of a 'swinging' suburban car park. 'It's by a bridge and it can hold about 20 cars, plus you can park the other side of the bridge. At night it's like a National Car Park, with cars pulling in and out . . . blokes walking backwards and forwards across the bridge at about 10.30–11 p.m. . . . . There's people doing it in cars down by the riverbank in the summer, there's a loo where I dread to think what goes on, which has been raided by the police . . . If I had a free evening, I'd shoot down in the car and pick something up, just like that.'

Jim has no intention of leaving his wife. 'But now she's fed up with the Mal situation. I think it's my guilt that makes me carry on with these threesomes rather than have a regular straightforward gay thing. But even though I could ring up a gay bloke I know, it's the fresh meat I go for, pulling something new. Afterwards, thinking how desperate I've been, the hairy situations I've been in with men in cars, I break out in a cold sweat and wonder what pushed me to such extremes when I could get caught and pulled by the law. I'd have no leg to stand on.'

Out in the open: Debbie ♀

'I loved Sue very much, but I loved her husband as well; they'd both been so good and so kind to me and Bill. I just felt too guilty to carry on with her. So we had a final weekend together and she said, "You're going all the way then?" I said, "What do you mean?" She said, "You're going to turn into one of them, are you?" I was upset; I hated her for saying that. Until that weekend, I'd been fighting it, and then I thought, I'm lesbian, I've got to face that . . .'

Debbie is a quiet, maternal, softly spoken woman of 40, who recently got divorced after fifteen years of marriage; now her children, friends, neighbours and colleagues all know that she is gay.

Debbie knew as a teenager that there was 'something different' about her: 'I used to have strong crushes on friends, and lots of fantasies about my science teacher: I used to save her from this fire and she used to cuddle me afterwards.'

Nevertheless, at the age of 22, Debbie married a soldier, Bill. 'I felt sorry for him and we used to have good times together; he was due to be posted abroad again and it was a dreadful post, so we decided we'd get married.'

Bill was posted out to the Far East. 'I remember this other married girl who was out there; we didn't have a relationship or anything like that, we were just very, very good friends. We used to swim and sunbathe together, and rub oil into each other. I remember the wonderful feeling I used to get, and I knew then that something was wrong, I shouldn't be feeling like that, but I didn't know what it was.'

Debbie's doubts about herself were confirmed by the difficulties she encountered in her sexual relationships with her husband. 'I didn't enjoy it at all. He wasn't experienced and neither was I. I honestly thought there was something wrong with me – I really did, it was awful. I thought we were doing it the wrong way, because it was so painful, so I trotted off to the doctor's and he said, "Oh, it's honeymoon cystitis; here's some cream – go back and try again." I got a book about it and read up about it, and we actually managed to have sexual intercourse, as a result of which I got pregnant.'

When the baby was born, Debbie and Bill moved house and found themselves living next to another young couple with a baby; Debbie soon became firm friends with the other married woman.

'Sue and I used to do everything together, and I think she got me through that first part of my marriage. We loved each other very, very much; we used to kiss and caress each other – nothing more than that. I thought it was beautiful, and I loved her more than I loved my husband.'

This went on for two years, then Debbie and Bill got posted back to England, where the marriage took a turn for the worse. 'Bill started making sexual demands, which I didn't like very much. We used to row an awful lot. I think perhaps if he'd been more loving, I probably could have coped, but I thought the sort of things he wanted to do were kinky; I said to him that I thought it would probably be better if we tried normal sex, so we had a go and I got pregnant again!'

The marriage hit a new low and it was decided that Bill should put in for an unaccompanied tour, while Debbie went to a transit camp. 'I think that was the best eighteen months of my marriage. I was really happy and contented there, it was super. They wanted volunteers to welcome new wives and they all came to coffee mornings at my house. I had a hell of a crush on one woman, and I even spoke to her about something being wrong with me – liking women more than men. "Don't be silly," she said, and just dismissed it straightaway. So I never ever brought it up again, because I didn't want to spoil our friendship.'

Meanwhile Bill was writing love letters back to Debbie. 'They really were beautiful, they excited me. But he came home and he was still drinking; he'd always been a heavy drinker. He used to spend all his money on drink and pornographic books; I remember one day I was so frustrated, I tore all these awful pictures out and stuck them all over his car. I just wanted to get my own back on him: the day before he'd beaten me up because I wouldn't play his sex games. Anyway he came home and he nearly killed me; I had to go to the doctor's – I had cuts and bruises all over my body. They sent a car round to pick up the children; I was taken from the camp down to my sister's and Bill was put in a psychiatric hospital. I didn't know this until I got a phone call from him saying, "Please don't leave me – come and get me out of this place."'

But it was to be several months before Bill was allowed to leave, and then they were posted abroad, where they went to see a psychiatrist who specialized in sexual problems. 'He used to give us things to do, like just touching and caressing each other. Each week it would progress, but Bill wouldn't cooperate. I used to want to try, though, I really did; I wanted us both to be loving and caring. We used to go back and say we'd done it, but it was just a big charade. This went on for eighteen months and I was under my doctor all the time, just taking more and more tablets; I was drugged up to my eyeballs – I lived on valium and librium.'

But at this stage Debbie was fearful of starting divorce proceedings. 'I would have had to give the children up; they'd have been put in a home and I'd have been put in another home until such time as I could find a place for us all to live. And I just didn't want to be separated from my children – it was as simple as that. So Bill and I went on to Germany and tried again.'

In Germany, by sheer coincidence, they met up again with the couple who'd been their neighbours in the Far East. 'It was lovely to see Sue again – we really hugged and kissed each other. She had us over for the weekend; she'd got me sleeping in her bed, and Bill and her husband were in the lounge. She started quizzing me about my marriage, and I was telling her about the kind of things Bill wanted me to do; it ended up with me in tears and her cuddling me. She went further and I was frightened; I thought, no, you can't do this, this is wrong, and yet I was really excited. She said, "Don't worry about it – just relax." So we just cuddled then and went to sleep.'

The next day the men went off together and the two women were left alone. 'I remember I had this awful pain in my shoulders, so Sue rubbed this special cream that she had into them, and her hands were coming through, touching my breasts; I can remember getting really excited and shaking all over. I'd never had such strong feelings before in my life and I ended up in tears; I sobbed and cried, and she took me into the bedroom and very gently, very lovingly, made love to me. It was the most beautiful feeling in the world.'

The two women had a clandestine affair that lasted more than two years. 'But we didn't see each other all that often – only about four or five times. I couldn't ever get away, and she was miles and miles away. We had to wait until both families could get together for the weekend.'

At the end of their tour in Germany, Debbie decided to start divorce proceedings. 'I knew I was just living a farce, I knew I had to get out. The children were suffering – I mean, they saw Bill beating me up – and I suddenly thought, hell, this is damn stupid. So that was it.'

So Debbie started divorce proceedings and a long, hard fight to set herself up in a new life: she wrote to everybody she could think of – including her local MP and even the Queen – and eventually found somewhere to live and a job.

But her troubles weren't over yet. 'I had a friend at work who was on the switchboard, and one day I was talking to her about Sue and about how much I loved her, and she got in touch with her. So the next thing I know, we're going to visit her for a holiday – oh my God, what a holiday, it was beautiful.'

But Debbie felt unable to carry on with the affair behind Sue's husband's back. 'He was a terrific fellow, a gentle, loving man, and I knew it was wrong, I knew I couldn't carry on with Sue any more. It really did cut me up.'

At this point Debbie, overwhelmed by everything that had happened, tried to commit suicide. 'I remember this doctor coming to see me and asking me why I did it. So I told him that too much had happened; I said, "I'm a lesbian." And then I felt great, I really felt great. I didn't mind once I'd come out and said it. I used to hate all the lying, all the deceiving. Now there's no more pretending.'

Debbie has even told her daughter, Yvonne, and her boyfriend, Nick. 'Yvonne said to me one day, "Mum, I'm pregnant." I said, "I know, love." Nick had been living with us and they'd been sleeping in separate beds, but I caught them sleeping together and I said, "No – no way" – I didn't want it done blatantly. We had the most frightful row about it – up until then, my daughter and I had had the most super relationship. So they went to live with Nick's parents, but the minute Yvonne became pregnant, they were out, and they wanted to come back to me. So I said, "I want to speak to you both first, separately." And I took Yvonne into the kitchen and I said, "Before you come back, love, I want you to know that I'm gay; I don't want to pretend any more." And she put her arms round me and hugged and kissed me, and she said, "Mum, I knew." Then Nick came through and I said, "How do you feel about coming back here to live, when I'm gay and will probably have women here sleeping with me?" And he just held me and kissed me and said, "I know you are, Mum" – it was the first time he'd called me Mum.'

The double life: Tony ♂♂

'If you like I really have two lifestyles now. If at some point in my life I reach a stage where I want to have a relationship with a man to the exclusion of my wife and children, then I have to make a decision: is that relationship more important than what I have with my wife and kids; is it sufficiently important to make me get a divorce?'

Tony is a trendy young music executive in his early thirties, who has been married for twelve years; he spends five or six nights a week with his boyfriend and the other one or two with his wife, Lyn, and two small children. 'I pop in most afternoons or early evening just to see the children, to see my wife, to do a few jobs around the house, look after the garden, that sort of thing. I still have a life there, I'm still essentially based at my house. So they see a lot of me.'

Tony has known from his teens that he was gay. 'I had one or two very close friendships with other boys, and obviously one gets to a stage where you start experimenting. I could see them growing out of that stage and talking about girls, but I knew I wasn't interested at all in girls. But I didn't know anybody who was gay, so I had no way of discussing or exploring it.'

So eventually Tony asked Lyn out; he'd known her since he was a child. 'There came the time when she sensed that something was wrong; I knew that I was getting into a relationship and it wasn't really fair on her. One evening we had a long, emotional discussion; I told her that I was gay, that I hadn't done anything about it, but I didn't see how our relationship could get any further. She was quite taken aback, because she didn't know anything about being gay and didn't really know how to handle it. So she said, "Well, we'll just have to see what happens."'

Tony and Lyn drifted on for a few more months. 'Then we had another session – she was talking about getting engaged. By that time she sort of treated it like something that might get better or go away if we had a good enough relationship. I was quite happy with that; I hadn't had any gay experiences to equate it with, so eventually we agreed to get engaged and six months later we got married.'

To begin with, everything seemed fine. 'We made a good life together, building our little home and this kind of thing; our sex life would sort of go in fits and starts – it would be quite possible for us not to have any sex for two or three months. But she hadn't had sex before, so she had nothing to compare it with, and I hadn't either, so it was OK.'

Then a couple of years later Lyn admitted that she'd slept with Tony's best friend, Roger. 'She was very upset; she didn't know what to do. She didn't want to do anything to hurt me, it was just one of those things. I was upset, because I hadn't expected this to happen. I thought, is this the opportunity I should seize, and separate and be gay?'

But Tony didn't. 'I saw Lyn as a very warm person, who was very interested in me and who shared the same interests. We are very, very fond of each other; we hold each other, we cuddle each other a lot.'

But he did become friendly with another young man. 'He looked on me as an older brother; he was fairly dependent on me. We used to go out to pubs, etc., and we'd come back, my wife would be out somewhere, and we'd watch television or something; he'd lie on the settee and put his head on my lap. It went a bit further than that, but we didn't actually sleep together.'

The relationship was initially an important outlet for Tony. 'It was, if you like, a safety valve that enabled me not to have a full gay relationship. If I hadn't had it, I'd have been incredibly frustrated.'

But it got to the point where Tony wanted more. 'It became more and more obvious to me that in fact my little gay friend was probably not gay at all. He needed affection and probably went along with anything more because that went with it and that was what we did. I began to feel I just had to get into some kind of gay relationship.'

The feeling was underscored for Tony by the arrival of his second child. 'It made the fence round a bit higher, it cemented me in a bit more. Suddenly I'd got two children, I'd got a wife, I'd got a house, and it was fine, but it wasn't going anywhere; this was me until I grew old. I felt I ought to have a gay experience just to check that I was actually on the right course.'

Accordingly Tony took himself off to a gay disco, where he bumped into a man who'd actually been working for him for several years. 'From then on I was on cloud nine, because I had somebody who was a close friend, who was gay, who knew about me, and I was able to get all sorts of interesting insights like, "Did you know I was gay?" "No, how can you be, when you're married with kids?" We had a marvellous time that weekend; we got plastered and cuddled a bit and that was nice. It was really the first time I'd been that close to somebody who was actually gay. And after I'd held him and kissed him, I knew what I hadn't got with Lyn.'

Lyn realized that something was up. 'She had been complaining that I didn't seem as bouncy as usual – well, obviously not, I was getting a bit uptight about the whole situation. So I'd been a bit withdrawn, a bit quiet, a bit sullen perhaps, and then suddenly I was all happy. Eventually she asked me what was wrong, and I felt this was the time to say something.'

Tony and Lyn sat up most of the night discussing the situation. 'I said it was the old thing rearing its head again; I was gay and didn't know what to do about it. Big scene all round. We talked through the various options. They were that we split up straight away, which neither of us wanted to do – I didn't know what I'd be splitting up to, and I didn't want to lose the kids, or her, particularly – so that was a bit of a mess, that option. The second option was that we didn't do anything about it and I got more and more frustrated, until possibly the whole thing went wrong anyway, when it would probably be too late for me to do anything. The third option was to stay together and try and get over it; we thought this was probably the best course, because neither of us wanted to break up the family.'

So Tony and Lyn decided to open up their relationship. 'She then started coming out with, "Well I've seen Roger a few more times and you know Tim, who always seems to be around, well he's a bit more than a friend", and this sort of thing. It turned out there were at least two people she'd been with on several occasions. I'm always working, I'm never there, so she had someone she used to go shopping with on a Saturday; it wasn't necessarily a sexual thing, but it was somebody to put in my place. And those sort of things obviously developed.'

Meanwhile Tony put the new arrangement to the test with a new boyfriend, Gary. 'Lyn knows that I always go out on a Thursday night, so I would see him every week, that was easy, but then he'd say, "How about Saturday night?" And I found it difficult to turn round and say to Lyn, "Look, I'm seeing Gary three nights this week and I'm only seeing you one or two, because I'm working the others", so I had to start a certain amount of camouflaging. I would say, "Oh, I've got an appointment in town", and in fact I would be going out with Gary."

Tony's double life has evolved to the point where he now maintains two establishments. 'Lyn knows I own a flat, but I've taken the precaution of letting one room with shared use of kitchen and bathroom, so I now have a perfect camouflage, in that no one comes looking for me at the flat. Gary and I go back to the flat when we've been out and spend the night there; in the morning we both get up and go off to work.'

Tony runs his double life seven days a week. 'Gary works all day Saturday and most of Sunday, so that's convenient from the point of view that I work Saturdays, so we're not saying to each other, "Oh you're always working at the weekend." Saturday night he spends on his own, because he has to get up early on Sunday morning, so then I'm at home; Sunday I have a family day, going to lunch with parents, which is very convenient for keeping up the front, and then mid-afternoon I meet Gary and we go back to his place for a bit.'

Meanwhile Lyn's affair with Roger has developed into a more or less full-time relationship. 'They sleep together most nights of the week, because I'm not there. Now we've even reached the stage where they sleep together when I *am* there, which I'm very happy about, because it was ridiculous for them to sleep separately before.'

Although Tony appears to have found the ideal solution to his situation, he admits to having the odd nagging doubt. 'I still love Lyn and I know that she loves me. She says she needs me and the children need me, and I think in a way she's clinging to that need. If anything, that upsets me a little bit. Sometimes I doubt that what I'm doing is really the right thing for Lyn; I have the nagging suspicion that while I'm still there in whatever context, she doesn't think, oh my God, I'm on my own, I've got to go out and find somebody and build a new life – which might in the fullness of time prove to be the right thing.'

4 The older gay

♂ 'I read Peter Wildeblood's book, *Against the Law*, when it came out in 1955, and that finished me off completely – the thought of going to prison for being what I am . . . The 1967 Act served as a complete release for me; I didn't analyse it too closely, but I just thought, well they're not going to throw me in prison if they find out I'm a homosexual. And within a couple of months I'd met somebody; until then, I'd never told another human being – not a single human being really knew.'

⚥ 'I was coming home on leave, and my brother had either *New Society* or *New Statesman* – I can't remember which – and there was an advert in it for the Minorities Research Group. It said, "Are you homosexual?" And I thought perhaps I am. So I wrote off for this leaflet, and it was fantastic – I got it in time for Christmas, and it was sort of like a present. I thought, well this is me, it's how I feel. It really clicked.'

In spite of the law, under which male homosexual activity remained totally illegal until 1967, older gays who realized and accepted their homosexuality were still able to lead a fulfilling gay life, although it obviously called for the exercise of much greater discretion than is necessary nowadays – or paradoxically, for a supreme and brave disregard for caution, with the aim of leaving others in no doubt about what they were.

But there were many others who, knowing no better in their isolation, suppressed their sexuality and led cramped lives that, while devoted to an ageing parent or spouse and children, or filled with frenetic activity, were in fact sustained by dreams of lost youth, memories of schoolday or barrack-room camaraderie and fantasies that more often than not took the place of reality.

Homosexuality was a subject of which there was little public airing; what media coverage existed was patchy, ill-informed and invariably sensational, sparked off as it usually was by a seemingly endless succession of petty court cases and show trials, in which homosexuals, from the humblest to the highest, were publicly humiliated as inverts and perverts, the manifestation of a social evil which, for the public good, had at all costs to be contained.

The dynamic of change heralded by the gay liberation movement was, by comparison, light years away; today's abundance of support and counselling organizations, as yet undreamt of; gay national publications to extend a line of contact to gays up and down the country, not even conceived.

And so sadly the lives of many older gays began in a climate of doubt, guilt and above all, fear.

The climate of fear

The fear of imprisonment had a paralysing effect on many older gay men. Homosexual activity was banned in the armed forces, and it is important to realize that many older gays fought in the last war or did national service, where early feelings of guilt or fear were likely to have been reinforced, or the awakenings of self-discovery doused by incomprehension or rejection.

⚢ 'I thought I've got to get away from home, so I took myself off and joined up. And my crushes on other women continued in the ATS; I think everybody thought it was a big laugh – "Oh Ann's got a crush on so-and-so." You'd hear the odd word, you'd hear a girl say, "She's probably a lesbian", and I would think to myself, I wonder what that means. And I'd go to the library and look it up in the medical books, and I seemed to fit in with what they said; I thought, well yes – that's me. None of the girls reciprocated, they were all quite normal. Then I had a crush on one who didn't like it, because I was always hanging around, and she reported me to the chaplain. He asked me if it was true that I had these crushes, and I said yes. He said, "Well you know, it's not normal", and sent me off to the medical officer. *He* said, "This is a load of rubbish; what you should do is go out and sleep with a man and you'll be completely all right." I said, "I have no desire to sleep with a man." And he said, "Well, you're not in the right place." The next thing I knew I'd been recommended for discharge.'

⚣ 'I was called up in 1942; in France during the fighting I was very attracted to a fellow soldier ten years older than myself, but I never felt able to express my feelings. Just before my demob I was at the 7th Armoured Div. HQ, where there were German waiters; I was attracted to one of them, but although many men were fraternising with German women and displaced persons, I could never pursue the man *I* desired. The nearest I got to having sexual relations with another man was in the middle of it all, when I was sent back to Brussels on a signals revision course for three weeks; I was attracted to this man, but all we ever achieved was wrestling on the floor of the classroom.'

For many older gays then, the years leading up to the 1967 Act were years of enforced isolation and sexual repression. Forbidden an outlet by the law for their natural affections and desires, and fearing blackmail if they should defy it, they crammed their days with interests and activities that would leave them no time to think about the sexual void in their lives, sometimes creating a pattern for life.

⚣ 'My great compensation for having no sex life used to be collecting objects, well beyond my means. I'm still a collector, but I'm not nearly so obsessional: I used to be in love with an object the way other people are in love with a person, and that was the way I was able to keep sane. That energy had to go somewhere – it didn't only go into collecting, it went into writing books and articles. I still am the victim of that pattern: I've always been frightfully energetic, I've always been a workaholic - I work ridiculously hard, I reckon.'

⚣ 'I used to play a lot of table tennis and when you're playing sport it's surprising how much time it takes up – you're practising, you're playing most weekends in tournaments and league matches – so it didn't worry me that I didn't really have a particular relationship. At the beginning my parents used to say, "Oh, you've got plenty of time"; eventually they said, "Isn't it about time you got married?" I always used to come up with an answer, so in the end I think they just gave up the idea. there was absolutely no point in my telling them – they had these set ideas: anybody who was gay used to come home, change into women's clothing and then rush out and chase three-year-old children. And there was no way you were going to change that.'

Duncan recalls the stifling oppression of those pre-Act years. A tall well-spoken man of 60, with an ex-public school air, he returned from the war to join the desperate search for a job; eventually he got one in an advertising agency. 'I recognised other gays under the surface; one of them was fairly obvious – he didn't try to disguise it really. He talked about it, which nobody did in those days. And there was another man I was very attracted to, whose wife was trying to divorce him, because she said he had a male lover and frequented the Turkish baths in Jermyn Street. He flatly denied it, of course, and I didn't dare do anything – I was scared stiff.'

One of Duncan's colleagues knew he wasn't married and behaved very aggressively towards him. 'Then this girlfriend of mine, whom I'd corresponded with right through the war, rang me up one day and got him by mistake. His attitude changed completely, because he thought, oh, Duncan isn't queer after all. It was never said, that was just the implication.'

The incident underlined for Duncan the ambivalence of his position. 'This girl got terribly frustrated because I wouldn't make any advances to her; she said to me, "Are you homosexual?" And I denied it; I didn't dare say it, you see – I didn't trust anybody, even someone I knew as well as her.'

Duncan then decided to go freelance and accordingly signed up with an agency. 'They were the biggest bigots imaginable. They hated the working classes, they hated the Jews, they hated the blacks and they hated homosexuals. They prided themselves on the fact that they could sniff out a homosexual as soon as he came in through the door. One got through the net, poor devil, and he was booted out as soon as they had a good excuse. Every time I went there, I used to listen to this bigotry and argue with them; I'd say, "Heil Hitler!" as I went through the door and they used to think it was very funny, but I meant every word of it.'

Overcome by a 'morbid fear of imprisonment and the pressures of a heterosexual society', Duncan eventually fled with his mother to the seclusion of the country. 'Our living together was a sound solution to our respective rejection by society; my mother was a divorced woman and she'd been rejected by the church. My agents were my only contacts; I had no friends, I never associated with anybody in the village, and my mother was a bit quiet – liked gardening and all the rest of it. We used to have relatives to stay – little old ladies – whom I used to endure for three weeks at a time; I wasn't particularly interested in them, but at least they were people.'

Duncan's isolation was not to be broken until the Sexual Offences Act, which at last enabled him to come out of his shell. In the meantime, other gay men and women, who had not been so profoundly affected by the climate of fear, ventured on to the underground gay scene and made the most of it.

The pre-1967 gay scene

The gay scene thrived long before the 1967 Act unwittingly signalled its commercial expansion; although much less overt than today and centred almost entirely in London, it was possible for gay men and women to circulate together quite freely, so long as they recognized and obeyed unspoken rules. Very often the gay man or woman got to hear of it by word of mouth, particularly if in the Forces where, in spite of the threat of dishonourable discharge and even imprisonment, a good deal of homosexual activity went on. For some young servicemen and women, hitherto unaware of their sexuality, that very considerable threat paled before the excitement of self-discovery.

⚥ 'There was a nucleus of homosexuals in my barrack room, and I used to think it very funny and rather nice that they used to sit on each other's beds and comb each other's hair. Then one day I was in hospital in a room with a married man; I heard him crying and I said, "What's wrong?" He said, "I've been married five days; I was taken ill immediately after the ceremony and I haven't slept with my wife yet!" And I put out my hand and pulled his bed over to mine, and just put my arm round him and said, "Don't worry, it'll be OK." We were affectionate with each other; we kissed each other and wanked each other. That was it; nothing ever happened after that between us, although we became very firm friends, but it

opened my eyes. I thought, *that's* what must be happening all
around me. So I stayed awake at night and saw figures going
from one bed to another, and I suddenly realized I'd been
offered opportunities by other people in the place. I decided
which ones I was going to take up; I felt excited and fulfilled.'

♀ 'I didn't even realize that I was gay until I joined the Army,
although I'd been living with a woman I was madly in love
with. But then I saw girls dancing together and carrying on in
the NAAFI; half the new recruits thought it was awful, but I
thought it was quite natural and nice and I realized I would
have liked to join in. It just made me think.'

Outside the barracks, the gay man or woman had to learn to
identify a certain look or style of dress, and become versed in
certain catch phrases in order to make contact with other homosexuals.

♀ 'Generally women didn't wear trousers in those days – I mean,
I never had trousers, I wasn't even allowed to wear shorts –
and the only way you could really tell the lesbian women, the
butch ones, was by their collars and ties, skirt suits, flat
brogues, thick lisle stockings and short hair, mainly Eton
cropped and Brylcreemed. You could walk up and down the
King's Road then and see these masculine women and think,
"Oh yes, she must be gay" – only it wasn't "gay" then, it was
"lesbian" or "homosexual".'

♂ 'You'd have had two or three drinks and you'd have made
sure the other person had had a few more, so that you were
mentally on beam, but of course it was never said – instead of
saying, "Are you gay?" you'd say, "Have you ever been *that*
way?" And you'd know if he wasn't if he said, "Er – what did
you say?"'

Gay men socialized with each other in a variety of places,
ranging from pubs frequented by service personnel to gentlemen's
clubs, which operated a strict 'members only' policy.

♂ 'In those days there was a recognized kind of transaction
between a certain kind of rather grand queen, and guardsmen
and sailors, to which the police turned a blind eye most of the
time. There was a series of guardsmen's pubs – the Grenadier

was one of them, and the Paxton's Head was another, always known as the Pax Head and exactly opposite Knightsbridge Barracks.'

⚥ 'In a lot of the clubs there was just drinking and looking and pretending not to look and being very haughty. They were smart places; you had to give your name and address, and you had to know a homosexual to get in. Then you could take out membership and bring in guests. The clubs were practically exclusively male, and nine time out of ten run by the most terrifying dyke, who used to sit in all her glory on a stool at the bar and ban you if you behaved badly.'

The gay scene for women was much less developed and was dominated by the Gateways club, well-known to gay women throughout the world.

Norma, now in her middle fifties, recalls how she and her girl-friend, Ursula, discovered the club back in 1947. 'Ursula didn't know anything about the scene, and neither did I really; we were both very innocent. She was just an ordinary office person that I would never have dreamt was gay; she didn't even know the meaning of the word, and she didn't know that I was gay. Sex didn't even come into our relationship until we'd been together for at least nine or ten months. But we went well together, we had a good friendship, we had a lot in common; we used to go to the pictures, the theatre, that sort of thing.'

What Norma and Ursula most liked to do was go to the Chelsea Palace, which featured variety acts like Ella Shields and Hetty King, old-style male impersonators, 'who used to dance Burlington Bertie from Bow in top hat, tie and frock coat', and who fascinated the two young women. The evening would not have been complete without a visit to the pub next door, the Lord Nelson. 'We didn't have any money in those days, so we used to share a shandy and sit and watch different people coming in. We thought a lot of the women were a bit like us; they seemed to be very close. We might see one touch another, hold her hand or something. Anyway we were sitting in there one night and a man came in and joined us. He said, "You two are obviously homosexual", and we said, "Well yes, suppose we are." He said, "You

ever been to the Gateways?" "What's that?" "Oh, it's a club where
people like you go." We couldn't believe it; we didn't know such a
place existed.'

The man arranged to take Norma and Ursula to the Gateways
the following Saturday; it was a night Norma will always
remember.

'We just walked down these stairs and we both sort of nudged
one another . . . The place was full, it was mixed – half men and
half women – and you couldn't move in there. We just stood with
this man, who signed us in, and we looked round and we saw girls
dancing together and boys dancing together – it was fantastic, we
couldn't believe it. We joined then and there; it was 2s 6d a year, I
think. It was about half the size it is now, and of course they had a
piano in those days – no jukebox or anything – it was foxtrots and
waltzes, that sort of thing. And there were all these masculine
women, sitting round in their skirts down to here and their bow
ties; the people they were with looked like prostitutes – they were
very heavily made up. We found out afterwards a lot of them were.
We talked about it all day Sunday and couldn't wait to go back; I
think we must have gone down there every night for two months.'

Norma and Ursula even took dancing lessons, if they didn't
exactly dress for the part. 'We had this enormous ex-Army
motorbike, which was dark green, and because there was no
clothing or anything for motorcyclists in those days, we went
round all these Army surplus shops and bought a pair of Land
Army breeches, a pair of Navy leather sea boots and Navy oilskins.
And off we'd go on this bike, the two of us, to the Gates, where
we'd dance the waltz and foxtrot, in all our gear!'

The 'Gates', as the club was, and is, affectionately known,
became the focal point of Norma and Ursula's social life. 'A lot of
the women who went down there were very rough-looking; we
found out that they were bus conductresses or worked on the
underground, but there were two middle-aged women we quite
liked the look of, so we got quite friendly with them and they used
to include us in their crowd. And on a Saturday night, after the
Gateways shut at eleven, there was always a party somewhere; the
word would go round, "There's a party – get a bottle from the
bar." So the Gates was our life from 1947 right into the sixties.'

As well as pubs and clubs, there were other, sometimes less

salubrious meeting places for the male homosexual like, for example, certain of the London Underground's public conveniences, which enjoyed a notoriety of which most passengers must have been quite unaware.

♂ 'You could get on at South Kensington, where there was a cottage before you went in, and then there was one at Gloucester Road, where you could get off the train but you didn't have to leave the station; Parson's Green, one, without having to go through the barrier . . . And having got on at South Kensington, you could either get off at Gloucester Road or Earl's Court, and nobody knew that you'd been all the way round the Inner Circle on your threepenny ticket. And you had all those possibilities of meeting someone; you knew which ones were so far along the platform that if any of the attendants were coming, you could see them through a little hole. But those have all been closed down now; they were the best – the others were at that time being watched by plain clothes policemen.'

And then there were the celebrated Turkish baths in Jermyn Street, frequented by public figures, foreigners, 'West End people who'd stayed up gambling all night', and any other gay man on the cruise.

♂ 'You went in and there was a cash desk with an old-fashioned masseur on it – nothing handsome, nothing even particularly gay; then upstairs there was a series of bunk beds and double compartments with curtains – rather inadequate curtains; downstairs, more bunk beds, but single; downstairs again, a long steam room if you turned to your right, and then there was a kind of open space where people were massaged, and a succession of increasingly hot dry rooms. People cruised everywhere, but where they got up to anything was in the bunk beds on the first level, which were in pairs. During the day the great place for hit-and-run sex was in the furthest and hottest room, because it was out of sight of the attendants. But the baths also ran all night, and then – certainly in the early period – there was a great deal of toiling and moiling and rolling around, until they finally had a raid and tried to tighten up and then, of course, the clientele fell off.'

An implicit, but nevertheless strict code of behaviour operated.

♂ 'If you were sensible, you could do anything you wanted – all you had to do was tip. If you were well-known and polite and you'd tipped your masseur, you were all right: he could walk past my bed and know that I was in there with somebody, but he'd look at the bed on the other side. But you could have a terrible time if you didn't have a massage or were rude to the staff, or just tried to do things and expected everybody to take it. If you wanted a service, you had to pay for it. It wasn't an enormous amount; I think at the time we started going, a massage was a pound and you tipped a pound, and for that – well, you had the freedom of the house.'

Away from the pubs, clubs, saunas, etc., gay men and women also socialized in the privacy and safety of their own homes; sometimes they met through contact ads, discreetly placed in the odd music or film magazine, or even national newspaper, to catch the eye of the isolated homosexual.

♂ 'The *Sunday Times* personal column was quite astounding, because about three-quarters of it was taken up with young men wanting travel companions . . . Anyway when I was 21, I inherited a very small amount of money and my mother said, "Why don't you take a jolly good long holiday?" I said, "I've got nobody to go with," and she said, very sensibly, "Why don't you advertise for somebody?" And I think we were both very surprised by the number of replies that arrived – hundreds of them!'

Pressure for reform

Meanwhile, in deference to increasing pressure from all quarters for reform of the law, the government of the day at last agreed to set up a Home Office inquiry into the state of the law; it was chaired by Sir John Wolfenden, and his committee's cautious conclusion in 1957 that homosexuality in private could be decriminalized was the signal for battle to be joined in earnest.

The late fifties and early sixties were formative years for the gay movement, in that they saw the founding of a number of homosexual organizations which, on the amber light from Wolfenden, became active in one way or another on behalf of gay men and women. The Homosexual Law Reform Society kept up a steady pressure for change in the law and chiselled away at the public and political consciousness about homosexuality; while its sister charity, the Albany Trust, in response to the desperate need of many isolated homosexuals for support and help, later widened its role to encompass counselling, education and advice. And for gay women, whose social outlets were particularly limited, the Minorities Research Group organized social evenings, eventually superseded by the more extensive activities of its breakaway offspring, Kenric.

⚢ 'What the majority of us in MRG wanted was more of a social life, and so it was decided to split up into groups, which could get together in their own areas. As we lived in Clapham, we got put into the Southwest London and Surrey group, and there must have been about thirty of us who met one day; a lot of the people seemed to come from Richmond and quite a lot from Kensington, so we called it Kenric and formed a committee of seven there and then. We drew up a constitution and I think we started off with two activities a month in different people's houses; we went as far as getting our own Kenric rings done, with the Kenric symbol, an old Latin rune – something to do with Sappho. It was really good, Kenric getting off the ground, because there was nothing else.'

The membership, which in the beginning consisted mainly of single professional women – teachers, nurses, civil servants, etc. – grew slowly, due in large part to the considerable reluctance on the part of the media to accept homosexual advertising.

⚢ '*The Times* wouldn't take our ad because we wanted to use the word "lesbian" – this must have been about 1965; we got in the *New Statesman* at one point, but we had an awful job for ages. I think the first to take our ad was *New Society*, but we had to badger them for a long time, and then we got into the *Spectator* and after that other papers. The membership grew and grew though, until about 1969–70 we must have had 500 members and our activities had gone from say two to four a month. Although it was London-based, people joined from all over the country to get the news sheet, so that if they came to

London, they knew there was something to go to.'

The experience of Kenric demonstrates that even in the permissive sixties, public attitudes to homosexuality were slow to change; the subject remained by and large taboo – witness the mere handful of television programmes, for instance, that addressed themselves directly to the issue before the change in the law. The two most memorable depictions of homosexuals of the time occurred in two films: *Victim*, made in 1961 but not shown on television until 1968, and *The Killing of Sister George*, made later but screened in the cinema the same year. Both reinforced gay male and female stereotypes: *The Killing of Sister George* was the story of an affair between a role-playing middle-aged actress and a younger, prettier woman; the older woman is in the end dumped by both the soap opera which has made her a star, and by her lover. Hardly radical fare by the standards of today, but sensational stuff at the time.

⚢ 'I'd been talking to my mother and I said, "Oh Isabel and I are having a week's holiday to be in this film", so she said, "What's it about?" I said, "It's called *The Killing of Sister George*", thinking she wouldn't know anything about it, and she said, "Oh, it sounds as if it's to do with nuns." I said, "Well it probably is", and I thought she'd forget about it. Anyway the film came out about eighteen months later and she rang me up and said, "This film you're in – it's disgusting, absolutely disgusting!" Of course it had been blazoned across the front page of the *Evening Standard*, and she'd been going round telling her neighbours that I was in this film and it had put her in a very embarrassing position. She just had to make out to the neighbours that I'd been offered a small part in a crowd scene in the film and I'd had no idea what it was about.'

The end of the decade also saw the appearance of the first relatively uninhibited gay male magazines like *Spartacus* and *Jeremy*; and for many isolated gay men the brave new contact columns of *Spartacus* and the 'underground' paper *International Times* in particular, acted as a springboard into an exciting gay life of which they had hitherto been unaware.

♂ 'I met this chap through *Spartacus* and he actually changed my life – I mean, I'd had the occasional dabble, but I hadn't met anybody through any gay connections at all. And we got on very, very well; he was very outgoing and had a lot of contacts, so we used to go to quite a few gay parties. We got friendly with a guy called John who used to have an orgy room upstairs in his house; on the first floor there'd be a party going on, dancing and all that, and on the top floor was a room with the floor covered with mattresses. John used to have these parties regularly; he used to go to the King William IV in Hampstead and say, "Come back – party", and everybody would go with a drink. I didn't really appreciate the risk he was running; he even used to leave the front door open.'

The passing of the 1967 Sexual Offences Act and the decriminalization of homosexual acts between males over 21 in private meant different things to different older gays. For some, it was no more than a rubber stamp on the life they had been living for years in the shadow of the law, but for many others it was the signal to give vent to that part of themselves they had for so long held in check.

Duncan, whose story we began earlier in this chapter, wasted no time in embarking on his first gay affair with a painter who was giving an exhibition at a local theatre. 'I sensed that he was the same as myself; he sensed it too, and we walked out to the foyer and had a conversation in which we never declared anything at all. We discussed painting, although we were thinking about something else, and I just said, "Come and see me some time."'

Thus began a two-year relationship which was to end in emotional turmoil, all the more painful for being experienced late in life. 'I had rather a rough ride; he was completely narcissistic, completely self-interested, but he was *somebody* . . . There was no love in it at all – just sex, which lasted until he picked up a very attractive young Scot and that led to real pain and agony. The whole thing fell apart and I was in a terrible state; I reached a point of depression where I was just a walking corpse. I really was absolutely in the depths because I felt I'd lost all contact again.'

In desperation Duncan telephoned the Samaritans. 'I just couldn't speak the first time – I was too choked, so I put the receiver down and waited till the next day. Then I rang again and I said, "I'm in a terrible state and I'm a homosexual", to which this Samaritan said, "Well, I can't give up smoking", which I thought was a strange answer. Anyway I went for a meeting with a very nice, sympathetic man, but by that time I was so overwrought, I burst into tears, which I didn't want to do really – I wanted to handle the thing much more coolly, but I couldn't; I absolutely let go.'

Years of pent-up emotion came tumbling out, leaving the Samaritan somewhat nonplussed – he confessed afterwards that he knew nothing about homosexuals and, indeed, had never met one before. But he did put Duncan in touch with CHE, known then as the Committee for Homosexual Equality, and early days though they were for the organization, it managed to introduce Duncan to a girl student 'who was running a sort of thing in her room. So I trekked all the way over there to my first meeting. I breezed in – some of them were cringing in a corner – but I felt completely happy and relaxed.'

Duncan's confidence in his sexuality was boosted by the meetings, which he continued to attend throughout various changes of premises. 'We had to give up meeting at this girl's flat, but she was a strong enough personality to go round the pubs – it needed courage – to find a place for us to meet, and eventually she got the functions room of this rather squalid pub: occasionally some of us used to get accosted just outside and called "fucking queer" or something like that. This went on for a while, until the landlady got a bit stroppy and then we started meeting in any pub that would take us.'

The optimism with which Duncan had turned to CHE gradually turned to disillusionment: like many another homosexual trying to make up for lost time, he was principally interested in meeting other homosexuals, in contrast to those who were more concerned with the structure and political aims of CHE. 'We had a youngster of about 23 – very, very pedantic; he used to lay out all the rules and regulations and sit there and reel them off, and you could see the utter boredom on these gays' faces – they wanted to pick someone up, they weren't interested in the politics of CHE.'

Duncan himself had a couple of affairs, one with a music student, 'with whom I got emotionally involved, as did he to a degree, but we both knew it wasn't going to last'; and the other with 'one of those people who would ring you up the next day and tell you what a marvellous time he'd had with someone else in the bushes, which I couldn't take. I gave up going to CHE meetings, because I knew I'd meet him; I believe in, and really I've yearned for, a very deep relationship with one person.'

Increasingly, in the next few years, Duncan's attention was to be taken up with his mother, with whom he was still living. 'My relationship with my mother was never Oedipussy – in fact we were just extremely good friends throughout the years. My mother was often attacked for not allowing me to leave the nest – this angered me, as it reflected on me being too weak to break the umbilical cord, and I had been away in the Army for four and a half years and my mother was adamant that I should leave her at any time I liked. She said to me once – she was very concerned about my welfare all the time, she was a very unselfish person – "Wouldn't you like to live with another man?" And I evaded it; I said "I'd rather live on my own." I absolutely adored her: I put all my love into her and she hers into me.'

And so they continued, happy enough in their own way, until senile dementia began to creep up on Duncan's mother. 'I didn't really notice it at first; when you're living close to a person, you don't notice these things, especially when you're doing a job, and it was only when she had a complete mental black-out at breakfast time, that I began to get the message. She was then 73.'

It got to the stage where Duncan worried every time his mother went out: 'She kept losing her key and I didn't know whether she'd come back again. It was almost a relief when the poor dear's legs got so swollen that she couldn't put her shoes on; that really gave me an excuse for keeping her indoors, which was cruel in a way, because she was a prisoner then. And she couldn't get her hair done and I tried to do it for her, and in the end, it looked as if I'd just gone round with a pair of scissors – I'm not good at that sort of thing at all, contrary to the belief that we're all hairdressers. I had to cook and all the rest of it; she wanted to do it herself – she was a jolly good cook, that was the sad part about it – but I just had to do the lot.'

Things got steadily worse, to the point where Duncan was at his wits' end to know what to do. 'I used to try and play Lexicon with her, and I was more or less playing with myself – she didn't know what the hell was going on. Then she could no longer do her crossword and literally she was doing nothing all day long and the poor dear was bored; I'd get nervy and snap at her and then I'd regret it, because she'd get tearful and I'd feel an absolute bastard.'

The pressures of looking after a senile mother and being isolated from other gays built up to the point where Duncan became suicidal. 'I went to the doctor and I said, "I have these hallucinations – I look at a row of knives and they seem to be intensified in colour and shape and everything else and they sort of draw me towards them; the flat roof outside my bedroom window draws me – I want to walk out and walk and walk, right over the top." And he put me on atavan and norval and told me it would take ten days to work. So I endured ten days; I'd dread getting up and facing the day.'

Then one night Duncan's mother fell all the way down the stairs. 'I came down and there she was, all crumpled up; I thought, is she alive? I called the ambulance and they took her to hospital. She was only in four days; she was covered in bruises – and they chucked her out – back to me! I thought, how the hell am I going to manage?'

That night, the same thing happened. 'I heard a thud in the middle of the night, and I went into her bedroom and she was lying on the floor; I tried to get her back to bed and I couldn't move her. I said, "This is it. I've had enough." I went downstairs – it was four o'clock in the morning – and I rang the doctor on duty. He came and helped me put her back to bed and he said, "I'll get her admitted to the geriatric ward tomorrow." He gave her a strong sedative and she slept right to the middle of the morning when the ambulance came and she was taken away unconscious.

'I felt guilty about letting my mother go into a geriatric ward, but I had to do it. And then for nine months I went in every day and saw her, but she didn't know who I was – she was very severely demented. And that was where I met Colin – he was on the desk when I walked in the very first day, and it was immediate: I said, "That's the man for me."'

It was a case of instant and mutual attraction that developed into a relationship which is still going strong. And yet Duncan still finds himself prey to the old fears. 'You feel that you could be physically attacked if it was ever found out; I feel it more for Colin than I do for myself, because he's more obviously gay. I feel terribly angry towards even people I love because of their attitudes to homosexuals. There's this woman who knows that we're gay, but she will not accept it and if she talks about other gays in the town, it's with bated breath, as if she were saying something rude. That kind of attitude is *rampant* out here. We've got a plumber a few doors up and he said to me, "Oh there was a couple of them lesbians living here one time", and I said, "Oh yes", and I found out afterwards that a couple of gay *men* used to live here . . . It made me laugh, quite honestly, but he also said, "I heard them at it all the time", and that inhibits me, quite frankly. When Colin's here and we're together upstairs, I'm scared stiff, because you can hear through these walls and I wait – I honestly wait – for rejection from my next door neighbour. It hasn't come yet; she still smiles sweetly at me.'

But Duncan is getting past the stage of caring. 'Two single girls have just moved into the street, so I said – deliberately – to the plumber, "That's unusual", and he said, "Oh well they're probably two of them lesbians." So I said to him, "I hope they are, and good luck to them – I've got lesbian friends", and his mouth dropped open. He still talks to me, too.'

Duncan thinks it would be unwise for Colin and he to live together. 'I've got to admit that I personally miss Colin's physical presence when he's not here; I feel I've lost out to a certain extent, because I still think that if we live together under this roof, it might be difficult.'

Profiles

The promiscuous older gay: Bernard ♂

'While there may well be a majority of miserable older homosexuals who feel they're past it, who feel they never get anything pretty, there is a proportion of older male gays who do very nicely, thank you, *because* they're older. A lot of my lovers, I've come to suspect, actually like me because I'm a substantially older generation: they somehow don't feel threatened by me; they can come and go as they please, and my ego doesn't get in the way of theirs – I've learnt not to hassle them.'

Bernard is 50, an urbane and witty man, who has what he calls an 'extremely well organized' love life. 'I'd always been a keen photographer and when I moved into this flat, I decided that I would advertise for models, on the cold-blooded assumption that people are always vulnerable to being admired – exhibitionists and narcissists. In the three years I've lived here, I've taken literally thousands of photographs.'

Like many other older male gays, Bernard didn't start leading a gay life until after the 1967 Act: 'I can remember thinking, oh well, perhaps I can get on with it a bit now.' And so Bernard began an affair with a politician that lasted all of eight stormy years. 'I was absolutely mad about Geoff; I couldn't believe my luck at having got something, among other things, that everyone else wanted, because in those days he was an extremely handsome man – and very conscious of his own good looks. You'd walk along the King's Road – in the days when the King's Road was still the King's Road – and Geoff would be purring and saying out of the side of his mouth, "Did you see him clocking me?" – and they were!'

Geoff lived with another man, something Bernard closed his eyes to, as he did to the affairs he knew Geoff was having behind his back. But so long as they weren't actually conducted under his nose, Bernard could somehow cope. Then Geoff began an 'enormous' affair with one of Bernard's friends. 'It became more and more obvious and he started to play me up more and more about times and that kind of thing, and eventually I said, "Look – I can't deal with this – can we keep one night when we'll just see each other." The first night of the new arrangement, so-called – how could I be so naive – he turned up with Chris, and we were going to a show and it became very obvious in the cab what was going on. We then went out to dinner, where it became even more obvious, and the next day I just wrote Geoff a note saying that he'd always had the keys to my house, please could I have them back – now!'

Bernard got his keys back, and he and Geoff even 'picked up again, but it sort of dwindled' into a very good friendship which has lasted to this day. Not long afterwards, Bernard's present pattern of relationships evolved. 'They write to a box number and I also ask for a photograph. It's a very interesting deal, because I

always make people come and have a meal and a talk beforehand –
I never go straight into the photographic session if I can possibly
avoid it, and that gives everybody a chance to get used to the idea
of everybody else. Sometimes you click partly, occasionally you
click completely. In a way they come here for therapy. It's a
liberation, to be able to act out their sexual selves with a non-
censorious and admiring audience – I never put people down
sexually, even if I think they're dreadful. I haven't been to bed
with everybody by any means and I haven't fancied everybody who
came; sometimes there've been evenings of disaster more often
perhaps than there've been evenings of non-disaster.'

But on the whole Bernard's scheme has paid off very well – so
well, in fact, that at the moment he's pulled his ads out. 'I
suddenly thought I've got such an accumulation of nice people in
my life, I don't actually need to go on recruiting. One of my
regular partners said to me, with deep gratitude, two or three
months ago, "Oh, I do like coming here for the evening – it's so
cosy!" It's a cat basket, as we say.'

Not that Bernard is totally free of the monogamous itch. 'I
suppose my real thing is that I have a lover who lives with someone
else; he was almost the only one of my models who didn't come to
me through an ad: somebody was dared by his lover to come here,
had a tremendously good time, rang another friend of his who was
trying to raise the fare to go to America and said, "You'll have a
much better time doing this than giving French lessons - why don't
you give it a try?" And Jerry turned up; at the end of it I said,
"Oh, I wish we'd gone to bed together instead of just fooling
around like this", and he looked at me and he said, "Well, as a
matter of fact so do I" – short pause – "Never mind, I'll come
round again and we'll do it properly."'

But much as Bernard may like the idea of a one-to-one relationship, he's got used to the single life. 'Even when Jerry's here
sometimes on vacation, I do occasionally trip over him and curse,
because I'm used to doing things much more quickly, and I can't
cope with having someone else around who has to have it explained
to them. And I now have an established pattern of having a lot of
lovers and being curious and expecting to satisfy my curiosity from
time to time.'

The solitary older gay: Joan ♀

'I'm on my own now. I don't see that I shall be going into any more relationships – I think I'm too old for that. No, I just think, well when I get older and can't be doing for myself, I'll have to go in one of the old people's homes. It'd be nice if there was a gay place for us to go to – I don't fancy going to a straight one.'

Joan is 56 and has retired early from the bank where she worked for twenty years. The big regret of her retirement is that she has no one with whom to share it: she still blames herself for the break-up of a relationship that lasted 18 years. 'Jackie and I had been so happy, and then I met somebody – I suppose our relationship might have been getting a bit stale, I don't know – but I was physically attracted to this woman and went off with her. Now I look back on it, it was a terrible thing to do; I destroyed Jackie – I mean, I've had a relationship since, but she hasn't. I'm the only relationship she has ever had, and she absolutely adores me still, and all she can talk about is going back, but it wouldn't work now.'

When Jackie realized she was in danger of losing Joan, she started beating her up. 'She did have a bad temper, but it wasn't really in character, and so I used to say, "Look, if only you'd understand – I've got a thing about Angela; let me work it out, because what I really want is to be with you." But she wouldn't see it that way and every time she thought I was going out, she would follow me in the car, she'd try to run me down – oh, it was terrible. And every time I went to see Angela, I'd have a split lip, a black eye or something, and eventually she said, "You've got to leave Jackie." So I was pulled between the two.'

But in the end Joan went to Angela. 'I'd gone back home after meeting her, and I think Jackie had probably been drinking – she took to drinking when I started going out with Angela – and she really beat me up; she said she could have killed me, and she got a pair of scissors and I was petrified. How I got out of the place, I don't know. I went straight to the police; they came back to the flat – Jackie had gone – and said I was to move out. They made me pack some things and I went to my father.'

Joan set up flat with Angela and they were happy enough for several years. Then Angela changed jobs: 'She wanted to go into some sort of social work and she got a job in July 1977; apparently the first person she met was gay and took a fancy to her, so on

Christmas Day 1977, Angela walked out on me. It was out of the blue – I was completely shattered. The day before we'd been out to a disco and she'd told me how much she loved me . . . I couldn't believe it, I just went to pieces.'

Joan was so upset that she didn't feel able to return to work. 'I phoned the bank up and said I was in a bit of a state; after about a week I thought, I'll have to do something about this. So I went to the doctor's. I didn't know what to say – I was crying – and he said, "Well, I can't help you unless I know what's wrong", so I said, "I'm homosexual; my girlfriend's walked out – I'm absolutely shattered." He said, "So you're homosexual – there's nothing wrong with that", and he put me on anti-depressants. I was so bad they thought I needed some psychiatric treatment. I must have been off work for about six months; after about three months, the bank wrote to my doctor to try to find out what was wrong with me; and they showed me the letter they got back: it just said I was grieving for the loss of a very dear friend – that's all they put.'

Joan believes firmly that 'one reaps what one sows': 'Angela leaving me was paying me back for the hurt and pain I caused Jackie. In fact I wrote to her just to let her know that I suffered as she did and that until you are on the receiving end, you don't know what it's like.'

This fatalistic attitude goes some way towards explaining Joan's apparent resignation to a lonely old age, much as the thought disturbs her. 'I don't like being out of a relationship; it's very difficult – I mean, I've always been in one and the people I've been with have been more extrovert than me. Jackie was always the centre of attraction, Angela was a great talker – I was a great socializer when I was with those two, because I would go off and chat to someone, but I always had someone to go back to. I still get invited to things, but I feel lost somehow.'

The married couple: Jo and Carolyn ♀♀

'We're like an ordinary married couple really; it's just that we're two girls. We've got so used to it now, we don't really think that much about it. It's nice 'cos you sometimes don't see people for years and then you meet up with them again; you go to parties and they come up to you and they always seem to be pleased that we're still together.'

Jo is 49, a large, comfortable, easy-going woman, and Carolyn is 50, taller, thinner and more loquacious than her partner. They have been together for twenty years. They met through Kenric; Carolyn caught Jo's eye because she was wearing long green socks. 'I was in a rather nice two-piece skirt and jacket and these long socks. Oh dear!'

About a year later they decided to live together. 'We used to know loads of people down the Gates, and this particular evening we went down there and told them that we were going to live together. And I suppose it's the nearest thing we had to a kind of engagement celebration – they all went mad, it was drinks all round. And from then on we sort of established that we were a definite couple.'

But it took a while for their families to accept them as such, particularly Carolyn's mother. 'She made our life a misery at first; she just used to pick fault with Jo. I bought her a nice imitation mink fur coat one Christmas, and she said I was just bribing her, because I wanted Jo to come and stay. But it's different now; Jo went to my cousin's wedding recently and now both my mother and father just treat her as one of the family.'

Jo and Carolyn's relationship has always been monogamous. 'We're friendly with a lot of people from the past that in our younger years we had our clashes and fights and things with, but they've always sort of turned up trumps as friends. So we like people; we can both say, "Oh I think that's rather dolly" or "I saw the most gorgeous thing today", and not get jealous – we don't worry about it.'

Jo and Carolyn think their relationship has lasted because they basically get on together. 'We do more or less agree about most things; there was only one thing that we ever clashed slightly on, and that was blood sports.' But they also see themselves as opposites. 'I'm extrovert and Jo's introvert,' says Carolyn. 'If something annoys me, I'll blow my top and then I'll come down. Whereas Jo tends to keep things in a bit more; don't you – sometimes I say, "Oh you're a right donkey", because she'll really put her heels in and won't budge.' 'It's only if I really feel strongly about something,' adds Jo; 'I am what I would call a typical

Piscean – I swim away from trouble. Whereas if Carolyn loses her temper, she really does – she's Scorpio.'

This complementariness is reflected in the division of labour about their house. 'Jo's very good at cooking, and she can get things done much quicker than I can,' says Carolyn, 'so I tend to tidy up and change beds and dust.' 'I'm the one that lays the tiles and puts the shelves up,' says Jo. 'I do the electric lights, the plumbing and the decorating.'

Jo and Carolyn cannot conceive of not spending the rest of their lives together, and have made plans for their retirement. 'We'd like to go to Yorkshire,' says Carolyn, 'and start a walking and climbing place up there, where people could come and stay. And we'd like my parents to sell their house and come and live with us, so that they wouldn't have to bother with looking after themselves; they're both getting on and not too well. That's what we'd like anyway, even if it's not for years to come.'

5 The bisexual

♀♀ 'I go through phases of feeling I'm being dishonest towards Jill, because really I'm heterosexual or I'm being dishonest towards Denis, because really I'm a lesbian. You sort of assume that you're being untruthful, because you should really be one or the other. Everything I've read is always about one or the other . . . it would be nice for someone to say it's OK, you can actually have sexual and emotional relationships with two people of different sexes.'

♂♂ 'Lots of my friends said to me, "Ah, you're going to turn exclusively homosexual – aren't you worried", and I never felt that, because it would be an aberration – like to be heterosexual is an aberration. I found myself being bisexual; if I became either hetero- or homosexual, I would have failed in who I am. I couldn't go back to being heterosexual and I wouldn't want to be homosexual. It's just that it's not a full way to live for me.'

The word 'bisexual' literally means having the characteristics of both sexes, but it has come to mean, more popularly, sexually attracted to both men and women. Even this usage is far from precise, tending to mean, as we shall show, different things to different people, depending on their view of themselves, their awareness and knowledge of their own sexuality and their own individual philosophy of human relationships.

The meanings of bisexuality

Many gay men and women who have come late to their homo-sexuality – perhaps after years of leading ostensibly heterosexual lives, to the extent of acquiring spouses and children – call them-selves bisexual in an attempt to make sense of the sexual limbo they feel themselves to be in when they are no longer practising heterosexuals, as it were, but have yet fully to come to terms with their homosexuality. Others use the word in much the same way to rationalize homosexual activity or relationships with a continuing attachment to a member of the opposite sex, whether sexual, emotional or simply affectionate.

⚢ 'I suppose I think of myself as bisexual . . . It's all still so recent; I've only just started having a relationship with a woman . . . I think I would identify myself more emotionally with being a lesbian, but the fact that I'm living with a man and having a sexual relationship with him suggests to me that I'm bisexual.'

Yet others use the word as a term of convenience, preferring the shelter of its comparative neutrality to the disapproval, rejection or even downright hostility that the much more committed label 'gay' can still invite.

⚢ 'I'm more confident than I used to be about how I feel and in fact I'm trying to be more open about it to people, although I'm not screaming out to the whole world, "Hey – I think I might be gay" . . . Even so, there's a part of me that says, "You are not gay; you are not going to be gay." I've just got this terrible thing about what people are thinking . . . You know, you hear them saying, "She's *not*! *Is* she? She doesn't look it . . . Oh well – you never can tell these days!" So I do still have these nagging doubts . . . I almost think "bisexual" is better.'

Hence many out gays' open disparagement of bisexuals, who they see either as closet homosexuals reluctant to join their ranks for fear of losing their claim to the benefits of sexual conformity, or as 'swinging' heterosexuals, who do not take the gay community seriously, but instead exploit it for their own sexual ends.

The word 'bisexual' is also used to denote a feeling of curiosity about or a sense of attraction to the same sex that has not actually been translated into sexual contact or if it has, only in sporadic form. Among those who espouse this meaning of the word are men and women who are sincerely committed to bisexuality both as a principle and as a way of life. For them, it is a more flexible and positive alternative to what they see as the rigid polarity of either heterosexuality or homosexuality; it offers unique opportunities for personal growth and new ways of relating to their fellow human beings.

♂ 'My bisexuality is my capacity to love fully both men and women. It would disturb me if I ever lost that capacity; I think it's wonderful. With my combination of relationships at the moment, there's more possibility for me to become a whole person. It's only through my bisexuality I can deal emotionally, sexually, spiritually with the two halves of myself: the need to relate to men and the need to relate to women.'

♀ 'I know that if I met a woman that I was really attracted to and the relationship developed until we were at a time and in a place where it was possible for us to go to bed, I would want to do it . . . I certainly couldn't face myself, knowing that I'd been too scared to do something like that. I like to think of myself as always sticking by my principles and it's certainly one of my principles that everybody has got the potential to be attracted to, and go through with, a sexual relationship with someone of the same sex.'

The importance of self-image

The theory that we are all, men and women, bisexually predis-posed or have a bisexual potential has always enjoyed a certain currency, not to say popularity.

♂ 'I no longer believe in homosexuality or heterosexuality: I believe in an infinitely shaded gradation; I also believe that people's sexuality is very variable, both according to social pressures and the mood they're in at the time. I find that if you explore the realities about people, not merely do you find surprising amounts of homosexual experience amongst heterosexuals, sometimes confined to the growing-up period – though not always, but also that among people who are gay, or are generally thought of as gay, you find quite a number who are closet straights, occasionally. I think it's a real cheek on the part of people who are militantly heterosexual and homophobic to assume this doesn't happen. But oddly enough, I think the militant gays also feel a bit sheepish about admitting they did actually go to bed with a girl the other night; they can't quite believe that they did it – but they did.'

This kind of bemused and embarrassed reaction basically arises from having caught ourselves out – from finding that our actions contradict our perception of ourselves.

♂ 'Which side of the sex divide you fall on, despite the stigma attached to homosexuality, is curiously enough much more to do with self-image, with how you see yourself, than with what you do in bed, or how often you do it, or whether you do it with one sex only, or with both sexes.'

From this stems the emphatic assertion of homosexuals or heterosexuals who from time to time stray across the sex divide, that they are nevertheless gay or straight. The reasons they diverge, if only temporarily, from the activity normally associated with their sexual identity, may be social, political – or just plain human.

♂ 'Lots of homosexuals, for reasons to do with cash, social prestige, saving their own skins, etc., can fuck ladies quite successfully . . . I think it's also to do with companionship and cuddliness; the actual basic human warmth of that kind of thing slips under the guard of the acculturation and there's that saying, a stiff prick not listening to reason . . . there just happens to be a place to put it there and then.'

♀ 'I think in a way, if you cut men out totally from your life, you can actually lose quite a lot of enrichment . . . I like to know what men are thinking sometimes – I know what MCPs are thinking just by looking at the newspapers, but although they might represent male attitudes, underneath all that there are all these individuals. I can do it politically, but emotionally I find it difficult to say men are all a load of shits and all women are wonderful. It's a bit silly, I think . . . So it's important for me to have some male friends and maybe occasionally to sleep with them; I think the sex sometimes just sort of happens . . . It's just pure lust – just a fuck, actually.'

A point of view that many heterosexual men who indulge in homosexual activity would no doubt endorse. Although married with children, they may nevertheless enjoy intermittent sex with other men, depending on circumstances and opportunity – whether it be a spell in prison or the services, a business trip or holiday abroad.

♂ 'I see there as being a large universe of happily married, straight-looking, straight-behaving men, who would like to indulge either their fantasies and get them out of the way, or their real desires and have what I would call healthy, straightforward, relieving sexual relations with other men. I found I could treat homosexual sex very much like a game of squash – you go out and play, feel good afterwards, have a pint of beer and go home. I bet you I could make a pass at, say, five out of ten men around where I work and if they were able to shake off their inhibitions, they would find that quite acceptable.'

But at the same time it would be unlikely to change their view of themselves as heterosexual; in other words, the ability to have sex with both men and women does not necessarily make a bisexual. The word is as much a label as 'heterosexual' or 'homosexual' and the individual who chooses to pin it on him- or herself, for whatever reason, is making as much of a statement about himself as the person who declares she is heterosexual or homosexual – even if it only amounts to saying that in his eyes, he does not fit into either category.

Sexual and emotional preferences

Many bisexuals lean towards either heterosexuality or homosexuality and cite a qualitative difference between relations with the opposite sex and relations with the same sex: one or the other tends to be more emotionally significant or sexually easier. An outwardly heterosexual man, for example, while seeking other men out for homosexual acts, may at the same time suffer from a psychological or cultural block preventing him from relating to his own sex on anything other than a purely physical level. This is in accordance with the traditional pressure on males in our society not to show emotion, particularly towards each other – an inhibition that it has been acceptable to relax only in the area of intimacy with women.

♂ 'I get immensely emotionally involved with women, even on the most casual contact; I'm always falling in love – the sort of ten-minute falling-in-love – and it's wonderful. I don't get that with a man. It may be because I'm resisting it; I've always wanted to hold that off, not to get emotionally involved with a man. I just don't feel I've got the mechanism to do so.'

♂ 'Making love to a woman is a very, very emotional experience; making love with a man is a very physical experience and doesn't have to have emotion attached to it – it doesn't even have to have tenderness: it can literally be a bit of athletics between you. This particular fellow I've had something with sporadically over the years doesn't like kissing, for example – that's something he obviously keeps for his wife – but still, we can get together, maybe have a quick drink, strip off, get down to it and have really sort of lustful, healthy, laughing sex. And afterwards we can both lie back and say, "God, that was fantastic", and start talking about books, cars, wallpaper, then put on our clothes and say goodbye till next time.'

Conversely, it has always been acceptable for women to have emotional friendships with each other, no matter how intense, but not sexual relationships – again, in accordance with the socialization of females in our society not to express sexuality: a taboo that to some extent the women's movement has been successful in breaking down.

♀ 'I would be terrified if I felt that I was close to having a sexual relationship with a woman . . . I don't know why . . . partly because of the practical aspects – what would we do in bed, that sort of thing . . . It's funny, because I've always seen myself as a very strong and brave person, who would try anything. But over the last year I've been to some women-only events, a couple of discos, bars and things and I have actively started thinking, which of the women in this room do I find attractive . . . and come to the conclusion that they all look quite amazing.'

The bisexual man or woman invariably makes a distinction between sex with the same sex and sex with the opposite sex; it tends to be easier, more spontaneous, with one or the other.

♀ 'I find sex with a man very hard . . . I have to really put a lot of concentration into it. If my concentration wanders, then I've had it; there's no way I'm going to have an orgasm or anything. I'll just lie there and say, "Well, help yourself and get on with it." Whereas with a woman, it just seems to come naturally.

♂ 'I enjoy sex with a woman, but it's harder to reach a climax for me . . . I do eventually ejaculate and one thing and another, but there's always a mental block when it comes to the climax.'

For many bisexuals, there is a deep reassurance to be found in making love with their own sex; it is a process they understand and feel at home with, in contrast to the feelings of alienation and insecurity they may experience in making love with the opposite sex.

♂ 'With a man I know exactly, because I'm one myself, the sexual mechanism. I am doing something which duplicates, whereas with a woman I'm doing something which complements. I don't know her sexual process; I'm doing something which applies myself to her sexual process and she's doing the same to me. For it to be successful, the chemistries should work. With a man, there's much more of a guarantee that it will, because when you masturbate a man, when you suck a man, you know, because you've had it done to you, exactly what the delight is. And therefore, when you're getting a response, one is much more secure, much more self-assured.'

♀ 'I just feel with men it's more or less bang, bang, bang . . . It's such a violent thing that I want something softer and warmer and slower . . . I mean, once a male starts getting really turned on, there's no way he can be slow. He just tends to get faster and faster and wham-o – that's it. Sex with a woman is more loving, I think.'

But in spite of their sexual or emotional preference for their own sex, many bisexuals opt for a permanent relationship with the opposite sex.

Outwardly heterosexual

The bisexual who is outwardly heterosexual may choose to appear that way simply because it is easier to abide by social and cultural convention than to flaunt it. But at the same time he or she may also be in a relationship with a member of the opposite sex of many years' standing: a bond of intimacy, affection and familiarity that it may seem inconceivable to break.

⚥   'One of the reasons I'm with Kevin is that I've known him most of my life: I've known him since I was 10. I know what he's like to live with; I know what sort of person he is to get along with. We all dream of our perfect partner and in understanding, temperament, etc., he's as near to perfect as I'll ever find. He suits me, if you like.'

If a bond of this strength is cemented by having children, then the bisexual may well consider that no other way of life is feasible.

Kathy is 27, a housewife who lives on a council estate with her husband Mike and two young children. As she puts it, she can 'dabble either side of the fence', but that doesn't make her bisexual, let alone gay. 'I don't really think of myself as anything . . . I've never really thought about it. I suppose you could say that I am heterosexual with bisexual tendencies.'

Kathy might not even have been able to admit this much if she had not at one time run a gay pub with her then boyfriend, Jay. 'I got very friendly with a lot of the gay guys; at first I was a bit frightened of the women, just from what I'd heard. Then my best friend came to work for us; at the time she must have been about 19. And one Sunday she came up to me and said, "Kathy, I've got something to tell you." She was crying and so I said, "Well what's wrong, Fran?" She said, "I think I'm gay." I wasn't shocked; I wanted to make light of the situation – she was obviously so upset. So I said, "What do you mean, you think you're gay?" "Oh I went here last night, went there, had a drink – and when I woke up this morning, I was in bed with a woman!" So I said, "Oh wow!" – you know – "What a terrible thing!" She said, "Oh, you're not going to give me the sack, are you?" I said, "Don't be so stupid." Anyway, that was it; Fran decided she was gay and started going round with a lot of gay girls and, of course, because she and I were always together, I came to know a lot of them. And the more heavily involved I became with the gay scene, the less repulsive I found it.'

It was Jay who encouraged Kathy to take things a step further. 'You know every man's fantasy is two women in bed – or most men's . . . One evening he said to me, "Go and get Fran." So I said OK and it was really strange, because there were no ifs or buts . . . Fran got into bed with us, so we started fooling around . . . and after ten minutes Jay had crashed out, but Fran and I carried on – without him. I was very nervous and it kept running through my mind, "I don't know if I can do this." But things just progressed . . . and then Fran and I started to have this thing whenever Jay wasn't there.'

This continued for several months. 'Then we just seemed to trail off and go our separate ways . . . I mean, Fran had her other friends that she slept with and there was no jealousy or anything like that; I didn't say to her, "Oh, you're going out tonight, you're going to sleep with so-and-so." The thing with Fran and me was more like a very, very close friendship.'

Then Kathy met and married Mike. 'We got along well . . . we didn't argue . . . Everything was smooth; things were good for us sexually and it was just a nice atmosphere.' But the affair with Fran had made Kathy see things differently. 'Before, somebody could say to me, "Look at that woman – isn't she beautiful?" and I'd just say, "Oh yeah" – not even look – whereas now, somebody can say, "I think that girl is really pretty," and I can sit and admire her and it turns me on. I think, "God, I could fancy her."'

So, eighteen months into her marriage, Kathy began to feel restless. 'The feelings got so strong I felt I had to go out and get myself a woman. I was in two minds whether to tell Mike, because I didn't want to spoil our relationship.' But in the event, Kathy's fears proved unfounded. 'The only reservation he had was that he didn't want me getting heavily involved with someone, bringing them into the flat and then disrupting our family atmosphere. He said if I wanted to go out to a gay place and stay the night with someone, that was fine.'

So Kathy looked up her gay friends and made the rounds of the gay clubs again. 'I had a good time, but I never got very far with anybody. I went to one club one evening and there was a girl there and she was lovely – I mean, I've never seen such a pretty girl in all my life. I was very strongly attracted to her – danced with her for most of the evening. But she had to go home and that was it.'

Since then, Kathy has seen other women that she's fancied, but hasn't done anything about it. 'I feel that my responsibility is basically to my children and whatever I do should not interfere with them. I live here in an ordinary working class environment; most of my neighbours are married with children – what is classed as normal families. And their attitude is very, very hostile – they're disgusted by homosexuality.'

Nevertheless Kathy is looking for a woman not only for friendship, but also for sex. 'I put sex with a woman in a class all of its own . . . With Mike, I'm not a very active bed partner; I like him to be masterful and take the lead and because I love him so much, it makes it different; there's a warm feeling that goes along with it. But with a woman, I take the lead . . . I don't know a lot about it really – I just do what my mind and my body tells me to. It's very soft and very gentle; it's something very special.'

Kathy's heterosexual male counterpart may find himself in much the same position. While indulging in extensive homosexual activity on the side, it may never cross his mind to abandon the matrimonial home to go and live with another man. For him, having a wife and children is not only the 'norm' from which it would be unthinkable to depart, but also – and sometimes just as importantly – a source of emotional as well as physical security, giving him an identity and a role to play – of husband, father, breadwinner – which he may always have aspired to or taken for granted he would assume and from which he may derive deep comfort.

♂ 'I always wanted to get married and I always realized I would, all things being equal. I regard having it off with a bloke as being something which is fringe, that I can accommodate alongside my much more deep-rooted ambition to relate to, or be associated with, a woman or women.'

Hugh is a well-dressed, well-spoken businessman of 41 who has been married nearly twenty years and has two teenage children. He also enjoys what he calls 'occasional bisexual relationships' with other men.

Hugh recalls his childhood as 'disturbed': his mother died when he was very young and he was put into care. Later he was placed in a boys' boarding school, where he had a number of homosexual experiences. 'Nothing very adventurous . . . I certainly enjoyed them physically, but I realised at the time that my ultimate aim would be to have a partnership with a woman. It didn't in any way make me think, "Oh, I'm homosexual."'

A year after he left, at the age of 19, Hugh had his first sexual experience with a woman, which he found 'every bit as interesting, exciting and gratifying' as his sexual experiences with boys. He then had a succession of girlfriends. 'One girl was very keen on performing oral sex on me and I found this immensely exciting. I recall at that time beginning to reflect what it would be like to perform oral sex with a man.' But five years later, Hugh had met and married his wife.

The next seven years were taken up with setting up home and having children. 'I suppose the next move forward sexually was a period I'm told is identifiable in a lot of people's lives; they start becoming sexually a little bit adventurous, maybe starting to have affairs, when kids are out of nappies, becoming toddlers. The stage of day-and-night dealing with a young baby is past; at the same time the husband finds it boring to wade around among toys and spilt bits of leftover breakfast on the carpet – home can become a bit sordid at that stage and often he starts to wander.'

Hugh's thoughts turned to having some more homosexual experiences and so, when the opportunity arose, he made an advance to a colleague he knew was gay. 'We had some business to do, which involved us travelling together . . . We booked ourselves into an hotel, transacted the company's business and did the usual thing of having a meal together in the evening. And I just made a straightforward pass, which he found extremely surprising, because he didn't think I was at all that way inclined. So I explained to him – he was a very nice, accommodating chap – that I wanted this experience, but I didn't want it to be anything other than just experimental – if he was game. And of course he was.'

It was an experience Hugh was to repeat with his colleague several times over the next few months, though not without

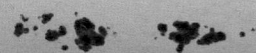

qualms. 'To begin with, I felt rather dirty and sordid. I found that in contrast to the post-orgasmic feeling with a woman, which can be extremely warm and satisfying – with a man, initially, I didn't like what I'd just done; you know, all I wanted to do was get out. But the most important thing was that he let me perform oral sex on him and to be absolutely frank, that was every bit – and remains every bit – as exciting and delicious as I thought it would be.'

At this point Hugh thought he might 'easily flip over and become completely gay.' To reassure himself that he would not, he took a renewed interest in his married sex life. 'I remember trying to make love with my wife on as many occasions as possible, having shortly before made love with my boyfriend, because to me it sort of re-established emotionally that I was, you know, married to her and all right.' At the same time Hugh began having affairs with other women. 'The sort of thing that happens when you go out to work, when you go out on your own – with colleagues, contacts, people in the business, people you meet at parties . . . But I realized I still had this homosexual inclination; I was really just waiting for the right person to come along again.'

Hugh's problem was that he really didn't know how to go about making contact with another gay or bisexual man. 'Whereas like most red-blooded men, I feel reasonably capable when it comes to meeting, chatting up and propositioning a woman, I had no experience of how to find an entrée into the gay world. I didn't want to go to a club, for example – that's not the sort of man I wanted to be with. I wanted someone like myself, with my kind of bisexual inclinations.'

Eventually Hugh met such a man, an American academic on sabbatical, married, like himself, with children. 'We were very compatible and it went extremely well. He helped me realize that the homosexual experience isn't something surrounded by guilt. It was largely coloured, I'm afraid to say, by the fact that I knew he'd shortly be departing; I didn't want the weight on me of a man who was always going to be around.' The circumstances thus enabled Hugh for the first time, as he puts it, 'to open the gates a little bit and have a much more all-round thing'; to relate emotionally, as well as sexually, to another man. 'I did get very, very fond of him . . . What he did was teach me to give much more of myself, unwind, relax . . . He was a very tender person – literally liked to gaze into my eyes, kiss, fondle – not necessarily let me get straight down to the business *I* wanted to perform. When he went, I felt very much of a gap.'

Hugh then decided to broach the subject of a threesome with his wife. 'We'd talked idly about this guy, a family friend, as being a candidate for some joint sexual experience and I had even said to my wife, "Look – you know, I sometimes get these gay twinges . . .". I then said – and this is where I went wrong – "Would you mind if I advertise to try and establish a relationship with another man." That she jibbed at, because to her that brought in the demimonde, the great world out there of herpes and horrible attacks and seediness. She felt she could accommodate it with this particular fellow, because in a way that would be all of us having a good time together.' Accordingly, a threesome was arranged. 'I didn't indulge in anything homosexual; I did what I'd always wanted to do and that was observe, and then follow, somebody making love to my wife. The nearest we got to any gay thing was when he'd withdrawn, I put a couple of Kleenex over his penis; that was just a gesture to a chum who was collapsing in a quiet heap on the bed next to us.'

Hugh's most recent homosexual experience occurred a couple of months ago, with a former colleague. They had had sex once before, when Hugh was on an extended trip abroad and had his own flat. 'He was passing through and we had a typical evening out on the town. We arrived back at my flat at three in the morning, a lot poorer, pretty well hyped up – but with nowhere to go, thinking that was that. Now I fancied him – he was a very fine specimen indeed, a very, very good-looking bloke and obviously not the slightest bit gay. But I'd probably had enough to drink to ask him – while we were sitting in the early hours of the morning, bemoaning the fact that we'd got worked up – if he'd accept the idea that he might be gratified by *me*. He did a sort of double take and I put it to him that my experience personally was that two men could enjoy sex as a sort of liberating let's-shoot-our-loads sort of thing, that it needn't be anything that wound him up; in a sense he could close his eyes and imagine it was a woman doing it to him and all that sort of thing; he needn't have any dealings with my body at all. I just put it to him absolutely like that.' Like a business deal almost, which was clinched a few minutes later. 'He said,

"Well actually I'm so horny – all right." So we turned off the lights and he pulled down his pants and jeans and I sucked him off. He then lay absolutely still and I could tell what he was thinking, so I just quietly left the room. When I came back the next day, there was a note saying, "Hugh, thanks . . .!"'

And that was that; over the next couple of years the two men had some business dealings with each other, but made no reference to what had happened. Until one day they found themselves in the same part of the world again and met for lunch. 'It was very nice – we just literally had lunch. But towards the end he suddenly said, "I've got to tell you – that was absolutely mind blowing. Would you care to do it again?" Anyway we went back to his hotel for a repeat performance.'

In Hugh's experience this kind of one-off homosexual encounter is much more possible with straight or bisexual men than with gay men. 'They want much more emotion and they appear to be much more in need of the comforting aspects of it, rather than just the straightforward thoroughgoing sex.' But Hugh remains wary of becoming emotionally involved with a man. 'I wouldn't want necessarily to relate to a man emotionally, because the samey-ness would be boring. To me, the male and female sexes are complementary; I need to have an emotional thing with women – to be balanced.'

Thus Hugh sees his life as continuing in much the same way: outwardly normal, but with regular homosexual sex on the side. 'I don't see, barring unforeseen circumstances, anything other than continuing happy marriage . . . At this particular time I'd like to have a fairly stable, occasional, discreet relationship with a like-minded bisexual male.'

Outwardly gay

Gays who go to bed or have relationships with the opposite sex do at least enjoy one advantage over their heterosexual counterparts: they are freer to do so, in that there are no social or cultural barriers to overcome; there is no taboo against heterosexuality. At most they risk the derision of militant gays. But while entertaining no doubts about their sexual orientation or the emotional strength

they draw from intimacy with their own sex, they may nevertheless feel uneasy about going out on a limb and cutting themselves off from 'half the population', as it is so often put.

⚥ 'If Martin and I finished, I think I would definitely be exclusively lesbian, but in the knowledge that if I actually found a man I liked, I would have a relationship with him . . . I don't know – in a way it sort of feels quite liberal to think you're actually responding to *people*, rather than saying, "Oh, I can't have a relationship with you because you're a man." So I think it's important that I keep myself open, even if I don't actually use the possibility.'

Those who translate the possibility into reality may do so not for political reasons, but out of a deep sense of insecurity, fostered by the heterosexual attitude that there is something abnormal about relating to the same sex.

Jude is 40 years old and a designer; she identifies herself as gay, but has 'odd now-and-then' relationships with men. This has been the pattern of Jude's relationships since her first gay affair at the age of 19. 'I still continued to sleep with men and so did my girlfriend. We didn't know any other lesbians, so we just had really good fun together and carried on as normal in the heterosexual world.' Jude then met a woman 'who was really very gay, into the gay world': 'I suddenly became cut off from my heterosexual friends and I didn't like that at all. I found it very claustrophobic, like a ghetto.'

The feeling disappeared when Jude went to university and met the man who became her husband. 'I thought, oh well, maybe I'm straight and I was quite glad actually, because it took a lot of pressure off me. It gave me security, acceptance and I also liked John very much – we were very good friends.' But after a couple of years of married life, Jude found the old attraction to women stirring again. 'I found this very exciting; I thought, I can have my heterosexual life *and* a bit of gay on the side . . . So I had a relationship with a woman and told my husband about it. He was a bit upset, but I was very clear about where my loyalties lay – to him – and it was all right.'

The relationship eventually petered out, leaving Jude feeling 'very schizophrenic': 'I felt very trapped by my husband, in the

heterosexual role of wife; I used to find heterosexual parties and dinner parties quite boring, because I was really more interested in making relationships with women. But at the same time I was quite frightened, because I didn't want them to pick up that I was gay.'

The conflict was resolved for Jude when she fell in love with another woman. 'John just went berserk. He said, "Oh I can't stand it any more, I'm not putting up with it." So I said, "Well I'm not prepared not to continue seeing her." So we agreed then that we'd have to split up, though it wasn't as rational as that – there were lots of rows and tears and God knows what.'

In the late seventies Jude finally came out as gay; at the time she had become interested in the women's movement. 'I felt very pressurized there to make a decision – and bisexuals are not liked . . . I can remember the first time I said that I was gay; I can't remember the circumstances, but I can remember the impact it had on me. It gave me quite a shock, I was quite astounded by it.'

Since then, Jude's relationships have mostly been with women, but she still seeks the company of men. 'I sometimes feel more at ease with a man socially than I do with a woman; I sometimes feel a bit self-conscious if I'm out obviously in a gay couple . . . That worries me a bit – not as much as it used to, but I still have flashes of it. I think one thing I find very difficult about lesbian relationships is really not being able to share them with somebody who isn't already a lesbian, say a colleague or whatever. So my life at times is very secret and I find that very oppressive.'

In fact Jude quite likes being with men, so long as they're not 'macho heavies'. She is attracted to 'slim men with nice bodies . . . a little bit feminine and interested in ideas and talking about relationships, films, etc.' But it is important to Jude that they accept her on her own terms: 'I can say to them, "I am gay", and they don't go, "Ooh God", but, "Oh fine."' Sometimes Jude sleeps with these men. 'It's usually when I'm feeling very turned on – but I mean I have to like them as well. I've felt sexually attracted to men and not done anything about it, but if I'm feeling particularly randy, then I might. I think it's a total fantasy really – like these dreams you sometimes have which are incredibly erotic and you're sort of on the verge of a huge orgasm and you always wake up just before you have it.'

Jude recalls the last time she slept with a man. 'He's actually married to a very nice woman; I've known him four years and when we met, we were very sexually attracted to one another. I was going through a bad time and he used to put his arms round me and I used to cry on his shoulder. But he was never sexually heavy with me at all. Then once, when his wife was away, he came round to my house to put my shelves up. And we were listening to some music, and, I don't know, there was just something in the air . . . We're very physical with one another anyway, so when he came up and put his arms round me, I just sort of knew that something had to happen.'

But Jude finds sex with men 'rather disappointing' compared to sex with women. 'Sleeping with women is much better than sleeping with men – I enjoy it more, I find it more exciting. I think it's the emotional bond . . . I tend to look for women who are a bit mothering, that I can be a little girl with.' But paradoxically, the kinds of relationships Jude has with women is one of the reasons she turns to men. 'I think it's got to do with roles . . . I tend to be attracted to women who are probably more feminine than I am; I tend to take on more of the – I don't really want to use the word "butch", 'cos it's not really like that – more of the dominant role. And sometimes I find that a bit frightening.' With men, as Jude points out, 'the mere sex act is far more dominating': 'I think it's something to do with looking for some sort of reassurance of my femininity . . . I think it's a bit neurotic and it's something I don't really like about myself in a way.'

But a gay man or woman may sometimes also form an intimate relationship with a member of the opposite sex founded on friendship and affection, while continuing to have regular contact with the same sex.

Terry is 39, an attractive, friendly man with an easy manner. He has lived with the same man for nearly twenty years. They are no longer lovers; for the last six years Terry's main sexual relationship has been with a woman. Yet, in spite of involvements with women dating from his teens, Terry has always thought of himself as gay: 'I never let it fool me for one minute.'

Terry was 17 when he experienced his first gay love and 21 when he got engaged to a girl. 'I used to go round in a crowd of gay guys

and Mandy used to be the only girl . . . And she came on holiday with us and she just used to slip into my bed and cuddle and I found myself getting very sexually aroused by her, so the next time we went away on our own for a weekend and had sex and that was it: I was engaged to her for about eight or nine months.' But Terry stopped short of actually getting married. 'I still had this dreadfully strong attraction for men; much as I tried to fight it, it was always there. There was nothing I could do about it; if I wasn't seeing Mandy, I would go out with a guy for the night.'

Then Terry met and fell in love with Graham, who was ten years older than himself. 'Within five weeks I'd given everything up and I was living with him. I had my own photography business in Manchester and was doing well, but Graham couldn't come and live in Lancashire because of his work in Yorkshire. So I sold the business and left home. And we had seven wonderful, fantastic years together – absolutely wonderful. There were no women, there were no other men – there was just Graham. I didn't go out very much; we had a nice apartment and I kind of stayed at home and did all the homely things – cooked, took the dog for a walk . . . And we had some wonderful times – I mean, times I'll never have with anybody else again.'

The bliss was broken when Terry found out that Graham had been having an affair behind his back for about a year. 'I found a letter on New Year's Eve . . . it was like some Bette Davis movie, it was terrible. It was a dreadful shock, because I'd always thought Graham was 100 per cent faithful. He said, 'Stick around – one of you will win, one of you will lose.' And like an idiot, I did stick around. Then Graham said, 'I'm giving him up,' and I said OK and we moved. But I could never ever forgive him for what he did and I couldn't forget it. I started to play the field to get my own back and in the end I hurt myself more than I hurt him and I had a complete nervous breakdown.'

When Terry got better, he took photographic assignments abroad, to try and put Graham out of his life. But they kept trying to get back together again, until eventually they settled for living together as friends. 'I can have dinner with him and his boyfriend now, very, very easily; I bring my lovers back as well and we all sit round the table together. There's no hassle, unless Graham gets a little bit pissed and doesn't like the particular person I've brought

back; then he'll let his feelings be known, but there's never been any threat to him, put it that way.'

It was through one of his lovers that Terry met Alison. He was then 33 and she 'a very immature 22'. 'She was like a little muppet – badly dressed, dreadful hair, but very intelligent. By this time I'd seen how stylish women dressed and I just transformed her in a matter of four months. I went shopping with her and told her exactly what kind of clothes to buy; we went out for dinner; I took her to a lot of concerts – Shirley Bassey, Johnny Mathis – and eventually we went on holiday together.'

It was on holiday that Terry and Alison started a sexual relationship. 'I hadn't been with anybody for two months and I was randy, so we had it off and it was very successful. But even then I was more attracted to men; I'd see somebody on the beach and think, "God, I'd really like to go to bed with him," and Alison would be lying by my side . . . It screwed me up; I didn't really want to get involved with a woman to that extent.'

So when they got back, Terry deliberately went to bed with another woman, to put Alison off him. She took the hint and on the rebound, got involved with a heterosexual man called Leslie. 'He was in the process of getting a divorce . . . He went to live with her and she told him everything about me; what we'd been to each other and how she was still in love with me. Leslie forbade her ever to see me again. But Alison sneaked out; she'd say she was going out with a girlfriend and we'd go round the shops on a Saturday afternoon or go to the cinema maybe one night a week.'

Last year Alison got pregnant by Terry and had to have an abortion. 'Leslie can't have children; when he was married, he had a sperm count and it was too low, so he'd have known Alison had slept with somebody else, who would obviously have been me. And her life with him wasn't as bad then as it is now . . . So we sat down and made the decision. It was horrendous; we would both have loved her to have had the child . . . But the time wasn't right.'

Terry doesn't know whether the time ever will be right. 'Alison and I are wonderful friends, absolutely wonderful friends . . . If I'm working late, I give her the keys to my place and when I get home, she's there. I go upstairs and have a bath; I come down; my drink's waiting for me; we sit and chat; we have a wonderful

dinner and nine times out of ten we go to bed and make love, as long as she doesn't force the issue and allows me to go to her rather than the other way round.'

Terry differentiates between sex with men and sex with Alison. 'Even though she's enjoyed it far more than I have, there's always this fantastic after thing, where I just hold her . . . Sometimes I've been to bed with guys and as soon as I've ejaculated, I've wanted to get rid of them so quick, it's a bit of a head spin. It's downright selfish, because they haven't meant a thing to me. I know it's a fact that I'm never going to see them again and they probably don't want to see me. They're using my body as I'm using theirs. But with Alison and myself, I'm not using her body and she's not using mine and that's the difference.'

Terry's homosexuality is something that Alison has come to accept. 'If I meet someone when I go out with her, as long as I arrange to meet them another night and see her home or whatever, everything's fine. We're going to go on holiday together soon for two weeks and she's put her cards on the table and said if I meet somebody and I want to go and screw him, go and screw – but come back. She said, "Over the last six years, you've always come back – you always will."'

But Terry is not so sure. 'I'd never give Alison up for anybody; I do love her, but I'm not *in* love with her and I am gay. I don't want to go to bed with another woman, although I deal with plenty of attractive women in my work. But I suppose if I met a really nice, decent gay guy that had a reasonable job, so long as he didn't want to live with me seven nights a week and I had my own independence – not sexually, but I could go out with my friends and have a good laugh and a joke – then perhaps I would revert to being completely gay.'

The avowed bisexual

In contrast to the homosexual who sleeps with the opposite sex and the heterosexual who sleeps with the same sex, there are men and women who genuinely think of themselves as bisexual. In other words, despite their sexual or emotional preference for one sex or the other, they choose to call themselves bisexual. In a society which categorizes people into either heterosexuals or homosexuals, this can sometimes be an uncomfortable position to uphold.

⚥ 'If you're gay, people accept you once they know what you are. But being bisexual, of course, you're rather in between and they don't know how to react to you. Basically you have to play the gay, even though that's not really what you want.'

⚥ 'I was always very, very confused before I realized I was bisexual. So I accept it, but I wouldn't say I was really comfortable with it, because there's not enough known about it. There's not enough faces out there – I can't go to a bisexual pub or something, there are no bisexual discos . . .'

This feeling of not belonging perhaps reflects the inner conflict that many bisexuals describe as experiencing within themselves.

⚥ 'I can't say if I had a choice, I'd be bisexual; it's not that enjoyable. Outwardly I've got to be totally heterosexual; on the other hand, I've got this other side of me that wants to be homosexual. And even when I'm having sex, I'm thinking, is this right; when I'm having sex with women sometimes, I'm thinking, well why aren't you having sex with men, and vice versa.'

Barry is a 27-year-old operations manager for a large firm and lives with his wife, Sandy and their three children, all under the age of 10. Barry classes himself as bisexual, having had homosexual experiences since he was a boy and throughout his marriage.

Marriage, for Barry, was something that more or less automatically occurred after he'd been going out with Sandy for about six months; it was hardly a love match. 'I went out with her because nobody else was and basically I felt sorry for her. I wasn't attracted to her sexually – there was something about her obviously I was attracted to, but what it was, I can't really remember.' Nevertheless Barry and Sandy have had sex twice a week for the past ten years – a rate well up to the national average. But Barry is quite frank about the reason for the apparent success of his married sex life. 'It was more of a selfish male thing – it was just a basic need. I didn't attach that much emotion to it, it was more mechanical. Basically I need more than just that, so I sought other types of sex outside.'

Barry was continuing a pattern that had begun at school, where he'd 'mucked about' with other boys. 'Thinking back on it, I tended to put a bit more into it than the others – something that obviously at that age I wasn't too sure of, but it wasn't just mucking about to me.' Barry went on to a seminary, where homosexual activity was 'part of the setup'. 'It was a very sort of spontaneous thing; it was a continual thing, like playing cricket. It wasn't exactly accepted by the college staff that that sort of thing was going on, but it was obvious.

By then Barry was also having 'heavy petting' with girls. 'I was quite attracted to girls, but that was all really . . . I still had this other darker side, which I did try to suppress, but which came out now and then.' Barry was still in his teens when he started going to public toilets and swimming pools and having sex with older men. 'It was all very secret; I think I was slightly confused, but I didn't dwell on it that much. I tended to split the whole thing down the middle in terms of the heterosexual side of me and the gay side of me. The heterosexual side was the outward, normal side; the gay side was the darker side, the sexual side – something I needed. It depended how successful I was on the heterosexual side. It even happens now, actually – if Sandy and I aren't getting on too well, I tend to look the other way.'

Barry has 'looked the other way' many times during his marriage. 'I'd say I've had sex with approximately forty or fifty men . . . With some it was more than once – especially if you went back to the same place; you virtually got the same crowd, particularly at public saunas.' As well as the saunas, there were the courses. 'I used to go away on courses and things and I'd always find some sort of involvement, usually with a male; I knew what to do and where to go, what to look for. In a group of say twenty men, even though I knew I fitted in with the heterosexuals, I could pick out the gay or bisexual men – well mostly it was gay. I didn't get emotionally involved with them, 'cos I knew it was just a week or fortnight's course and that would be it anyway.'

Sandy knew nothing of Barry's homosexual life. 'There were lots and lots of times when I would like to have said something . . . As a woman gets moody at a certain time of the month, so I would get these moods and become very, very unliveable-with; I'd try and cause an argument, so that she'd say, "Oh get out," and I

could go. And then I'd have to make excuses about where I'd been
. . . It was not very pleasant, you know – it was very, very
difficult.' But Barry was unable to resist the urge. 'There is something in you that says this is what you must get; you try to divert it,
try to suppress it. Sometimes you don't want it to come out, but it
does. It's not nice, going round trying to get picked up; it makes
me feel pretty cheap, I don't enjoy doing it at all – much nicer if I
was in a relationship.'

Barry has accordingly decided to abandon these 'sordid little
forays' and look for a male partner, 'someone who can fulfil me
emotionally.' By comparison, he sees Sandy as more of a wife,
mother and friend. 'I tend to take out from each of those which,
again, is rather a selfish thing. I like to be mothered, that sort of
thing . . . I like that closeness of the mother business, whereas on
the homosexual side, it's more of a dominant thing; the man's
more dominant with me.'

Then Barry met a man at work who helped him see his situation
in a different light. 'At first I didn't think Ian was at all gay, but
there was something else about him which I recognized in myself.
It was only when we used to talk down the pub that I realized what
it was, because he used to be quite open about bisexuality – and
that was something I hadn't actually thought about, being
bisexual.'

The two men became firm friends; Ian, like Barry, lived with a
woman and had two children. And for about a year, they had a
sexual relationship. When it ended, they continued to see each
other. 'Mentally we're on the same wavelength the whole time
anyway; I feel a certain closeness to Ian, which I don't with Sandy.
I feel better and easier and I can actually say or do anything,
whereas it's more strained with Sandy.'

Sandy noticed the difference too. 'We all went down the pub for
a drink and she said I was touching Ian more than I would another
man; not actually holding hands, but I'd put my hand on his
shoulder and there was something in the way we were looking at
each other . . . I wasn't even conscious of it.' And so Sandy found
out about Barry's bisexuality. 'Having her know was a big relief.
It's made us closer in a way; things are on a much more even keel
now between us.'

So, although there was a time when Barry was going to leave

Sandy, for the moment at least, he is staying. 'The children are an added complication; basically they're of an age when they want to know where I am when I'm not there, and obviously you do love your kids and you want to be with them. And being someone who doesn't like complications, I always go for the soft option – as long as I can carry on, you know.'

In this Barry is deriving considerable support from a bisexual group he has started to attend. 'It was worth going just to see other bisexual people; I knew there must be others about, I knew I couldn't be the only one. It's so mixed, it's unbelievable – every sort of age group . . . from every walk of life . . . just to discover that was worth it, even if we'd just sat round and said nothing all night.'

Barry now feels happier with his bisexuality. 'I don't mind being bisexual now; it's OK at the moment, but it's not something that one really likes, because you've got this imbalance, one thing fighting against the other all the time. I don't think I'll ever find the ultimate relationship, because I don't think I could ever be committed to either a man or a woman.'

In contrast to Barry, who hovers somewhat uncertainly and uncomfortably between either sex and is committed to neither, there is the bisexual who is committed to both.

Profiles

The committed bisexual: Robert ⚣

'I'm only just beginning to understand myself, who I might be. My life's task at this stage is to explore the separate strands of my bisexuality, the possibilities of different types of relationships; as I come to maturity and fulfilment in these or fail, whatever it comes to, my task is to integrate all these into the whole person. And the whole person includes my homosexuality and my heterosexuality: anything less for me is to be a cripple.'

Robert is 35 and for the past five years has been living with a woman, Paula, but describes himself as 'involved with a combination of men and women'.

Robert's background is Scots, Jewish, lower middle class and at the time 'seemed largely heterosexual'. It wasn't until his mother showed him some old family photographs, that Robert realized there might be more to his background. 'These were the first photographs I'd really seen of my father. And one of them, when I masked off the dreadful old forties hairstyle and just took in the centre of the face, was the photograph of a very beautiful sensitive gay man. I have the feeling there were more gay influences in my background than I realized until recently . . . But it's impossible to know because my father was in hospital when I was 4½ and that was the last time I saw him before he died.'

It was taken for granted by his family that Robert would marry. As Robert puts it: 'A nice young Jewish boy would want to get married; it was just a question of a nice Jewish girl.' Throughout his twenties Robert had relationships of varying lengths with women. 'There was always a thought in the back of my mind that it might just be possible that in certain circumstances, I could be physically attracted to a man. But the whole concept of being emotionally involved with a man was sick, it was disgusting. And it was that way for many years.'

Then Robert met Paula; at the time they were both inspectors of taxes. 'It started off that we met each week at taxes training centre and I got talking to her. And within about four weeks I'd invited her back for a coffee. We went to bed, but we didn't fuck . . . then I saw her two weeks later and in that time, we agreed that she was going to be my Tuesday night fuck, effectively. But it didn't work like that; I just asked her to move in and she said yes.' Robert had fallen in love. 'It was the same for Paula; it was just very deep, very intimate, very good sexually and emotionally. We were completely and consciously monogamous; we wanted to be with each other, we were very, very wrapped up in each other. We were very happy for about two years, just very cosy – two in a small flat.'

But then Robert and Paula began to feel a need for new sexual and emotional partners. 'It just grew on us . . . We've always been very honest and direct with each other, but it took us six months to get round to saying, "Look, you aren't everything to me; at the very least, I'd like the sexual excitement of a new partner." So we agreed that I'd go out and look for a girlfriend and she'd keep an eye open for a man to get involved with. I know from discussions afterwards that Paula envisaged my just finding somebody to fuck once or twice a week or whatever. But I knew I wanted much more – still from a woman. That was consciously.'

But a funny thing happened to Robert when he went out looking for a girlfriend: he joined a men's group. 'I got involved in some crèche work and came across a magazine of anti-sexist groups. And there was an advert in it for a therapy group just for men to communicate with themselves . . . and I was really interested in the idea of finding new ways to relate to men – nothing homosexual, you understand; I just wanted to get a feel for what it was like to relate to men differently from the way I had. Even though I was looking for a girlfriend, this is what I was doing, this is the way I was thinking.'

The first time Robert went along to the group there were about half a dozen men; this narrowed down to two or three. Then one day they were joined by a new member called Andy. 'I opened the door on him and it was instantaneous. I looked at him and said, "*Wow*," and he looked at me and said the same thing. Then I got into: "Come in, we need a new member, who are you, tell us about yourself – oh you're gay, that's fine." "I'm completely heterosexual", I told him, and he believed me as well. I meant it, it was completely sincere. My only concern was, would he come back next week. And that's the honest truth. It never occurred to me he'd be my first male lover – I mean, the guy was gay for Christ's sake.'

The next time the group met, Andy talked about one of his previous lovers. 'I felt a real twinge of jealousy when he said he might see him in the near future . . . At the time I pushed it aside, completely unwilling to deal with it, because I thought, I don't think like that, homosexuals think like that.' The following week just three members of the group turned up – Robert, Andy and another man called Alan. Andy got Alan and me to sit opposite each other, eyes closed, smoke some dope and just touch each other. For me that was a real shock. I had freedom to touch Alan – Andy knew what he was doing – and I was touching his legs, his thighs, and I realized I couldn't have told if they were a man's legs or a woman's legs. I wasn't sexually attracted to Alan, it was just nice – the feeling of flesh in tight jeans was nice.'

Then Andy suggested that they all say what they felt about each other. 'Andy said he was attracted to me, but he could handle it, because he understood I was heterosexual. When my turn came, I started to say that I was attracted to him, then – it's actually a very common reaction in me at very intense moments – I couldn't talk. And I realized I couldn't talk not because I couldn't acknowledge I was sexually attracted to him; that was no problem – I mean, anybody can be sexually attracted to anybody – but because I knew I was emotionally involved with him already. It was the shock of that that stopped me talking. My instinctive understanding was, my God – there's Paula, I'm committed to her; my God, I feel all this for this guy . . . I don't even know him . . . don't tell me I'm homosexual . . . What in hell is happening, it's all so complex.'

Robert and Andy made an arrangement to meet outside the group. 'I went round for a meal, but he was too nervous to cook and I was too nervous to eat. We had a cup of tea and we went upstairs and we made banal conversation for about an hour. Then – well, we just did the whole seduction scene . . . Andy kissed me – which was strange, very strange, to be kissed by a man . . . not bad, just strange . . . And I wanted a relationship with him and I was just going to say, "Look – are we going to do something," when he said, "Do you want to have a relationship with me?" And I just said yes and it was sealed.'

But Robert had yet to have sex with Andy. 'We went to bed the following weekend . . . I smoked a lot of dope which relaxed me . . . and it was really sensual, it was fantastically sensual. I was frightened of his body at first, but the feel of it against me, especially the feel of his cock against me, was really good. But the biggest sexual experience of all was the first time I sucked his cock: that was fantastic, I've never had another feeling like that.'

By this time Robert had told Paula about Andy. 'She knew . . . she'd seen that I was going to get involved with Andy; she could hear it in the way I said hello to him when I picked up the phone. At the time she wasn't terribly upset . . . Our sex life improved a very great deal . . . I was bringing in a fresh sexuality to our relationship; no longer did the standard heterosexual thing of a bit of foreplay leading to vaginal penetration apply. I had been so locked into that when I thought I was heterosexual, but gay sex really opened up my understanding of sex. We had a lot more sex which was just physical contact rather than being based on penetration and . . . really enjoyed that.'

Yet there were problems. 'Paula felt I would become exclusively homosexual and not stay involved with her, or what was happening with Andy was opening up new areas that would lock her out. We did have some difficulty in adjusting in the first few months, as I began to spend nights with Andy, but it was just something we came to terms with. And I made it clear to Andy from the beginning that I was living with Paula and she was my prime relationship.'

Robert's relationship with Andy lasted about fifteen months. 'It was a really great time; a whole new area of my life was opening up. Suddenly there were twice as many people to be attracted to, there were all sorts of possibilities. I had to cope with homosexual guilt – Andy was very good for me in fighting that, he had a very positive attitude to being gay. And there was, how do I conduct myself at work? Why are all these men suddenly flirting all around me, which I'd never seen before?'

It was with one of his colleagues that Robert next got involved. 'Steve's 24, very street-smart, working his way up . . . We got talking; it was a very difficult phase in my relationship with Andy and I needed a friend, somebody to talk to. I went round to see him; we got more and friendly and all the time I was picking up gay vibes . . . I primed him to know that I was bisexual: I let him know I had two lovers; I talked about Paula, but I never mentioned the name of my second lover. And eventually he asked and I said Andy. He was filled with an identity crisis – was he gay or heterosexual. I said, "That's shit, only idiots think like that – you're bisexual, why fight it?" And that was very good for him, because he realized he didn't have to choose between one or the other.'

Robert split up with Andy and started a relationship with Steve. 'He was into going out to gay discos . . . terrifying, mind-blowing . . . But I just really love men relating to other men when there are no heterosexuals around – they do it so differently, they're so free . . . Forget all the camp stuff and the clones and the leather gear – just when men relate to men in gay bars and clubs, there is a gentleness about them in their approach to each other; they brush against you, they touch you; it may be sexual, it may not. It's a gentleness that heterosexual men just don't know how to begin to deal with, they don't know it exists.'

Robert has an ambivalent relationship with Steve. 'To begin with, we went to bed a few times, but that wasn't successful for either of us. Although it was very emotionally intense, not much sex took place. Now we don't go to bed . . . we wrestle a bit, we occasionally kiss . . . It's not something we can handle, because neither of us is ready to deal with the emotions. We're having to find another route to deal with that.'

The route Robert and Andy have chosen is, in Robert's words, 'a little complex'. He explains: 'Steve lives with Karen, I live with Paula. Paula met Steve and they had a sexual relationship. This caused a lot of dramas, which have been smoothed out. I suggested to Steve the possibility of my having a sexual relationship with Karen, 'cos I knew she was interested. And he said he couldn't bear to happen to him what he did to me.' But then all four of them got together one evening. 'We went out for a drink first of all and we were sitting in this pub – Karen, then Steve, then me, then Paula. And there was a lot of sexuality floating around, most of it focused on me. Steve was even pawing me – he undid my fly . . . Paula was all over me . . . Then I left those two to get together and sat beside Karen. We started kissing . . . Steve and Paula had a talk for the first time in ages – oh, a lot of sexual possibilities were flowing around. We stayed together for twenty-four hours. No sex happened, we just talked, but I became aware that I could have a relationship with Karen and Steve could have a relationship with Paula.'

So they all got together again to discuss how it could work. 'We agreed everything would be open, nobody would get hurt by this; if anybody did get hurt, we'd try to take it into account, there'd be no subterfuge, no secrecy – we'd try to be as open as possible. We each had to be concerned about the other three, 'cos we were interdependent: if Steve's miserable and pulls out of it, we all lose 'cos we can't keep the balances. And there was a lot of commitment from all of us to the group, a unit of four.'

Through the group, Robert and Steve hope to unblock their own relationship. 'One of the things Steve said was that he felt that our relationship was emotionally and sexually blocked and through his involvement with Paula and mine with Karen, we would become lovers. And when I've been fully sexual with Karen, I'll be open for another man and that'll be Steve. At least I hope it will, if it all works out.'

But as far as Robert's concerned, the potential is there. 'I am entering a very exciting stage in my life with this combination of the four of us; I feel more alive, aware, fulfilled and pleasured than I ever did before.'

The feminist bisexual: Maggie ⚦

'Since I've been with Sue, I haven't had any relationships with men apart from my relationship with Pete. But it does confuse me, because when I first started having the relationship, I thought, I'm a lesbian, it's obvious; like, give up the whole present, past – just throw it out the window, it's no longer relevant – I'm a lesbian. But after the initial surprise of having that relationship with a woman, I've now decided that yes I am, I think, bisexual – physically, even though emotionally and politically I think I'm more a lesbian.'

Maggie is 26 and has been living with Pete for about six years. But for the last year she has also been having a relationship with a woman. Maggie was already living with Pete when she went up to university. While there, she went home every fortnight or Pete would come and visit her. 'I did have other emotional and sexual relationships with men on campus, but they were only ever brief affairs. When I finished university, I moved in with Pete again – that was about three years ago – and we lived together as married; I had no other relationships.'

As a student Maggie hadn't really been aware of women. 'It's amazing – all the time I was at university, even though I've always got on very well with women, for some reason I didn't get involved with the women's group. I just had this one woman friend who was very close for the whole three years and that was all. I didn't think of women other than sort of colleagues in seminars . . .'

Maggie's first job was with her local council and it brought her into direct contact with women. 'We had lots of women's groups hiring rooms, we put on exhibitions by women, and I became very friendly with lots of women in all different situations. And I suddenly realized what I'd been doing; how for some reason I'd purposely not been making friends with women; and I actually liked women a lot more than just to chat to. I found a sympathy there . . . I wasn't trying to impress them . . . cool . . . I wasn't putting on any act for them – I was

Then Maggie went to work for an all-women production company. 'I was working all the time with women who were very aware, very political . . . some of them were bisexuals, some lesbians, some heterosexual . . . so the whole time your politics and sexuality were in the office – it wasn't something you just spoke about when you went home. And I became very emotional about the whole thing, I was terribly excited; I suppose it was at that point I actually thought it would be quite interesting to have a relationship with a woman that was beyond a close friendship.'

Then a woman temporarily joined the company whom Maggie had met in her previous job. 'The minute she walked in, I recognized her, so it was, "Oh hello" – immediately we knew each other. And that was the first time I became conscious that I was actually physically drawn to this woman, that I found her very attractive, visually as well as personality-wise.' The woman, Sue, turned out to be gay and to be living in a permanent relationship with another woman. But she and Maggie became very friendly. 'I suppose I became aware that she was acting towards me in a certain way, but it completely flummoxed me – if she'd been a man, I would have known instantly what she was doing, but because she wasn't, I kept thinking, no, no, I'm completely misunderstanding this and I'm doing her a great injustice; I'm putting on her all these ideas I have in my head about macho come-ons, as it were, and I'm being very unfair to this woman.'

But then Sue invited Maggie out for a drink and back to her flat afterwards for coffee. 'And it was the same situation . . . . I was actually quite nervous about the whole thing and thought, no, I can't handle it, and sort of got up and went home . . . only for her to phone up a day later and ask me out again. I said yes and it was at that point that I knew I had made a decision; that I would have to phone her up and say no, if I didn't intend to stay the night with her, because I knew that was what was going to happen and I couldn't walk out of her flat again. It freaked me out, I was terribly, terribly nervous . . . because I didn't know if I wanted to really or whether I was just being voyeuristic or what. It got me very confused.'

Those feelings of nervousness and confusion were still with Maggie when she actually went to bed with Sue. 'I was completely floored . . . being 15 and going out with your first bloke . . . you think, how do I kiss? . . I thought, Christ, what am I supposed to *do*? Even though you know your own body and know the sensations in your own body, to actually try and recreate them on someone else, I found very unnerving. So I sort of left it to her and just imitated what she was doing. She knew I was living with a man, but she didn't realize she was the first woman I'd slept with.'

Maggie found that the relationship she'd begun with Sue impinged on her relationship with Pete. 'We went through quite a difficult period sexually – it wasn't that I suddenly found his body repulsive or anything, it was more that there was so much emotional energy going into the discovery of what a woman's body was like, I somehow almost didn't want to be bothered – I *knew* what a man's body was like, I didn't want to know any more.'

But it was difficult to explain this to Pete. 'I wanted to be terribly open with him, because it was quite important to me that this had happened, so I explained that I had got very involved with the women's movement and it was a natural extension of that. That was fine, but Pete was terribly upset by the fact that I was giving some emotional energy to someone else. I tried to explain it was a different pool of emotional energy that was going to Sue, it wasn't actually taking away from the emotional energy he'd always had. But he couldn't cope with it and became quite jealous and things at home got quite uneasy. He would go into moods and want to know what it was I wanted from my relationship with Sue and what did that say about my feelings for him.'

Likewise, Sue feels threatened by Maggie's relationship with Pete. 'Even though she knows that when we're together, I'm actually obviously very involved with her, she does get very jealous of my sexual relationship with Pete. She would be far happier if I was living with a woman: she feels it would be much easier, because her emotional jealousy – of my being with someone rather than with her – would be the same, but she wouldn't have that sexual jealousy.'

It is no easier for Maggie, in the middle between Sue and Pete. 'I go through phases of being terribly anxious and tense, because I want to see Sue more than one night a week, but can't because of the woman she lives with and because of Pete. It sort of comes and goes . . . she's very involved with h⬛⬛⬛⬛⬛⬛⬛⬛ans she goes away for two or three weeks at a time, so then I think, we're going to have to cool it; we're going to have to calm it all down so that we can both actually handle the primary relationships in our lives. But of course, when she comes back, the emotion is so strong, that doesn't work.'

Maggie confesses to feeling 'exhausted' sometimes by the two opposing emotional pulls on her. 'Because I've only known Sue one day a week for a year and Pete seven days a week for six years, I'm automatically, I think, closer to him emotionally: I've known him so much longer and we've been through a lot and done lots of things together; it's more relaxed emotionally, it's much calmer – there's no real shattering peaks as there are with Sue. It becomes quite fraught with Sue, because it's terribly intense and then I have to take it away: when I go home, I have to try and switch it off, because if I don't, I think I'm being very unfair to Pete and bringing Sue into our relationship.'

In fact Maggie has had to play her relationship with Sue right down for the sake of peace at home. 'I suppose in the end I copped out . . . Without actually saying it, I implied that sex had virtually ceased between Sue and me and that we were just very close friends . . . That's the only way I seem to have been able to play it.' Conversely, Maggie doesn't feel she can be open with her women friends about her relationship with Pete. 'I'm a real schizophrenic . . . when I go places like women's bars, I always go with a load of women, but only my very close friends know I live with Pete. I don't say to the others that I'm *not*, but I don't actually make an effort to explain my situation; I keep quiet about it, because I don't feel I've got it worked out enough in my head to be able really to justify it to someone attacking my views.'

But for the time being, Maggie sees no change in her situation. 'I can't see myself leaving Pete to go and live with Sue and equally I can't see her leaving either . . . I can't imagine being without Pete, but then I think, oh well, is that just because I'm used to him . . . At the moment he's the only bloke I really feel comfortable with and want to see; I don't feel I want to go out of my way to make more men friends. I feel that I want to put all my energy into friendships, existing and new, with women. In a year's time maybe I will change, but at the moment I don't think I want to bother emotionally

6 Gays at work

♂ 'If we as gay people are to be accepted as not being security risks, then we have not to hide these things. That doesn't mean it's plain sailing by any means, but at least if you're honest about it, you've got some personal integrity, some self-respect, and they can't complain about you deceiving them. Who you tell, after that, is entirely your affair; I think you've got to tell who you feel comfortable telling – and tell them naturally, be yourself.'

♀ 'On the one hand I think I shouldn't shelter them from it – they talk about their boyfriends, I listen to that all day, so I talk about my girlfriends; I won't keep it all hidden and undercover. But sometimes they try to find out more than I'm willing to tell them and then I don't talk about it; I only talk about everyday things that I would talk about if I had a boyfriend. I'm not prepared to discuss all the ins and outs of it, just so they can learn more.'

The majority of gay people work with and for heterosexuals and so must decide whether to come out or stay in the closet: to make known to their employers, colleagues or workmates that they are gay or keep it to themselves. Some gay men and women do not actually have a choice – those who work in the armed forces, for example, where to admit to being homosexual is automatically to be discharged. Some are in occupations where to declare their homosexuality is to forfeit promotion or access to certain posts; others are in jobs where to be gay is to be deemed unfit to practise their particular vocation.

Yet gay people have no recourse to the law if they are dismissed, demoted or passed over on the grounds of their sexual orientation; there is no legislation that protects them against the whim or prejudice of an employer. Particularly vulnerable are those gays, especially men, who work with children or young people who are commonly thought to be in greater danger of assault from homosexuals than from heterosexuals, in spite of statistics to the contrary. While there are growing signs of enlightenment among employers and unions alike, there exists, as yet, no across-the-board pro-gay policy on employment in the security of which gay people may come out without fear of losing their jobs or jeopardizing their careers.

In coming out gay people may also have to contend with everyday heterosexual prejudice ranging from outright homophobia through varying degrees of ostracism to curiosity verging on the zoological. In part such attitudes are a reflection of the state of the law whereby, for example, almost any kind of sexual activity that takes place between two men except behind closed doors, is an offence; in part, a legacy of repressive ideas about sex that linger on from Victorian times.

While today's greater openness about and tolerance of homosexuality mean that these attitudes are changing, they are slower to do so in some work situations than in others.

'I used to work on a tree-felling gang and in a manual job like that sex is talked about an awful lot more than if you work in an office . . . They were a rough lot; they used to discuss in intimate detail over a cup of tea what they did with women, and that was a pressure and a strain. Being gay was quite often mentioned; they had a sort of working man's attitude to it, which was pretty anti – they called gay people "queers" generally, that sort of thing. One of them once asked me if I ever fantasized about men – he was sort of doing a come-on – and in that kind of situation, I'd never trust anyone, because your life can be absolute hell, so I just denied it completely; it just wasn't worth it.'

By contrast, coming out in certain professional circles, for example, may be a matter almost of indifference.

'One of my colleagues and I were having a drink one lunchtime and I said I was going on leave to Germany, which is where my lover lives. He said, "That must be difficult, being involved with somebody in another country." I said yes. He said the obvious thing: "Why don't you marry her?" I said, "It's not really possible, it's not really appropriate." He looked puzzled, said, "The fact of the matter is, it's a fella." And h̶e̶ ̶... ...ightforwardly. In government service, if you're in a fairly senior position among people who are well-educated, middle-class professionals – and therefore by and large liberal – you don't get the same hassle. But there are no hard-and-fast rules; coming out is of necessity a personal decision, the timing and consequences of which are for each individual gay to judge.'

David is a 31-year-old college lecturer, who has 'deliberately come out of the closet with an absolute bang, so that everybody knows.' He started coming out while a university post-graduate student; the turning point was reading E. M. Forster's *Maurice*. 'I picked it up in a bookshop and I read the first forty pages and I couldn't believe it; I'd never read anything positive about homosexuals before in my life. And you need only to read one thing that's positive and then you know there's no going back; there's only one way out – you have to live the reality. Even if you perceive the cost as losing all your friends, the hatred of your family, the end of your career or whatever, you think, I will make it work, because it is more important to go to bed once with a man than to have all this falseness.'

It took David about two years altogether to come out, a process he completed in his present job. 'I thought well, either I start here on the right basis or I don't bother. And within a week somebody had approached the department asking for a lecturer to address the GaySoc. So I volunteered and of course posters went up all over the college. The first impression everybody had was what an amazingly liberal-minded fellow, and one of my colleagues, a great pal of mine, came into my room and sat down and said, "I see you're addressing the GaySoc, then – ha, ha, ha!" I said, "Ye-es . . ." She said, "Oh really? Oh sorry, sorry – didn't realize." From then on, there's never been any problem. I discovered that one of my other colleagues is gay and that the head of the department is gay: he's an older guy in his fifties and one effect my presence has had is that it's made him more relaxed about his sexual activity; he talks more readily now about being gay.'

David's openness about his homosexuality has also had a positive effect on some of his students. 'I've had a handful of them come to me over the years who've felt ▒▒▒▒▒▒▒▒ity to talk to me about being gay. And I've ▒▒▒▒▒▒▒▒▒▒▒ thing, because I know how they feel and I am here for them.' The reaction of straight students, David has found, is initially 'somewhat negative': 'I remember an occasion when I went to put the key in the door of my room; the corridor was crowded and as my hand came down to crutch level – 'cos the lock is at that level – the men backed away very fast. That was quite funny. But it doesn't take them long to calm down; they don't want to be negative.'

Being 'in the front line', as David puts it, does occasionally set him up as a target for malicious heterosexual gossip. 'There is a certain kind of straight woman who looks upon me as a challenge and one student – a very affected Sloaney type – decided she was going to have a bash at me. And I never see this coming, I'm green about this, even though I'm very aware of my homosexuality. We were sitting in a gay pub, just to make it very plain, and she made an enormous play for me, which eventually ended up with her saying that some student had said to her, "What would you do if David straightened out then?" And she turned to me and said, "I said I'd go to bed with him, because I think you're very attractive." I had no answer; I just don't know how to handle that. What the hell can you say?

'Unfortunately she tends to weave a web and says things which are outrageously untrue and I got hassled about it. Then I noticed that my colleagues were pulling my leg a lot over it, and it suddenly occurred to me that no one was taking her seriously, which is fortunate; it's probably the best way to deal with it.'

Heterosexual harassment is something that gay women are even more vulnerable to, on the double count not only of being female, but homosexual as well.

Angela has been an air stewardess for eight years. She applied at the age of 21, for much the same reason as many other young women: she wanted 'to be paid a lot and travel a lot'. At the time she had not yet come to terms with her homosexuality, resisting it as something 'strange and frightening'. What changed her mind was seeing the film, *Emmanuelle*: 'That really had a drastic effect on me, because there were women loving each other all the way through and having sexual relationships and treating it as a normal thing. And I suddenly decided it wasn't this awful thing I'd been fighting all

Not long after, Angela started a sexual relationship with one of the other stewardesses on the training course, with whom she also shared a house. 'Julie epitomized to me what *I* should be looking like: she looked so cool and confident, she was blonde and I thought very pretty, and she dressed really well. I just admired her, I thought she was fantastic. And we were having a dinner party and smoking pot and having lots to drink; I was desperately in love with Julie at this point, because I'd lived with her for quite a while and I think I was upset because her boyfriend was there. I got very, very drunk and went to bed in tears; she came to console me and somehow we moved up into bed with this boyfriend and he got totally left out.'

Angela and Julie had a 'fling': 'It gave me real confidence, because I knew that's what I wanted; it was all so clear after that.' Then the job forced them apart; there were other realities to face too. 'The thing with flying is that most of the people we look after are men. So constantly they're chatting you up, throwing cards at you, saying, "Give me a ring – I'll be at this hotel." Not only have you got to put up with all the passengers propositioning you, you're flying with a lot of straight men as well; you're working together in a very confined space, galleys, etc. and a lot of men touch you up, grab you, kiss you and things like that. Occasionally there'd be a really dirty old man – I mean, the pursers are getting on a bit – and you'd just have to say, "For Christ's sake, Bob – don't do that." Even a lot of the straight girls would go berserk.'

In addition Angela had to deal with prurient interest in her homosexuality. 'The reaction of straight stewards or even captains to finding out that I was gay was one of incredulity. They thought all gay women looked like lorry drivers and I was going to be terribly unhappy; I used to say that you felt more comfortable just being with a woman. But they really wanted to know what you did; I didn't really like talking about it, but what I tried to get over is that we weren't all leaping about with great big dildos and things like that.'

The reaction of other stewardesses was similarly unenlightened. 'Although they didn't say anything to my face, apparently they said quite a lot behind my back, things like, "Oh well, I'm not going in the galley when *she's* there." The were really insulting, because often you wouldn't hav   bargepole;

there's no way you fancy every single woman.'

Angela coped by making light of the situation. 'This famous golfer was on a flight once and I was in the galley and he came in and said, "I think you're gorgeous, will you marry me?" I said, "No, and if you don't get out of my galley, I'm going to throw you out." And he said to the CSO, "Gee, you get some really great girls on your flights these days."'

The golfer wasn't the only passenger to appreciate Angela's unorthodox approach. 'One said to me once, "It's good to see girls like you on the flight," and I said, "What do you mean by that?" He said, "Well I'm not one of the best people to fly, in fact I'm petrified; I hate flights where they're all pretty-pretty stewardesses, because I don't feel safe. I feel as if I'd have to save *them* if anything happened, whereas you seem as if you could help me."'

Angela thinks he has a point. 'The thing about a gay woman is that no matter what she looks like – no matter how feminine – there is something butch about her; what I mean by that is that there's something very capable about her, she's got a strength. But that means that to do a job like a waitress is difficult. Whereas a little feminine woman likes being servile and a lot of gay men enjoy it; you can tell they enjoy being doily queens, as we call them, making everything fancy and pretty and all that. But it's not the ideal job for a gay woman.'

Sadly, some of the most suitable jobs for gay women and men are also those in which they are most likely to encounter opposition to and misunderstanding of their homosexuality.

Verona is 24 and has done some form of community or social work since she left school at 16, the age at which she also had her first gay relationship. But it is only in her present job with a voluntary child care organization that Verona has come out; in previous jobs she has run into difficulties because of her homosexuality.

In her last job as a residential social worker in a children's home, for example, Verona was actually taken off a case she had been on for a year because she was known to be gay. 'I was allocated a 16-year-old girl, a very tough case; we got on extremely well, but she got into a lot of trouble and was sent to a girls' assessment hostel. And obviously she wrote to me and I wrote her back. She used to wr   you and I miss you and I'm sorry I didn't listen to you," and I used to sign my letters, "Lots of love, Verona," like I would to lots of people I don't even know very well.'

But unknown to Verona, the letters were intercepted; the first she knew of it was when she was called to a meeting with her boss. 'I was asked to resign from this girl's case; apparently she had quite a crush on me. And I was very annoyed, because I was told, "We know you're gay and we're trying to protect you." It sounded really shitty. But I agreed that I would not be the girl's case worker, although she came back several times to see me.'

Verona was so disillusioned she handed in her notice and applied for the job she currently holds: to prepare boys and girls of 17 and upwards for the outside world. 'I was so determined to get the job that I went along to the home a couple of weekends before to let them see me, knowing that I don't interview very well.' The interview did indeed turn out to be quite an ordeal. 'This particular guy was asking me very leading questions: had I worked with adolescent girls, how did I get on with them. I think he had a feeling that I was gay and wanted to know how I handled them. I said I got on with adolescent girls far better than I did with boys, I could relate to them far better, but I didn't actually explain any situations I'd got into. I didn't feel at ease and felt I couldn't say very much.'

But the interviewer wasn't satisfied. 'A burst of light hit me; I thought back to my previous visit, when two girls had been standing at the door. One of them had looked very butch and I'd thought, that girl's gay, and maybe I represented something she didn't want to be and she had said that she didn't want me coming there. My mind went back to that and I sat there and then I said, "OK yes, I am a lesbian." And I explained the problems I'd had in my last job and then I sat back, feeling very relieved – a big burden was off my shoulders.'

Verona had taken her interviewer by surprise. 'He didn't say anything; he just sat there and looked at me. Then he said, "Well, we'll give you a ring." I rode home thinking, I don't know if I've got it, but I've done it. I felt quite happy with myself.' Verona was even happier when she heard she'd got the job. 'I felt really pleased. I'd taken the risk of opening my mouth and I'd got it, my way.'

Not long after she started the job, Verona found that her honesty had indeed paid off. 'The interviewer and I were talking and he told me why he'd pushed me. It *was* because of this girl who was having an identity crisis; he said, "Had you not said what you did, you probably would not have got the job. It's important how you handle yourself and how you perceive other people." I felt quite chuffed.'

Verona was fortunate in that her homosexuality did not count against her in the end and she was able to continue in her chosen career. Others have not been so fortunate.

Bill was, until four years ago, the deputy headmaster of the local secondary school in a small provincial town. He was then 40 years of age and had twenty years in education behind him; he was also gay, but lived quietly at home with his parents. Literally overnight his life changed when he was arrested by police agent provocateurs in a public lavatory. 'It happened at about 11 p.m.; I had to go to the post office with some letters I wanted to catch the first post and I went into the toilets quite honestly for a pee – cottaging* isn't my scene at all. They were in darkness and I couldn't see anyway, because I'd just come in from the street, but I was vaguely aware of another man at one of the stalls. Then after a while he turned round, produced a warrant card and said, "You're under arrest." And another officer came out from one of the cubicles, again not in uniform, and they said that I'd turned to the first policeman and was masturbating, which was totally untrue.'

Bill was 'absolutely astounded': 'I'd said and done absolutely nothing. But I was marched out with my arm up my back, hustled into a car, taken to the police station and interviewed by a couple of policemen. They said, "We're used to dealing with prostitutes and homosexuals," and started asking me questions about my private life: how many times had I performed buggery, had I had sexual intercourse with women. I was totally open and said, "Yes, I am gay."' In due course Bill was charged under the then notorious section five of the Public Order Act with insulting words or behaviour likely to cause a breach of the peace.

On his own initiative Bill then informed his education authority

*Gay slang for the practice of going to public toilets to meet and/or have sex with other men.

of what had happened and was duly suspended. A colleague of his had recently been arrested on a similar charge and although he had been found not guilty, had been sacked by the authority and had subsequently suffered a complete nervous breakdown. 'I thought, right, you're not going to do this to me, I'm not going to give you the satisfaction; I will hand in my resignation. So they didn't sack me; I knew jolly well they would do, no two ways about it, but it would be after going through a quasi-interrogation, star chamber sort of thing and I thought, No, I've done nothing to be ashamed of.'

Bill accordingly decided to plead not guilty. 'I think it's the only time a magistrate's court has actually been adjourned to a public loo, because the policeman in the cubicle had said that he was looking through a hole in the door and could see what was happening. So they had to get permission from the council to close the toilets; there was a policeman at the door stopping anyone going in and inside there was the clerk to the court, my solicitor, the prosecuting solicitor, me, the two policemen and the three magistrates, two women and a man, who went into the cubicle to peer through this hole. I know it sounds incredible, but it's absolutely true; I said to my solicitor, "Shall we pull the chain and declare this loo well and truly opened?"'

They all went back to court and Bill was found guilty. He then instructed his solicitor to appeal and they decided to go on to a crown court; in doing so they were directly challenging the police not only on the facts of the case, but on the point that the charge against Bill was an inappropriate one. 'It was an absolutely frightening experience; I was ushered into the dock with two prison officers . . . Anyway, we actually lost there – I thought we'd won. In fact it was touch and go; I think the judge wasn't quite prepared to make such an important decision at that level.' So Bill took his case to the Royal Courts. By now he had the backing not only of the National Council for Civil Liberties and *Gay News*, but also of family and friends, whom he found 'terribly supportive'. And finally his persistence and courage paid off; his conviction was quashed and the judges ruled that it was indeed inappropriate for the police to bring such a charge against homosexuals. Bill had thus won an historic victory, as a result of which the police were no longer able to prosecute homo███████████████ five of the

Public Order Act; in addition, any homosexual so convicted in the six months prior to the ruling was able to appeal and have his conviction overturned.

While Bill is pleased that others have benefited and he has cleared his name, out of the last four years he has worked only fifteen months and he has not taught at all. 'Teaching is really the only thing I know, the one thing I love. It's difficult to explain when you've been teaching for twenty years and not in high-class areas, but ordinary down-to-earth kids, some of them the more deprived, those in trouble. To say just because you're gay, you're not fit to teach, although they won't put it in writing is really, I think, the biggest blow you can ever be dealt.'

Bill also thinks it is 'absolutely ridiculous': 'Yes, there are perverts in the gay world just as there are perverts in the straight world. But to me, gayness is not equated with perversion; the affection I have for people of my own sex is the same as that between a man and a woman, which is difficult for straights to understand. I feel for youngsters exactly the same as any father would.'

Despite his experience, Bill's advice to gay teachers is not to deny their homosexuality. 'A lot of education authorities now are prepared to say well yeah, so what. My personal advice is prove your reputation first and weigh up the ground; don't be outrageous, don't think, oh yes, I've got to be the great martyr and go standing on the school gates saying "I am gay", etc. But if you're asked, be honest: "Yes, so what?" It's surprising how many people respect that honesty.'

But for some gay people honesty is not really an option; to come out in their jobs would actually be to lose them or if not, to be cruelly ostracized.

Lyn has been in the police many years; she knew she was gay when she joined, but she had no idea then of the attitude to homosexuals within the force. 'I don't think you're aware until you're actually in the job of the bigotry of police officers – even the policewomen are bigoted. It's the job that makes you like that and you really have to guard against it. The police are supposed to be compassionate and understanding and they are to a degree, providing they're dealing with som... ...thing to do with homosexuality or colour . . . unless you're big and hairy and sweaty and drink pints of beer and have a pot belly and shag a woman every night, you're a poof.' Gay women are also dismissed with contempt. 'The word is "lez" mostly, or they might say, "She's a bit of a dyke," or, "She's butch." If you're butch, you've got to be gay – they don't realize that some of the most beautiful women can be homosexual.'

As a young policewoman, Lyn was frightened by this attitude. 'I started to get very wily, very crafty; I thought that if I was going to stay as I am, and I didn't know what else to do – I couldn't go out with men just for appearance's sake, it just wasn't me – then my private life must remain even more private than ever.'

But despite this resolution, Lyn was discovered at one point to be involved with another policewoman. 'I knew that she was particularly interested in me and at the time, I was going through great traumas with an affair that I was having, which was virtually at an end and which had knocked me for six, because I'd given everything to this particular person. I think I clutched at straws; when I knew that there was someone there that wanted me, I grabbed it. But unfortunately, I happened to write a letter to her, which you should never do, and it was found by a colleague. There was a hell of a kerfuffle about it; luckily I had a boss who was very sympathetic, very understanding and I wasn't sacked – but I could have been, very much so.'

Although she kept her job, Lyn nevertheless paid a high price for being discovered to be gay. 'Everybody knew about it; my life was hell. I knew that I was being laughed at and pointed at; even though it's not actually done like that, you can tell from someone's attitude what they're thinking. They made a ten-foot barrier round me, they didn't come anywhere near me – especially the women. I mean, no woman *dared* be in the same room as me – in case this great big terrible ogre was to jump on them, you see, and rip all their clothes off and rape them. I used to find this quite funny; I used to want to say to them, what the hell makes you think *I* fancy *you* – you're ugly, for Christ's sake, look at you.'

Lyn found her sudden isolation almost unbearable. 'I didn't have any friends, no one telephoned me; I used to sit there and I was so lonely and devastated by what had happened, that I wanted to commit suicide – I just didn't want to carry on any more.' But somehow she did. 'I went out and did _____ n't going to let them beat me. They would have liked to, I think; they didn't go out of their way to make my life hell, it was just that I was something they didn't understand; I was an alien being from a world that belonged to the dark side of sex. Luckily I've got a tremendous sense of humour and no matter what happens to me, I can always see the funny side of it: I saw the stupidity of those people and that's really what kept me going, I think.'

But it was hard. 'I did try to go on a promotion board and I knew even before I went on it, it was an absolute waste of time – I wasn't going to get anywhere. I wasn't told why – nobody ever tells you that sort of thing, because it isn't talked about – it's shoved under the carpet like prostitution.'

Lyn now 'doesn't trust anybody' and is out only to certain girlfriends in the force. 'I've made it known that I'm not a social animal as far as policemen are concerned, so I tend not to get invited to police parties or if I do, I make some excuse. It's never been easy inasmuch as I've always lived in police property, in an area where there's a lot of other policemen, and policemen's wives are the worst in the world for chattering – if you're single and you've got loads of men going in and out of your house, you're a trollop and if you haven't, you're queer or a bit odd. So I've had to go to other people's houses to do my courting; I've rarely had anybody at my house. It does put a lot of pressure on a relationship.'

So much so that Lyn conducts her present relationship almost like an undercover operation. 'We've got to be careful, because if I'm seen with her, near where she lives, then people might put two and two together. And because we know that car numbers are checked by certain colleagues of hers, I have to leave my car in a car park, so they don't suspect.'

Despite the difficulties of being gay in the police force, Lyn still thinks it's got a lot to offer a gay woman. 'It isn't a job for a gay man, not unless he's very big and butch and macho. Even so, you're expected to go out and drink with the lads after your two to ten shift or whatever, and if a man didn't do that or he started eyeing someone up, he'd soon be found out. But if a gay girl's got the ability and she's really career-minded, she can get on very well. A lot of senior women police officers tend to be homosexual: to be a success in , you've got to be unmarried – you can't do it with a family, because there are too many demands on you – and you've got to be able to push to get where you want, because it's a male-orientated job. So I would say it's a good job for a gay girl – so long as she's discreet.'

Sometimes gay people are discreet at their place of work out of fear or guilt about their homosexuality, feelings that may be exacerbated by the attitude of their heterosexual colleagues.

Joe is 29 and has worked for the Post Office for seven years. He is still coming to terms with his homosexuality and feels ill at ease in the overtly heterosexual male environment of the sorting office in which he spends much of his time. 'The rest of the men are mostly very macho – football supporters, golfers, etc. and I think they'd rather not be associated with gay people.'

Joe is not out, but his colleagues know he is not one of them. 'I don't think they picked it up consciously – I don't think I was transmitting it consciously either. But I think you do transmit anxiety or fear and maybe that's what drew their attention to me.' Joe's colleagues started making jokes about poofs in his direction. 'I used to get embarrassed about it; my face just used to go bright red, and I was very aggressive in a passive way. I can only explain it by saying I just used to create an atmosphere; I didn't want anybody to say anything, and the striking thing was that they eventually stopped the name-calling altogether – even in fun.'

But there are other incidents that serve as a constant reminder to Joe of the discomfort of his situation. 'We face up all the mail on what we call the facing table, so that it can be put through the machine, and just last week one of the cards was of two naked men embracing. And someone picked it up and started passing it around; curiously enough, they never showed it to me. But this bloke said, "Look at that, the dirty bastards – absolutely disgusting." I remember thinking at the time that it wasn't really that disgusting. But prior to being aware of the gay side of things, I could never see that two men locked together could be anything other than repugnant. But having become aware of the emotional side of the relationship between two people of the same sex, it was completely different.'

It's even worse for Joe when pornographic gay magazines land up on the facing table. 'That's a nigh͟͟͟͟͟͟͟͟͟͟͟͟͟͟͟͟͟͟͟͟ st go from hand to hand; ones showing homosexual intercourse are stuck up on the wall. All work stops and everybody gathers round to have a look. They're fascinated, but it's a send-up more than anything else – it's a laugh.'

Joe confesses to feeling 'threatened' by all this, but he also concedes that his heterosexual colleagues feel similarly threatened by his undeclared and unexplained homosexuality. 'People want to be my friend, but they don't want to be associated with homosexuality at the same time – I can see them struggling with that. One thing I've noticed is that anybody who's been with me for any length of time – walking down the street or having a cup of tea – has to go back to the security of their friends and make them aware that nothing else went on.'

But Joe is inhibited from coming out by fear: 'Fear of being rejected, ostracized, even though I've been ostracized anyway to a degree. I'm sure it would make it a lot easier for me if I did and it would make it a lot easier for them; it's the unknown quality that they're afraid of. I think if gay people are really open about their homosexuality, they're less of a threat. But I haven't got the courage.'

Coming out invariably does involve a degree of courage, and never more so when it actually involves putting a career on the line. Heterosexual reaction cannot be guaranteed to be positive.

Peter is in his mid-thirties and joined the civil service as a graduate entrant thirteen years ago. At that time the security aspect of the job gave him no cause for concern. 'It was a matter of routine to be positively vetted, because you could be in an appointment where it was a requirement. But as far as I was aware, and as far as they were aware, I was completely heterosexual. They review the position every five years and I didn't know I was gay in the first quinquennial review, but by the time of the second, there'd been this change.'

Peter was still under no real pressure to declare his homosexuality, because he was not in a security-sensitive post. Nevertheless he decided to do so. 'I had reached the point where for me not to have been honest about it would have been so lacking in moral integrity and self-respect as to make me feel I wasn't worthy to fill the j⬛⬛⬛⬛ ⬛⬛⬛⬛⬛ ⬛⬛ Because if there's one thing a public servant should have, I believe, it's complete personal integrity, and for me to have lied would have been against that principle. It would also have been a complete negation of all the sense of gay pride. I didn't have to think really; I'd got to the point where I wasn't ashamed of it and I wasn't scared of anyone knowing and I was damned if I was going to lie about it.'

In this Peter was fully backed by his union, who agreed he should be 'completely honest'. He accordingly made a declaration along the following lines: 'Since I've last been reviewed, I've had a number of sexual relationships with other men and I now consider myself, by orientation and preference, to be a homosexual. I don't consider this has any bearing upon my fitness to do my job, but I am aware that you will want to know this.' On the advice of his union, Peter added, 'I know you will take this matter further, and I wish to be informed of the outcome,' in order that if necessary, he could appeal.

But it didn't come to that. 'In fact the response was not unfriendly, not unhelpful and since then I've got promotion and my career looks reasonably good. There are potential problems, but I can live without filling certain posts. The last thing I would want, for example, is to be posted to a country with virulent and draconian anti-gay laws, like Pakistan or Iran; I would find it oppressive to be obliged to go there. But one's got to get this thing in perspective; it's an enormous organization, the civil service, and there is an awful lot of work to be done that does not require these kinds of special clearances.'

Even so, Peter admits, it is easier to come out officially from a position of seniority. 'Perversely, it's argued that it's more difficult the more senior you are, but in fact I think it's more difficult the more junior you are. I know of people who are quite junior and who have been either summarily sacked or moved to other areas. They can get away with it with a junior – they don't fight. With my seniority I can fight it; when you get to a certain level in the civil service, you're considered to be a three-dimensional human being whose needs have to be taken account of – below that, you're not considered to be a person of any great importance, frankly.'

Peter has also come out 'quite a lot' unofficially – 'Usually quite nonchalantly, in a completely haphazard way' – and was cheered by the reaction of colleagues when ▪▪▪▪▪▪▪▪▪▪▪▪▪ his lover.

'One of the women in the office said, "Are you all right – I was a bit worried," and another came and saw me a couple of days later and asked how things were. I thought it was really rather sweet; they were supportive and they were positive. I didn't expect the men to say anything, but one colleague who knows did his best to be helpful and said, "Look, you know, today is the first day of the rest of your life" – I mean, it's a corny remark, but it's a positive thing to say. And some other colleagues were suitably sympathetic – typical male camaraderie, pats on the back sort of thing. It wasn't anything to do with the fact that I was gay, it was simply that I'd been jilted; it was rather nice. In fact I think it's quite good when you can get that kind of response from people, where they are treating you just like a mirror image of themselves – it doesn't follow that you are, but when they perceive you that way, it's much better.'

7 Gay relationships

♂ 'After Dean left I was living on my own and I didn't like that. I was used to his company, which I missed very much . . . I felt rather lonely. Loneliness – or solitariness – is pretty awful, a pretty heavy burden to bear, a very difficult thing to deal with unless one is very strong.'

♀♀ 'It's interesting that I didn't mean to have a relationship with Anne: it happened quite by chance and what was most striking about it was that we were already friends, so there was a basis for the next step. No matter what happens in our lives, I can never see myself not being her friend, because no one has ever truly accepted and understood me in the same way.'

Relationships are a source of endless fascination as well as a matter of acute concern to us all, gay or straight: there are very few of us for whom to be alone is not eventually to be lonely; who don't need someone else – to share with, to give to and take from, to love and be loved by; in short, to give that emotional dimension to our lives without which they would be that much the poorer.

Gay people put a particular premium on relationships, for several reasons. It is still not as easy for them to make contact with each other as it is for heterosexuals; they cannot assume that the person working next to them or sharing a seat with them on the bus or train or drinking at the next table is also homosexual. The only places where they can be sure of meeting their own kind are gay pubs, clubs, discos, etc. and these are, in the main, with their noise, lights and emphasis on show, not the most conducive to forming relationships, let alone those of the lasting kind.

Many gays, too, harbour within themselves varying degrees of insecurity, attributable in part to society's still guarded acceptance of them and in part to their own doubts and fears about themselves, which can sometimes infuse their relationships with a brittleness that can make them particularly vulnerable to life's ups and downs.

Unlike heterosexuals, gay people cannot enter into the institution of marriage or look to it for guidance: there are no recognized vows that they can publicly take to bind them to each other; no established role models to help structure and discipline their relationships; no legal or social sanctions to stop them from straying; and no children to hold them together in the way that they do, for good or ill, some heterosexual couples.

Gay people must look to themselves and themselves alone to keep their relationships going, whereas there are various incentives for heterosexuals to stay together.

⚥ 'Just consider a difference such as this: if I fell in love with an American girl, I could marry her, and that would give me the freedom to go and work in America and to be with her, if she didn't want to live in this country. If I fell in love with an American male, no such luck. Well, I know of a number of gay relationships which have been really severely messed about simply by things like passport, visa and green card problems. That's a perfect example of straightforward inequality.'

A married couple may well be deterred from splitting up by the thought of having to face divorce proceedings, which far from being the automatic 'quickie' affair they are sometimes assumed to be, are more often a time-consuming, messy, expensive and painful business. By contrast, there is no such legal process that gay people have to undergo when they break up, although they may well have complicated joint financial arrangements to sort out. So it is easier for gay people to part than it is for heterosexuals. Nevertheless, the fact that one in three marriages ends in divorce should go some way towards putting the belief that gay relationships are especially short-lived in a proper perspective.

A decade or so ago, when gay people were not so visible and therefore not so available to each other as they are now, they were more likely to form relationships on the bond of homosexuality alone. But now, with a much more developed gay scene and a more open climate, gay people have a much greater choice of partner and a much better chance of establishing a permanent relationship.

The permanent relationship in any case is coming back into fashion; economic recession and the new political conservatism throughout the western world have made their mark on sexual mores: the eighties is the decade of sexual as well as economic retrenchment. People are more prudent about their investments – emotional as well as financial – and a relationship is now seen as a safer bet than a one-night stand.

While gay people may not have the framework of marriage to support their relationships, this is something that can work for as well as against them. They are much less likely to find themselves trapped by the legal or social structures or the role restrictions imposed on heterosexuals, and so their relationships tend to have a more natural life – to come to an end when there is no good reason for them to continue or, conversely, to last because they are inherently worth maintaining, not because they are propped up by tradition, convention or law. Thus gay relationships tend to be characterized by a greater fluidity and versatility than heterosexual relationships, and if anything, to call for a higher degree of personal commitment if they are to be successful.

⚧ 'I think a quality relationship is one that is worked on – and I really mean worked on – by two separate individuals in their own ways, from introspective points of view; and it is from the introspection that those two people come together. You can only have a quality relationship when both people have looked into themselves and have recognized what they're all about, what it is they want or need from another person and what they have to offer. I think gay people are much more likely to do this than heterosexual people. That isn't to say I don't think heterosexual people look at themselves, but because gay people have to question much more what they're all about, I think it is much more likely that they will come up with a quality relationship.'

In gay relationships, the fact that both partners are of the same sex provides a ready basis for effective communication.

⚧ 'I think because the element of understanding in a homosexual relationship is greater, our expectations are higher – we expect a woman to say, "I understand you because you are a woman," or a man, "I understand what my lover's all about, because I know what it's like to be a man." Whereas heterosexual relationships are usually supported by both partners' same-sex frien   eterosexual woman who says, "I don't understand what my husband's about and he hardly knows who I am either, but we've got the kids and the house and we go out to dinner together. But I have my girlfriends and he has his mates that he goes down the pub or shooting with." So I think you're much more likely to get some form of emotional mirroring in a homosexual relationship by virtue of the fact that you've both got tits or willies, you both have periods or you both produce sperm, you both have orgasms in the same way.'

Mirroring; adolescent and age-gap relationships

In some kinds of gay relationships, such as adolescent love affairs and relationships where a significant age-gap exists, mirroring, or a degree of reflection of one partner by the other, may form the essence of the attraction between the two people.

⚥ 'I have always felt that in youthful homosexual relationships there is an awful lot of mirroring, in that the young boy is looking very much in a narcissist way for his own reflection, and I think you're going to find this much more in homosexual than in heterosexual relationships. The young boy goes maybe for his dark counterpart who likes the same sort of thing that he does, and I think you get the same mirroring in two young girls.'

Gary is a slim, good-looking young American who fell in love for the first time at 17 with a boy a year older than himself. 'Phil was very much my mirror image; I was very infatuated, interested and attracted, because he was at the time how I thought I would like to be. He was very beautiful – androgynous, smooth-skinned, beautifully kept, beautifully groomed, quite tall – and he moved very well; he had a very nice body, in that it was very angular and very lean.'

Gary and Phil began seeing a lot of each other and eventually moved in together. 'We were both students, but we were both having trouble with school in so far as attendance and things like that were _____ ____ __ __ We ____ very similar in every way: our interests were very similar, our habits were very similar, our liabilities and assets were very similar.'

But in that very similarity lay problems for the two young men. 'We became too competitive: because we were so alike, there was a constant comparison between us which I began to dislike intensely, to a great degree because of insecure feelings in myself – fear that he was running over me, I guess.'

Sexually there were problems too. 'I was, and I think he was too, quite sexually naive at the time. Our sex life consisted of him being the passive partner and me being the active partner, mostly because he had a very passive nature sexually – not that I had such an assertive nature, but I didn't have a comfortable passive nature; I wasn't open to being the passive partner, even though he occasionally wanted me to be.'

But socially it was Phil who took the lead. 'He knew more people than I did; he was more active socially than I was, more comfortable with people than I was. So I felt quite under his wing – his sidekick – to a certain extent.'

The relationship began to falter. 'I moved out and I became very dogmatic: it was a case of me saying, in my actions and even in my words, that we have a relationship on my terms or no terms at all. He became simpering and pleading; he was *my* sidekick and I had him under *my* thumb, and obviously it didn't last very long.'

Among heterosexuals, age-gap relationships have always been common between older men and much younger women or girls. Likewise, among homosexuals, age-gap relationships are well established between older men and much younger men or boys, and are increasingly found between older women and much younger women or girls.

♀ 'I think if an older man, for example, has not had a homosexual relationship when he was younger, you may find him having a mirroring relationship with the sort of young boy he once was himself. So again, you have that narcissist interaction. I don't find as many women go for women outside their own age grouping, but I do think you get that mirroring in an older woman who, again, has never had in her teens that kind of the-only-way-that-adolescents-can-love affair with a young girl. I also think with a woman who hasn't had a child because she's gay, the mother[...]fined, though not necessarily in her own mind, as, "I want to have a young lover/baby." This applies to gay men who don't have children too, and I think that conditions our need for mirroring.'

If we resume Gary's life-story, we shall see how an age-gap relationship works from the younger partner's point of view. About a year after his relationship with Phil had ended, Gary, now 20, met a 39-year-old artist. 'He was definitely the older brother, who had the reins in his hands. I had got myself into a situation where I did not have much clout of any kind; I lived with him, but I didn't pay rent and things like that, so the situation developed into one where I was a houseboy really.'

Gary was drifting, on the rebound from his previous relationship: 'I didn't want to be in any kind of committed or possessive relationship.' Inevitably there were problems. 'All of the household duties were handed over to me, and he'd become upset because he was constantly having feelings that I was not doing enough, not paying my dues. At first it was sort of interesting; I was in a very glamorous physical setting and that appealed to me. It soon wore off though, and I started to reject it. What basically happened was that as soon as I really started to look after my own concerns and lead a broader life, he found it unacceptable and the situation no longer functioned as it did before.'

After only a year, Gary moved on. Then at the age of 23, he met Ray, 17 years his senior, with whom he still lives. 'To a certain extent I'm attracted by his age, but it's also what he has along with his age, which is a masculinity, assertiveness, confidence, a nurturing nature, kindness, compassion, honesty, trustworthiness – he has all of those things, which is amazing to me, because I find myself in a situation now where one of my real fantasies has come true: I have the perfect daddy. He takes care of me, has real concern for me, is very attracted to me physically, is very potent sexually, is lenient and considerate and gives me a love I'm absolutely sure of.'

Gary is aware of wanting to please Ray much as a child would its father. 'But I've also come to realize that here I am again in a similar situation in many ways to my last relationship. This one is definitely 1200 per cent better, but it's also perhaps the worst situati   e it enforces and solidifies many of the things I see in myself as liabilities, that I want to conquer: because it allows and encourages me to be dependent, I *am* dependent. I'm in a situation with this very dynamic man that makes it difficult for me to express other sides of my nature, because he is so powerful.'

Ray's power is partly economic. 'He's in a business where people frequently write him cheques, and some of them are just made out to me and I put them in my bank account. I don't feel in any way like an employee or a child on an allowance; there is the feeling that what is his is mine, although of course that isn't absolutely true, because he is really in control of the finances.'

In Gary's words, Ray takes care of everything; the shopping and the chores are shared. 'That's never really been an issue between us, but it is a slight problem because I'm not good at cleaning things – I just don't like it. He isn't very good about it either, but occasionally he gets preoccupied with it and would like things to be better, despite being understanding of my nature.'

Gary is in an age-gap relationship where he does not feel patronized because of his youth and lesser economic power. 'Usually older men who do patronize young men just need it to be very, very clear that the younger man is a beautiful possession, an object, something to reflect the older man's image. Ray may do that subconsciously to some degree: he definitely likes being with a younger man, but it's just from a very real sincerity. He nurtures me rather than keeps me; I do not think of myself as kept.'

Nurturing forms an element of many kinds of relationships, age-gap or otherwise, to a greater or lesser degree, but in mature relationships it is usually in some way reciprocal.

☿ 'I think when people say, for example, ''Ooh I could eat you'', it means ''I could eat you because I want to be more whole'' – in other words they're saying, ''I want you to feed me'', ''I want you to nurture me'', ''I want you to mother me'', because mother feeds. I think it's very dangerous, because we're talking about an imbalance, a baby needing to be fed, rather than both of you balancing and finding one another. As you grow older and learn to nurture and be nurtured, whether you're two men or two women, I think that we're talking of a certain element of mirroring, but I do feel that it should not be something that you strive to having a masturbatory relationship. I think we're talking of balance, and balance means that you have someone that isn't *quite* your mirror.'

In finding this balance in a relationship, two men or two women may face difficulties arising out of the fact that they have been conditioned into similar roles more appropriate to heterosexual relationships (just as a heterosexual couple may encounter problems because they have been conditioned into different and supposedly complementary roles into which they do not necessarily fit).

⚢ 'There are problems if there are two mothers in the home; it's enormously difficult if two people suddenly want power in that area. There was a time when Jackie was writing a book and I took responsibility for the house and children. And I was really quite comfortable: at that point Debbie was five months old, it suited me to be mother and it obviously suited Jackie to take the time to write the book. So we worked out our roles, if that's the right word, really well there. But I had difficulty giving up that power, because you get used to being the person who says, "Well we'll have three lots of soap", or whatever.'

⚣ 'An awful lot of men are brought up as little princes and when you've got two little princes in the same household, it can cause a lot of domestic irritation. I think many relationships break up over the small things – they make you so angry with your partner, you go off and fuck with someone else.'

Promiscuity

Gay people are often assumed to be more naturally promiscuous than heterosexuals, an attitude founded to some extent on a general lack of understanding of – or prejudice against – homosexual lifestyles. Gay people, as we have already pointed out, do not enjoy the same ease or freedom of association as heterosexuals, and this can lend their sexual activity an edge of urgency which might well be missing if their sexual partners were as accessible as those of heterosexuals. In addition, the sexual behaviour of gays, while subject to disproportionate legal penalties if overt, is not bounded by the same social conventions as that of heterosexuals.

If there is any divide where promiscuity is concerned, it is more likely to lie not between heterosexuals and homosexuals but between men and women. The nature of male sexuality is such that promiscuity has always been more endemic among men than among women, gay or straight. For men sex is more of a physical act, compartmentalized away from the emotions; it is still much more socially acceptable too, for a man to have multiple sexual partners than it is for a woman.

Women, on the other hand, have been deeply conditioned to see sex not as an isolated act, pleasurable in itself, but as part of the reproductive process, and thus to place great store by fidelity and monogamy; while this is also true of many men, it is much harder to abide by in a gay male relationship.

> 'I think the hunting instinct makes it very, very difficult for male gays, even if they are extremely fond of each other and even if they have a principal partner, to be faithful, and if a premium is put on fidelity, as it generally is, then even though they would do anything rather than break the relationship up, break it up they do, because they just cannot resist that grab of the passing pleasure – and they get found out.'

Jim is a big, well-built man of 50 who works for his local council as a decorator; his eight-year relationship with Alistair well illustrates the point. Looking back, the way they met might almost have been an omen of the way they were eventually to part.

Jim was out for a walk one evening when he literally bumped into Alistair: 'He smiled and said hello – I said, goodbye! On the way back he was still there, leaning up against a bollard, and still smiling. We got chatting and he invited me over to dinner.'

The two men spent a pleasant evening together and arranged to meet again. 'Alistair was obviously very keen; I didn't know whether I was or not. I suppose I was fascinated – I must have been, because I saw him several times over a period of months. A relationship grew and ultimately we moved into a flat together.'

Jim describes it as a very full relationship, not least because they were both very involved in the dog world; in fact it was when

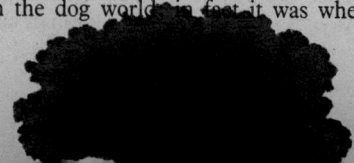

Alistair withdrew from it that things began to go wrong. 'He had to have a hobby, he had to involve himself in something, and he used to have the house literally crammed full of pot plants, on every windowsill, on every floor – even in the spare room there were plants. I was a bit house-proud and I liked things all nice, and there were these bleeding plants everywhere. He used to come home of a night, have his evening meal – which I prepared, he never used to do much housework – and then water all the bloody plants, hour upon hour. Then he'd say it was time to go to bed!'

In spite of their domestic disagreements, Jim and Alistair had a good sex life – but it wasn't enough for Alistair. 'I found out he was cottaging on the way home from work. I didn't bring it up for quite a few weeks – I was upset, but I wanted to bide my time. Then I found a piece of paper on the floor with a name and telephone number on it, so I rang it up. This very cultured voice answered, and I pretended I was Alistair and asked if I could come over. He said yes, so I went to this address and he turned out to be a film director. I put my cards on the table and he said, "Oh yes – that was the guy I met in the cottage last week; I wasn't really interested, but he pestered me to see him again." I took a dislike to him; he made a play for me and I thought anyone was his game, anything would do any time. So I left.'

That evening Jim confronted Alistair with his evidence. 'He said, "Well, what can I say – it's true." I said, "I'll tell you what you can say – you can fucking well get out." He said, "Don't take it like that." I said, "Well I happen to know that you cottage every bloody day on your way home from work." He said, "Well so what – there's nothing in it." And I said, "Well maybe there isn't to you, but there is to me. You're going behind my back, you're deceiving me. If I wasn't enough, why didn't you have the guts to tell me, and then perhaps we could have come to some arrangement: I could have gone out and had something on the quiet if I'd wanted to, and we could both have lived together under those circumstances if that's what you wanted. I haven't looked at anybody else since I've known you – for a whole eight years: I've not even thought about it, it's not even entered my head." I said, "That really has hurt me, I don't want to know. You've just killed something in me: whether there was something there or not, it's dead, and I can just never forgive or forget that – and I'd rather us just finish now."'

And finish they did. It wasn't until Alistair had moved out that Jim discovered he'd been through their photo albums and cut himself out of all the pictures of them together. 'It was so petty. I was prepared to forget and in a way forgive, but not live with him. I just couldn't do that – I just couldn't condone that kind of conduct. I don't think it was because I didn't satisfy him; he just wanted the excitement of catching something else and he wouldn't alter.'

The itch for the new, the unconquered, is a characteristic of the sexuality of many gay men – also of some gay women – for which explanations range from the disarmingly frank to the more psychological.

♂ 'I think a feature of a lot of gay male sexuality is Don Juanism – how many have I had; I think it's a variation, often not expressed in an aggressive personality, of the desire to dominate combined with a very strong curiosity about other people.'

♂ 'I discovered that I could give myself a great deal of pleasure from these relationships, and I decided it was something that perhaps I should indulge in as much as possible; it seemed only rational and right. And I think underneath that lies the promiscuity of a great many homosexuals.'

Adrian is a 34-year-old musician who has been living with Tim, about the same age, for the last five years. The account he gives of the life he led before he settled down with Tim provides a revealing insight into gay male promiscuity.

It begins in 1970 when, at the age of 20, Adrian left the council estate in the Northeast where he'd lived all his life and moved to London. Already he was acutely aware of a difference between himself and his contemporaries, as though his life, as he puts it, 'had a completely different root from theirs', and had had several homosexual encounters.

In London, Adrian took a bedsit in Bayswater. 'It was wonderful – it was cosmopolitan and, coming from the North, I used to find foreign-looking chaps attractive, olive-skinned, hairy-chested creatures. Then a gay drinking club opened called By Appointment (to her Majesty the Queen) i░░░ ░░░░ Bayswater

Road – Notting Hill Gate, somewhere round there – and it was terribly exciting, because all kinds of people got there, people who didn't call each other Olive and Mavis and Gladys – interesting, stimulating people from the arts and all over. And I was very pretty, it was when long hair was in; I was liberated, I could do what I wanted and by God I did. Sometimes it would be twice a day with different people.'

Adrian was elated by his sexual prowess. 'I knew I had the ability to pick up just about anybody that I cared to, which was a nice feeling of power in a way. I was always nice: I used to say I had a mini-affair with everybody I met; I got to know their names, at least at first.'

And so Adrian became promiscuous. But he puts it down not just to his 'pulling power', but to the heady sense of freedom he experienced on leaving the North, where he was 'always having to make excuses' about his sexuality, together with having a tremendously high sex drive. 'I never thought of settling down because I was living for the instant: I wasn't living for tomorrow, I wasn't planning for next year – it was now, this afternoon, this evening. I found new lips and new bodies so stimulating, and you know the adrenalin hook – you get a taste for the adrenalin rush you get when you make the first eye contact, then the adrenalin rush when you eventually get in the hay. So you're getting all these adrenalin boosts all the time and you get hooked on it.'

But after a few years the promiscuous life all of a sudden palled on Adrian. 'I got pissed off, for no apparent reason; my drive went totally and the hunt bored me – sex bored me. I wanted nothing to do with it.'

For a year Adrian was virtually celibate, then he became 'casually promiscuous, in a way you'd expect of someone not permanently attached to one person, but not in the wild two-a-day manner.' There followed a serious affair which, looking back, Adrian sees as paving the way for his relationship with Tim, 'a cheery little chap from the same background: I felt at ease, I felt comfortable; I immediately knew that I'd clicked in a big way.'

Adrian had no difficulty, despite his promiscuous past, in staying faithful to Tim. 'I think sex gets better with someone with whom you have a strong relationship, because there's the wonderful feeling, a kind of sexual excitement, of going to bed with someone whose sexual tastes you know and whose body you know. It's a wonderful kind of comfort, which grows even though the "adrenalin rush" sexuality has diminished.'

Adrian looks back on his twenties as a phase he almost had to go through in order to emerge a 'sensible adult'. Much like his heterosexual counterpart really, sowing his wild oats before he settles down, but the heterosexual man's promiscuity is held in check by penalties that simply do not apply to his gay fellows: for example, common though adultery may be, it still contributes to grounds for divorce; and if a heterosexual man makes a woman other than his wife pregnant, he may literally have to pay the price.

In the United States, the spread of AIDS, while checking the sexual activity of many promiscuous gay men, appears simply to have heightened the thrill for others. One gay man, who has recently returned from a visit there and who describes himself as both 'promiscuous by instinct', and 'like everybody in Britain, terrified of the AIDS scare', reflects on the current situation in America:

'I saw gay friends out there and discussed it with them and I've been in correspondence with others, some of whom are on the militant side, and I thought that although there is a small core which is very concerned – the political activists – the rest of the gay world, after drawing in its horns a bit, rather terrifyingly has gone right back to doing what it has always done: it's just as incautious, the back rooms still flourish, people still go to the bars and fuck their brains out and so it goes on. I think people have simply decided that it will never happen to them or, to put it another way, gay sex is an addiction like heroin. Once people are accustomed to having a lot of it and accustomed to having it very highly spiced, they can know there's a risk and often they can know there's a fairly high risk, and they are yet utterly incapable of giving it up. So in that sense all the whole disease business has added is a strong edge of desperation: I'm going to go to hell in my own way – if I catch it, it's just like playing Russian roulette.'

While there is evidence that the number of AIDS cases in Britain is beginning to follow the American pattern of doubling every six months, the incidence in this country is still comparatively low. A sexually active gay man, well-informed about AIDS, reflects the feeling of many British gay men.

⚣ 'Most of my sexual partners are people I know and have known for some time; they're rarely people who are on the gay scene, they very rarely have a more active sex life than I have and we very rarely indulge in full sexual intercourse. All that being so, I see no reason to change my lifestyle, because I don't think I'm at risk. If I went around the pubs and clubs and picked people up casually a lot, then I think I might change. But I've never done that; it's not been my way. It doesn't mean I'm not afraid of catching something – when I was sick with flu recently, in my morbid moments I thought, oh my God, I'm dying of AIDS, but by and large I don't really feel that way.'

Promiscuity among gay women invariably lacks the anonymity, immediacy and frequency often associated with gay male promiscuity: for most women, gay or straight, sex is inextricably bound up with emotion.

⚢ 'For me to have some kind of affair with someone, I have to feel something for them; I've only ever slept with someone for the sake of it when I've been out of my head, and then the next morning I've woken up feeling horrible. I don't think I could particularly handle going to bed with someone and then carrying on as normal; it must be quite ideal if you *can* detach yourself, but I can't – I get very emotionally involved with people I care about.'

⚢ 'Sleeping with someone for one night is very easy initially; it's a sort of deal – you're going to do *that*, and you'll get out of it what you want physically. But more and more I realize it's more physically gratifying to have sex with someone you know; to have a wonderful relationship with someone you know is better than having a one-night stand with a stranger. It's like conversations on trains, you know: I can remember them and they're interesting, but they don't have much to do with my life.'

But there are promiscuous gay women (just as there are promiscuous heterosexual women), whose sex lives are just as rampant and episodic as those of their male counterparts.

Kim is a 31-year-old nurse, tall and attractive. Although she is now in a monogamous relationship with another woman, she led a promiscuous life from an early age. 'One day I read an article about the number of lesbians in the Army and my heart went bang, bang, bang; I thought, oh my god – lesbians, so off I charged into the Army and had this wonderful time for six months, seducing all these women, until they threw me out.'

Kim then moved in with a girl she'd met in the Army, who stayed with her for two years before she left to get married. It had been Kim's first real love, and it was in a very disillusioned frame of mind that she then came on to the gay scene. Not yet 20, she became promiscuous in much the same way as Adrian; indeed she even recalls it in similar terms. 'The hunt's the same – or even more highly charged. If you fancy someone sexually, then you're on a high – it's really exciting. It's a real physical feeling; it's like you just want to go over there and screw the backside off somebody; you don't particularly want to know them or speak nicely to them, you just want to be in bed with them. What used to get me was breakfast the morning after – I mean, OK, it's nice to go out and find somebody and chase them and pick them up and get drunk and go off somewhere and fuck all night long, but then the next morning you've got a hangover and you want to eat, and you've got so fed up with this person you've got to have a conversation with and you don't even know them.'

Sometimes these encounters would turn into desultory relationships, where Kim would live with someone, but still have affairs on the side. 'The other person never in fact knew about it at all; I had a job where I occasionally had to stay overnight, so I had access to a bed, and in one year I had about five other lovers. I just used to go to bed with them; it seemed quite simple and it was good fun.'

But, as in Adrian's case, the sense of fun eventually wore off. 'I think I just got fed up being in bed with various women; it was completely and utterly sexual, and I just didn't feel that it was fulfilling any need whatsoever. It's like trying to ride a bike – once you can do it, fine, but then you don't do it unless you have to. I

mean, the fight was always to try and get somebody into bed, almost to find out if I was attractive enough to sleep with all these people.'

Kim views her switch to monogamy with a mixture of resignation and cynicism. 'Now, if I see someone I fancy, I can sort of contain it and think of other things, because I'm older; what happens is that the feeling of horniness carries on until I get home and then it redirects itself to the woman I'm with.'

Monogamous and open relationships

For many gay people monogamous relationships are synonymous with marriage, from which they are excluded by virtue of their sexual orientation. Hence their preoccupation with open relationships. But monogamy remains the perennial model of human sexual and emotional intimacy, aspired to by gay and straight people alike.

♀ 'In many ways it's like anything else – the more restrictions you place on yourself, the easier it is to operate, whether you're on a diet or living in an I-have-given-you-a-promise-that-I-won't-sleep-with-anyone-else monogamous relationship. I think we need certain restrictions to keep ourselves together; it's a bit like comparing the person who goes to work with the person who lies in bed until midday – the person who goes to work has a discipline, and I think monogamy equals a discipline.'

♂ 'I think the best kind of relationship is a genuinely equal partnership; I've occasionally met people – usually people who've been together a very long time – who really are happiest in each other's company. I would go so far as to say they were still in love with each other, but they are also each other's best friends; whatever hang-ups, horrors and neuroses they have, they are each other's support, they always have someone to talk with, they have the same sense of humour. And the result is that one is always happy to be in their company, because one for the moment shares that kind of togetherness.'

This is no doubt why people tend to be drawn to couples who have spent most, or a good part of their lives together, like Jo and Carolyn, for example, whom we profile in The Older Gay; they consider themselves as married as any heterosexual couple, and remark on the delight their friends take in their twenty-year union.

As well as the permanent monogamous relationship, there is serial monogamy, or the practice of going from one monogamous relationship to another. Veterans of this kind of relationship sometimes wax a little cynical about it, much as a heterosexual man or woman might about a third or fourth marriage.

'The second year of a relationship is a wearing down into a sort of run-of-the-mill thing; it is still quite fun, you can get good moments out of it, but by the time the third year comes along, it's all just hurtled downhill, finding other people attractive and wanting to get away. It's like in the middle of the second year you say, "Great, we're into the second year, this must be something really fantastic; I really love this person, I really enjoy being with them and what I want is to go out and buy a house with them." It's as though every relationship reaches its peak when you decide you're going to set up home together and it's just old hat, you know – here I am again, I'm going to set up home with another woman. And from that moment on, the interest suddenly goes – you've got what you want. I always think a change is as good as a rest, I wouldn't want to be with that person in ten years' time anyway.'

Then there are those whose relationships encompass both the promiscuous and the monogamous.

'I have two sorts of sexual relationships; I have steady sexual relationships and periods when I like sleeping with lots of different people. The two work equally well, but they don't work together. I feel it is wrong to have a long relationship with someone and then sleep with someone else and not tell them. It's bad manners to the person you're with – call me middle class if you will, it's bad manners. It's being unkind, ungiving to the person you're with; it's saying, "I can treat you lightly." You can't have a sexual relationship with someone which is quite deep and then say, "Look, I fancy

that person, so I'm going to go off and fuck them – OK with you?" Because it's not; because there are two types of sex – "fling" sex, and sex which is very much to do with giving yourself absolutely, where you don't mess around.'

But inevitably there are those who are unable to make the distinction, or who don't see why you can't have your cake and eat it, or who simply can't make up their minds. Hence much debate about the open relationship, the relationship which opens out to let in a third party who can bring something to it which is considered to be missing, or to have gone, or waned.

Open relationships tend to be more common among gay men than among gay women, and the trigger is usually sexual: one or other partner's sexual desire or interest can no longer be kindled or satisfied within the relationship. The truly open relationship calls for a considerable investment of time and energy on the part of both partners; even so, it is a difficult thing to achieve, involving as it does the delicate synchronization of at least two people's sexual and emotional needs.

♀ 'I think an open relationship is a very difficult one to make work if you're living full-time with someone; I think it's much more likely to work if your main partner and you don't actually live together, because then you're not rubbing each other's noses in it. After all, you could be considering not just one or two people's feelings, but four and possibly more.'

Commoner is the one-sided open relationship (see Profiles: Robin and Tim), in which one person is not happy with the situation, but puts up with it, even at the cost of much misery and pain. There is always the risk with this kind of relationship, as with the truly open, that it may suffer irreparable damage. It's a gamble a lot of people are not prepared to take.

♂ 'I've been to dinner parties with gay couples where they say, "Oh, we've got an arrangement", and I can't understand what they mean – are they friends that live together and screw elsewhere and screw each other when there's no one else? What is an "arrangement" if you're living with someone? It doesn't make sense to me. If you're going to sleep around – fine, sleep around: live by yourself and sleep around, or share a flat with someone and sleep around. If you've got a relationship with someone, I don't see how you can screw around – because if you do, you're leaving all those doors open that wreck relationships.'

But there have always been those who are interested in experimenting – even if only verbally – with new ways of relating to each other.

♀ 'There's a lot of talk about monogamy versus non-monogamy, but if I went to bed with Gill tonight and Kate tomorrow night, that's still *serial* monogamy. I think we've been approaching it the wrong way: we've been saying, "Well yes, I'll be with you tonight", but what about if you were a loving *group*? I'm of the opinion that we oughtn't to have two women in a bed, but three or four. Now that sounds scary, I know, and I certainly haven't got there yet – maybe only single women could handle that one, I don't know – but it might be the best way through. It wouldn't be a question of saying, "This is the fucking room", it would be a question of knowing that each night, every night, you all slept together in a monster bed.'

A way-out alternative to the monogamous relationship maybe, but it probably stands more of a chance of working with gay than with straight people, not only because, as we have already pointed out, gays are less restricted by structure and role models in their relationships, but also because their actual pattern of relationships tends to differ from that of heterosexuals.

Friends and lovers – surrogate family

Many of the primary relationships of heterosexuals revolve around their families, and when they marry these are expanded by a whole new web of kin relationships with in-laws, etc. This is much less likely to happen with gay people who are, in any case, sometimes estranged from their families by virtue of their homosexuality, and so the place of relatives for them tends to be taken by friends, who together make up an elaborate and extended support system.

♂ 'Homosexuals are socially out-turned; they have a network of friendships which isn't arranged in a family tree way, and

through this network they can actually spread out. They meet more people than heterosexuals, I reckon; they're socially much more mobile. And what you find you depend on when you get yourself into trouble as a homosexual – trouble of any kind – is your friendships. As I did, for example, when my mother was ill. It was very instructive to me that my friendships stood up to the very considerable strain of that kind of thing, that is, somebody who was eight months in hospital and nearly three years in a nursing home. I think homosexuals are also very often capable of having friendships with each other without illusions: they are more accepting of each other's faults and they confabulate, they lick their wounds – I have people who ring me up every day, or whom I ring up every day.'

In the gay world, where incest and other taboos do not hold sway, friends become lovers and lovers become friends with a speed and ease that may well amaze the heterosexual onlooker, whose sociosexual behaviour is much more curtailed. It is quite common for the social circle of gay men and women to be made up in part of people with whom they have, at one time or another, had a sexual relationship, as if homosexuals are bound to each other by sex, love and friendship, in place of blood. The gay world is a small one, something of a sexual and emotional hothouse, where lovers jostle ex-lovers and friends switch loyalties in an incestuous melting pot of love and lust.

⚥ 'If you take a new lover into your life, he has to cope with all these other relationships and that's not easy. I mean to say, you don't come on your own, and homosexuals – even more than heterosexuals – have got to sort out whether they're going to keep the love affair *exclusive* of their existing relationships, or whether they're going to introduce everybody round and see how it works.'

The changes of status in gay life, from friend to lover and lover to friend, the conflicts that can arise from striving to keep new lovers happy while not losing touch with their predecessors, can make for a delicate balancing act and occasion much soul-searching.

♀ 'The three women that I've had long-lasting relationships with, including the one I'm with at the moment, are always going to be in my life. There's just no way that the other two haven't got access to me and if the person I'm with can't handle that, it's my problem. I hurt because (a) I don't like having hassles, (b) I'm inflicting obvious pain on someone I love very, very much and that's very, very hard, and (c) it just makes for bad feelings all round which overflow into all sorts of other things. But the whole point of not being heterosexual and falling into the heterosexual norm of monogamous relationships is actually to form values that are yours. Whoever comes into my life next has to take on board what has made me *me*, and I am me because of other people that are still part of me, so they buy me or they don't buy me.'

♂ 'I had an affair with a South American called Alberto once, and I've kept in contact with him. He occasionally pops back into town; after two years I'll get a phone call and yes, it's fabulous to see him. But it's very difficult – you remember what it was like, and if you haven't met them for a long time, all the attractive qualities they had when you first met them are still there, plus the knowledge of their bodies. And apart from the sex you have feelings left and the feelings were usually hurt somewhere towards the end of the affair. So I find it very, very difficult.'

Gay people sometimes refer, half-mockingly, half in earnest, to their circle of friends and lovers as 'the family', but there are also more conventional families within the gay community, in which children play an important and coveted part.

Gays and children

It is often not fully appreciated that some gay men and women want children as much as some heterosexuals, and make just as good – and sometimes better – parents.

It is becoming increasingly common for gay women to resort to AID (artificial insemination by donor), like Linda, whose story we tell in Gay Family, and in America gay men can even take advantage of the practice of surrogate motherhood. In California, where gay couples are barred from adoption, increasingly desperate gay men are even buying babies in Central America and smuggling them back into the United States.

Gay people, then, have to go to considerable lengths to have children. Tragically, this is often the case even if they already have children by a previous heterosexual relationship. They are still, for example, frequently refused custody of their own children by the courts and even, in the case of gay men, denied access to them.

All too often behind these judgments lie deeply ingrained prejudices that are seldom questioned and for which no real evidence has ever been produced. Among the most common are that a gay household is in some way inferior to a heterosexual household, even though the relationship between the adult members of the former may be much more stable, affectionate and harmonious than that in the latter; that a child brought up by gay adults will, willy-nilly, develop a homosexual orientation; and most pernicious of all, that such a child will be under constant threat of sexual molestation by its parent's lover, although this is much more likely if it is female and the latter is a heterosexual male. Underlying all of these assumptions is the notion that a child of a gay household is in some kind of 'moral danger' from which, although unspecified, it must nevertheless be protected.

New professional research gives the lie to much of this; for example, the recent study by the Institute of Psychiatry in London concluded that being brought up in a lesbian household does not in itself lead to a child becoming homosexual, or in any way put it at psychiatric risk.*

As judges are made more aware of such research, the present situation is likely to improve and indeed, there are signs that this is already beginning to happen. But it is still by and large the case that it falls to the homosexual party in a custody case to demonstrate that her or his sexual orientation will not influence the development of a child to its detriment.

Thus to be involved in such a case is invariably to undergo a deeply harrowing and traumatic experience.

*Children in Lesbian and Single Parent Households: Psycho-sexual and Psychiatric Appraisal, by S. Golombok, A. Spencer and M. Rutter, 1983, Journal of Child Psychology and Psychiatry, no. 24, pp. 551–572.

♀♀ 'I found myself having to answer very detailed and embarrassing questions by my own barrister about my sex life, and both my lover and I had to file very detailed and distressing affidavits about our backgrounds. We became more and more aware that had we not been professional working women, the possibility of our winning the case would have been very slender indeed. What seemed to matter was our status; our saying, "We are this, we are that, we are graduates, we have a nice home, we've got such-and-such an income." And we found ourselves having to answer to a court welfare officer who came and looked round the house. We were very fortunate in that we had a very supportive and experienced solicitor who'd dealt with lesbian custody cases before. And basically we realized that had we not been homosexual, there wouldn't have been a case to answer: had I been living with a guy and saying, "I want my son", there'd have been very little to go on.'

The chances of gay men obtaining custody of their children are at present poor: not only do they have to contend with the natural bias of the courts towards women in this area of the law, but also the great prejudice against male homosexuality. In general they have to content themselves with access to their children, and sometimes even this is granted only on an understanding that their lovers or gay friends will not be present during visits. Even if this is not the case, such is the legal and social paranoia surrounding homosexuals and children, that gay people frequently feel inhibited anyway about behaving normally towards their partners in front of their children.

♂ 'I see my children for half of each school holiday; John is often with me – he gets on well with them – but I haven't told them about the situation. When the four of us spend the night together, John and I sleep separately; we also forego terms of endearment in front of them, although they know that we go on holiday together and share the flat. It worries me, because it's unnatural. But the situation is under threat anyway by my ex-wife at the moment; she's the kind of person who has to have everything spelt out, and sooner or later she's going to say something to them. So John and I will probably increase our affection at home and let the children learn that way.'

Certainly if gay parents act as if they have something to hide, their children will assume that homosexuality is some kind of shameful secret; if on the other hand they explain that they are gay and what it means, their children are much more likely not only to understand it, but to accept it.

Jenny is a pretty, pert woman of 33, divorced with two young children, a girl of 12 and a boy of 10, and now living with another woman.

Although Jenny had been leading a gay life from the age of 17, she got married at 20 because she was unable at the time to resolve what she saw as a conflict between her religious faith and her sexuality. 'I was brought up in a Christian family, and heard a lot about the natural thing that man is made for woman and woman is made for man, and I thought I was perfectly capable of carrying on a day-to-day relationship with Paul, who was a great friend. And he understood; he said, "It could work quite well – I'll go my way and you can go yours." It was the sixties and anything went.'

And anything did for the first three years of the marriage. 'We had a pub at this stage and he used to go out with his friends and I used to go out with mine; we hardly ever went out together, although we lived together and slept in the same bed.'

But then the children arrived within two years of each other, and for the next seven years Jenny had no time for her gay life; she also found herself drifting further and further apart from Paul.

Then one weekend Jenny went to a Christian rock festival, where she was particularly moved by the words of one evangelist. 'He talked about reconciliation and how God really loved you, just exactly the way you were – you didn't have to change, he just wanted you to be yourself. And that was when the penny dropped – I burst out crying, because my faith does mean a great deal to me and I'd been fighting this on and off for years. And finally I didn't have to be anything I wasn't; I could be just exactly how I was and still be acceptable.'

Fired by the revelation, Jenny made two decisions: to find a gay church and to come out again into gay society. So she went along to the Metropolitan Community Church,* joined the Gay Christian Movement and called a family conference with Paul. 'We got Philippa and Douglas in and sat them down and said, "Now look – Daddy and I don't love each other any more, we're just friends now; we can't go on living together, because we don't get on, we keep fighting." We worked it out so that the children would have the best deal. And that was, that I left; Paul retained the house, and we had joint custody of the children, but he had official day-to-day care. This means that he pays the school fees, so the children still go to boarding school; I see them for all their breaks during the term and for a period during their school holidays; I also buy their clothes and Paul pays for all the extras.'

Jenny moved out into a flat. 'To start with, Philippa used to say to me, "Never mind, Mummy, you'll find somebody," and she and Douglas were anxious to try and find me a new husband. I just kept on saying, "Look, I'm never going to get married again" – "Yes, you will, you wait and see." "No look – I'm never going to get married again: get used to that fact, I'm perfectly all right as I am, there's nothing that I need a man for." They just wanted me to be happy really.'

Then Jenny met Sue at a party. 'I got her telephone number and asked if I could come and talk to her. I told her that I was gay, but I hadn't been out for seven years; I wanted now to come out and I needed to talk to somebody.'

Jenny and Sue began a relationship; then came the time when the children were due home for the weekend. 'I wrote to them saying that we were going to spend the weekend with a friend of mine and we'd come and collect them. Right from the word go, it was, "This is my friend," and "Of course we sleep in a double bed together." And on the Saturday morning they bounced in; Sue and I were sitting up in bed drinking coffee and they sat on the end of the bed. At that stage the dogs were allowed on the bed, so there were three dogs, two children and two grown-ups – all in one double bed! It just went from there really. It was just all perfectly normal and natural.'

*The Universal Fellowship of Metropolitan Community Churches (UFMCC), a gay Christian church, was founded in 1968 by the Reverend Troy Perry in Los Angeles. Today it has over 200 branches throughout the world with a total membership of nearly 40,000.

Since then, they have all been on holiday together, and if Jenny can't go and pick the children up from school, Sue does. 'She picked Philippa up on her own recently and Philippa said, "I'm really pleased that Mummy found you." Sue said, "Well, I'm glad too – why in particular are you?" "Well, if she hadn't met you, we'd never have seen so much of her and we wouldn't have the lovely weekends that we have and we'd never all have gone on holiday together."

Both the children know that Jenny and Sue are gay. 'Many moons ago we had this long conversation about what was a homosexual, and I've always brought them up to understand that gay people are perfectly normal, natural people who just love people of the same sex – that's what "gay" means. So they've always known. I said to Philippa recently, "You do realize Mum loves Sue very much" – "Oh yes, of course – I think she's lovely too."'

In accordance with her policy of being open with her children, Jenny has explained to them why she and Sue are not allowed to pick them up from her parents' home. 'My father's perfectly civilized, but my mother is not at all. She won't have Sue in the house. So I have just had to say, "Grandma doesn't like any of Mummy's friends; she doesn't approve of them and she doesn't understand. So she's not going to be terribly interested if you tell her what a lovely holiday you've had with Mummy and Sue." We've had long conversations about how everybody should be able to choose their own friends and after all, I am grown-up and no other grown-up should tell me whom to make friends with or anything like that.'

Jenny and Sue now plan to buy a house together. 'We sat down and seriously started planning the future, with the thought that when the children leave school they might want to come and live with us.'

As Jenny points out, this involves a considerable adjustment for Sue. 'They're not her children; she hasn't had a part in bringing them up from babyhood. As an independent person she's never had to deal with silly things like not having an inch of space to yourself – things that all mothers know, like not even being able to go to the bloody toilet without a kid banging on the door and saying, "I want a tissue and I can't reach the box." But she likes children; she gets on very well with them and she's got three godchildren of whom she's very fond. And she'd like to be a parent. She's gradually becoming more dominant with the children; instead of saying to me, "Do you think such-and-such", she's telling them herself. And the kids are delighted that we're all going to live together in one big house.'

Profiles

Gay widower: Frank ♂♂

'Kevin was in hospital for seven days – they were bloody horrible days. There was a series of Fridays – he first had his haemorrhage on a Friday, he died on a Friday and he was buried on a Friday. And for quite a long time after that, every Friday was really horrible for me. I can remember two things: the Wednesday before he died, sitting up in bed and saying, "Kevin, let me go. Let me go!" and then after he died, saying, "You fucking bastard – how *dare* you die and leave me alone!"'

Frank is 61, trim and well-dressed, and has been alone since Kevin's death over three years ago. They met when Frank was 28, Kevin 27, and for the next twenty-seven years they were inseparable. 'I fell in love with Kevin the moment I saw him. I can remember the time when we didn't have a lot of money and we'd exchanged signet rings and he went to a pawnbroker and sold our typewriter, the rings and our evening dress suits in order to get the money to pay the rent.'

But times got better, Frank's business prospered and eventually he decided to make over half of it to Kevin; he also decided to destroy every memento of his life before he met Kevin. 'The only thing he was jealous about was my past, and it was a question of making a great sacrifice and deciding which was more important. One night I made a big fire and burnt every photograph, every letter and every diary that I'd had before I met him.'

Some of these, no doubt, made reference to Frank's promiscuous past, but he and Kevin, who had also been promiscuous, remained faithful to each other for the first few years of their relationship. 'For seven years, if either one of us looked at anybody else, the other would react; I've knocked Kevin across the road more than once, and he's hit me on the head with a saucepan. But Kevin was a two-way guy: to put it very openly, he liked to get fucked and he liked to fuck. Well I don't, but I began to realize that if I didn't let him fuck somebody else, I was going to lose him. So we started going to the Turkish baths. The agreement was this: I said, "I don't care who you have and you don't have to care who I have, as long as we don't meet somebody in the street and they come up and say, 'Hello Kevin,' and I have to say, 'Who's that?' Before I go with anybody, you can know who it is and I'll say, 'Do you mind?' and vice versa." Eventually we bought a house in Agadir in Morocco, which we used to visit five or six times a year, and that provided plenty of extramarital love/lust. In fact we used to vie with each other in finding suitable partners for each other. Kevin gave me the most beautiful birthday and Christmas presents: he used to go out and find lovely people to give me.'

The words belie the initial difficulty Frank experienced in coming to terms with the situation. 'I was jealous of Kevin because I wanted him and I didn't want him to have anybody else. But I knew that he needed something that I couldn't give him, and because I loved him, I wanted him to have it, to make him happy. It brought us much closer together, because we were able to be much more honest with each other.'

And so the relationship blossomed, with each spoiling the other. 'I wanted to give Kevin the best life I possibly could; I just wanted to be able to give him everything he wanted. Instead of shutting the shop, I'd carry on working, so that if he said, "Oh let's go to Morocco next week", I could get the tickets and cancel all my appointments. I never ever said no to him. But he pampered me like mad. For example, in the mornings, he always used to get up and make the breakfast and bring it to me; then he'd say, "What are you wearing today?" I'd tell him and if it was something casual, he wouldn't let me wear it – I had to have a tie on every day! And I was never allowed in the kitchen: he used to come home from the shop and say, "Get into bed and put the television on", prepare me a meal and bring it to bed. Kevin had a wonderful sense of humour and he was nice; he taught me a kind of tolerance of all sorts of things, and I taught him to enjoy opera and ballet and classical music. We were extremely happy . . .'

. . . Until one night in March 1980, when Kevin was suddenly rushed to hospital. 'He went out at a quarter to seven one evening to get a newspaper, and at five to seven I turned round and said, "C'mon, it's time we went home." And he was unconscious. I thought he was kidding. So I said, "I'm going to ring for a doctor." And I did, but it was his weekend off. Then I said, trying to frighten Kevin, "I'm going to ring 999 for an ambulance." He didn't answer, so I knew then that something was wrong. I did ring for an ambulance and they took him to hospital. They told me he'd had this massive brain haemorrhage and there was probably no hope at all, or else he'd be a vegetable. He was in hospital for a week, and I went there two or three times a day. I put my hand out to him and there was no reaction at all; he couldn't feel. He didn't even know it was me.'

Kevin had had a 'black Irish premonition' of his death. 'On 19 January I went out to have my hair cut and that took about an hour; during that time he wrote a letter to me care of our solicitor, saying, "In case anything happens to me, I want you to carry on; I want a quiet funeral, and I want you to tell people that flowers are for the living and to give flowers to someone that they love. I don't want a notice in the newspaper, because it'll be so much better for you to tell all our friends little by little and talk about it. And as soon as you possibly can, find yourself a new friend and make sure that he is not as dictatorial as I was." That was my wonderful friend – and the only times he was dictatorial were for my own good.'

For about a year Frank was 'useless': 'I went into the shop every day, but I didn't do very much work. I just wanted people to leave me alone. I drank too much and I ate junk food, except when I was with friends. And I had this awful need to look after somebody, because I'd looked after Kevin so long. I started picking up the most horrible people, lost souls, who needed me more than I needed them.'

But some time after Kevin's death, Frank got a 'terrible impulse' to go to the church where he and Kevin used to rendez-vous after a row. 'I *had* to go there and I don't really believe in life after death or anything like that, but afterwards I got a very strong feeling of a kind of comfort, as though he'd said, "OK, you came."'

The experience may have signalled some kind of release from

the past for Frank; in any case he began slowly to recover, helped by becoming godfather to the baby son of close friends of his and Kevin's. And he started to look for the 'new friend' that Kevin had urged him to find. But while 'missing the sex, and the affection, like Kevin's hand reaching out in the middle of the night' if he was having a bad dream, Frank was frightened of someone wanting him for what he had and not for himself. His friends counselled him to look for someone his own age. 'They told me he had to be at least 50, otherwise it would be disgusting. And I just turned round to them and said, "Y'know, you read in the papers all the time about so-and-so who's married a 26-year-old girl – do you call that disgusting?" The trouble is, I don't feel my age – I've kept myself fit, my hair has stayed brown; my beard is white, but I shave every day through vanity, I suppose.'

Frank now has a lover who is forty years younger than himself – a 21-year-old unemployed technician called Ewan, who came down to London from Scotland when his mother could no longer stand having him around all day. When Ewan's money ran out, he took himself off to Piccadilly Circus, where he met a boy who introduced him to a man with whom he later had sex for £30. By the time Ewan met Frank, six weeks later, he was earning a living as a rent-boy. 'It was very funny,' recalls Frank, 'he was sitting next to me in my local and I clocked him. I thought, there's a nice pretty boy, and he took one look at me and he said to himself, "There's a punter." Then he said to me, "You got a light?" I said yes. A little while later, "I'm a bit short – do you think you can buy me a drink?" I knew then that he was rent, but I liked him and I took him home. When we got there, I asked him how much he charged. He said, "£60 for two hours." He nearly dropped through the floor when I actually gave him £60. Then I took him out to dinner.'

To Frank, Ewan is like a 'lovely little puppy-dog', who has also given his ego a boost: 'I'm very happy that a younger person can give themselves to me and not feel disgusted.' Frank hasn't lost his head over Ewan, although he reminds him physically of Kevin, and in fact has already advised him to go back home, get himself a job and grow up with a gay man his own age. In the meantime, as Frank philosophically puts it, 'Ewan's making me happy and he's got nothing else to do.'

In the closet: Sally and Helen ♀♀

'You couldn't talk about our relationship, because it was strange and different – I didn't know what it was. You couldn't say to someone, "I'm having this thing with Helen." Most of the women we knew were heterosexual anyway, and we went to discos and occasionally danced with creeps. When we were away from each other, it was like schizophrenia, we were like different people; then behind those closed doors we became lovers again, but to the outside world, we were just two friends. It was frightening in a way – frightening, but lovely.'

Sally is 31, bright, attractive and friendly, and has recently split up from Helen, with whom she was in a totally closet relationship for ten years, more out of sheer ignorance than fear. They met when they were both nursing; shortly afterwards they took jobs as nursery assistants at a holiday camp. 'It was the most horrifying thing I've ever done. We shared a very small little room – it was like a cupboard and so cold – and you could hear through the walls. On one side was a married couple having it off every night; on the other was some Australian Charlie knocking the hell out of his bird every night; and over the way were a couple of studs always getting drunk, pulling the birds in, peeing up the wall and God knows what – I've never seen anything like it in my life.'

In this brazenly heterosexual atmosphere, Sally became very protective towards Helen, without really knowing why. 'In fact one bloke tried to pull Helen and I went berserk – I put my hand through a window, because he was in a chalet with her. I was possessive, I wanted her; she was my – I didn't know what she was, but I didn't want anyone messing around with her, she was part of me.'

Even so, no one took Sally and Helen for anything other than two girls working the season together and keeping themselves to themselves. But when they moved on to jobs as hotel chambermaids, it wasn't so easy. 'All the chambermaids used to congregate in a little corner and talk about some pop star and say, "Oh yeah, he's nice." And you had to say something, otherwise after a while they'd think, "Well, what about you."'

And so the dissembling about their relationship began, and quickly gathered momentum, so that by the time Sally and Helen were working at a nursery, they both had 'boyfriends'. 'I knew a guy called Michael who was a plumber, and I fictionalized that I was going out with him, so to people at work he was my guy; fortunately he was married, so that made it a little bit easier. Helen was "going out" with a guy who was an electrician – he was modelled on someone who actually came to the nursery one day to do some work.'

That kept the girls at work happy, but Sally then had the problem of what she told Michael, a real friend whom she did actually see from time to time; at this point she abandoned half-lies for pure fiction. 'He'd ask me who I was going out with, and I used to make up this story about this bloke who worked in the karate studios down the road – who didn't even exist! That's how stupid it became.'

Yet Sally still did not know who she was or why she was attracted to Helen. 'At the time I wanted to have a sex change: I'd been reading a book about a girl who had a sex change, and Helen and I just felt that that was perhaps what I was – a man trapped inside a woman's body. I thought that if I had a sex change, I could relate to Helen in a way that society, our families and even I could accept – because it didn't seem right that a woman loved another woman. I thought maybe then Helen and I could get married, because I wanted that – I wanted much more for both of us. I even felt quite hurt that I couldn't have a baby with her, I loved her so much.'

Sally's agonizing eventually eased when she bumped into an old friend, considerably further along the road to self-discovery than herself. 'Intellectually it was so stimulating to be with someone that actually talked about feminism, women's lib, etc. Ann knew that she was gay, and she made me question my sexuality and what had been happening: it was her that actually made me face that I was a lesbian. It was incredible – here was someone who was very positive about enjoying being with women. And from then on I went to loads and loads of gay clubs: I had to find my sexual identity.'

In so doing, Sally left Helen behind, in more ways than one. 'She was staying at home; she didn't want any part of it. There was a lot of hostility and anger coming from her; I was starting to find myself and I was losing her. It was like being on the other side of a bridge, knowing that once you've crossed over, you can't go back and she didn't want to come with me, so I had to do it without her. It was sad because that was the start of the rows: all of a sudden I'd become "one of them people in the club – your lesbian friends", and I just used to say, "What the fuck do you think we had then?" She saw Ann as taking me away from her, but it wasn't that – Ann helped me, but so did other people and I wanted to be with them, because that was what I was and I wasn't ashamed of it.'

Inevitably Sally and Helen parted, although not without a wrench on Sally's part. 'I felt that Helen had been my life for the last ten years – my family, my friend. I knew she cared for me, and she always would care. But I haven't now got someone reinforcing all the time that what I'm doing is bad or dirty or wrong. I feel much happier.'

The one-sided open relationship: Robin and Tim ♂♂

Robin: 'It is becoming quite common: the actual affair may finish, but you continue to have an affectionate living-together relationship. I think it's difficult to adjust to: on one level, when Tim goes out to see someone, I say, "Give my love to so-and-so", and I'm quite happy about it; on the other, there's a nagging feeling at the back of my mind – sometimes I resent it. I think that's natural and it's something I'm coming to terms with, but I don't think I've completed the process yet.'

Tim: 'I quite often feel resentful that I can't lead my own life in the way that I would like – for instance, I think it would be nice to be able from time to time to entertain people *not* as a couple. On the rare occasions Robin does go away for three weeks, I do have a tremendous time because I'm able to entertain my other friends in *my* place rather than always having to go to theirs. I do tend to resent the fact that I haven't got that freedom basically to be selfish.'

Robin is lanky and thoughtful, Tim is slim and athletic-looking, and they have been together since they met at a GLF disco ten years ago, when Robin was 24, Tim 21. At the time Tim was still coming to terms with his homosexuality, a process that had been speeded up, as he puts it, by someone spiking his drink with acid a couple of months before. 'Robin was also into LSD and smoked dope and things; he was very much more experienced in – oh, everything. He was like an elder brother even from the start, but I fell in love very deeply, very intensely with him.'

Robin was slower off the mark, viewing the relationship, to begin with, as a 'very close friendship, but not exclusive'. But that's what it quickly became, and Robin and Tim eventually set up flat together, for all the world like any married couple. 'The only difference that ever struck us between what we were doing and getting married was that we didn't get any wedding presents: we thought that was terribly unfair, 'cos you can stock up a house with wedding presents.'

But Robin's parents knew and accepted that their son was gay, and tried to treat him and Tim no differently from their other son and his wife. 'They find us washing machines, fridges – things that we can't afford; they're second-hand, of course, but if I say, "Well you must have a fiver or a tenner or something", they say, "No, no, no, of course not – we do a lot for Steve and Margaret and this is something we can do for you."'

When Tim, on the other hand, tried to tell *his* parents about him and Robin, the reaction was 'very sort of what-are-you-talking-about' – so much so, that Robin wrote to Tim's mother. 'It turned out to be a very valuable exercise. I think I tended to be a bit too melodramatic, but I was pushing the GLF point of view that there was nothing abnormal – it just happened to be different, and Tim meant a great deal to me, trying to explain to her in as simple a way as possible just what was going on. I didn't get a personal response, but I gathered that she appreciated it immensely. I would go down and visit and was made to feel extremely welcome, but I think they simply treated me as one of Tim's friends – they didn't really want to think or talk about it.'

In the meantime, the initial sexual intensity of Robin and Tim's relationship had worn off; Tim had decided he wanted to explore his sexuality and embarked on a series of 'fairly meaningless' one-night stands, of which Robin was uneasily aware. 'I'd become conscious, obviously, that he was going out – not terribly frequently, maybe only once a fortnight or so, often with an excuse, not really telling me where he was going. Maybe I was just naive or something, because usually I'd believe him. But I found it very difficult to cope with and I didn't like it.'

Robin and Tim eventually started sleeping apart, Tim claiming that their double bed was 'bad for his back'. But their relationship survived, due to 'mutual affection, familiarity and the convenience of the flat', and wasn't really threatened until Tim met and fell in love with another man, Graham. At first Robin tried to be philosophical about the situation: 'My reaction was, OK, if you two being together makes you happy, I will try and deal with this myself, but obviously it will cut me up no end, if it doesn't mean the end of the relationship. I was prepared for Tim to have a relationship of sorts with Graham, so long as it didn't impinge too much on me and take Tim away from me too much.'

Things came to a head when all three of them went on a picnic one day. Robin recalls that the outing began amicably enough. 'We drove down the motorway and stopped at a little pub; it was all very friendly. At that stage I didn't quite know how serious their relationship was; I didn't quite know what Graham's attitude was. The picnic went OK until he started pawing Tim, knowing that I could see. I got cross and walked away in a huff; I made it clear that I had not only seen it, but I didn't like it, and I thought it was taking liberties and being undiplomatic. They stopped and I came back. We all got in the car and went back to the flat. And then, having had this on the whole very pleasant day apart from that little episode, Tim said, "I hope you don't mind, but I'm going back to Graham's tonight." And I did mind – I was furious: I don't usually break things, but I just threw these empty beer bottles at the grate, just to make a noise, just to indicate that I was wound up and upset. I was *really* furious; I suppose that's when it came home to me just how serious their relationship was.'

Graham in fact wanted Tim to leave Robin for him, but Tim balked at this. 'I was very dubious about moving in with someone else, knowing how long it takes and how difficult it is to build up a living-together relationship and a good domestic scene: you've got your cats and the hi-fi and all the things you've bought together, and I decided that I didn't want to go through all that again with someone else.'

Robin hoped desperately that the relationship with Graham would come to an end, and he and Tim could go back to how they'd been before: 'In other words, Tim would have other friends, casual pick-ups that he would sleep with, but he wouldn't be away every single weekend from Friday evening to Sunday afternoon.'

Very much on the rebound, Robin answered an ad in a gay magazine. 'I thought, well even if our relationship does survive, I've got to get out more and meet new people.' The upshot was an affair with a man with whom Robin had 'good sex and enjoyable times', but he wasn't someone he would have considered leaving Tim for.

So unhappy was Robin with everything that was going on, that he told his family about it. 'They were immensely sympathetic, to the extent that Tim and I went round together one Sunday lunchtime, as we did quite regularly, and my father took Tim off for a drive in the car and just said, "You've got to make your mind up, you mustn't play about like this – it's obviously making Robin very unhappy." Tim took it quite well; he said that he entirely agreed, he did feel a worm for doing what he was doing, but he was enjoying it.'

Until one evening when, in Robin's words, Tim and Graham came to grief. 'It was a very strange evening. They'd arranged to go to the cinema together, and I felt more and more fed up. I was very much into the tarot at that time, and I made a little wax model and stuck pins in it with as much venom as I could. I was really angry, and I really did put a great deal of energy into it. And Tim locked his keys in the car and had to come all the way back to the flat to get my keys, and I don't know – he and Graham had apparently always had this arrangement that if the end came, they would just shake hands and part – and they did. That was really happening at the time I was sticking my pins in; I really wasn't doing it thinking that anything would happen, I was just getting rid of aggression on a little manikin. It *is* just coincidence . . . Anyway that was the last we heard of Graham.'

To this day Tim remains confused by the events of that night. 'I don't quite know what happened, but I think that Graham went off with someone else. That wouldn't have been so bad if it hadn't been for the fact that he was meant to be meeting me.'

With Graham out of the picture, Robin and Tim were able to take stock of their relationship; at Robin's suggestion, they re-arranged their four-roomed flat. 'One room was the shared living room, one room was my study, one room was Tim's bedroom and the other room was my bedroom plus the TV lounge, as it were. And that seemed to work extremely well. I just felt tremendously pleased it was all over and willing to compromise far more in other respects.'

Tim was also relieved that the situation had been resolved. 'I found it was much better to have a few good friends whom I could sleep with, rather than fall in love and have the difficult time that that seems to entail.' He made it clear to Robin that although he meant a great deal to him, he didn't turn him on any more.

Robin took all this on board. 'I just had to accept that however much I needed Tim in a physical way, I wasn't going to get it. I just had to say, "You feel the need to go out quite regularly and score – I don't particularly like it, either emotionally or even morally, come to that, but I've got to recognize that it is your life."'

Tim urged Robin to get out more, but Robin preferred to 'have someone come round for a meal and watch TV', and so tended to stay at home. 'There were times when I felt I wouldn't mind him going out so much if I got some of it, but I thought that if I protested, I'd just be making a nuisance of myself and I'd probably precipitate a disaster.'

So Robin and Tim settled back into the domestic routine which they'd always found comfortable. 'I tend to do the dishes more and clean the bathroom floor a little more often, but Tim provides the van and keeps it clean, and he's handier with a paintbrush than I am. We both enjoy cooking, especially if people are coming round – we're not too keen on cooking for just the two of us, although Tim will get a piece of beef from time to time and we'll have a nice meal.'

And so Robin and Tim lived together happily enough, until Robin went off to Greece for three weeks, whereupon Tim seized the opportunity to have an affair. 'Fairly soon after I came back,' recalls Robin, 'I was told about this very nice person called Ed, who had invited us round for a meal, and in my blinkered way, I just thought, well this is another of Tim's friends: doubtless he sleeps with him quite a bit, but it's just like Tom or whoever that I've got used to. And Tim sort of assumed that I must realize everything, and was very pleased and told Ed, "It's all right, Robin knows everything." Well I didn't know anything. Anyway it eventually dawned on me that Tim had done his usual thing of going a little bit over the top to begin with – as he'd done with me, as he'd done with Graham – and what was going to happen now – would he take off this time. That's when it started hanging me up a bit.'

Nevertheless Robin again put a philosophical face on the situation, as Tim acknowledges. 'I used to go back and talk a lot about Ed, and Robin was wonderful about it. He would really encourage me and hope that I was happy and not to worry about him. I know now that he was very cut up, but at the time I didn't – he's very good at bottling his emotions up. As soon as he starts to open up, I tend to get uptight and say, "Well it's really got nothing to do with you."'

But Ed had just split up from his boyfriend and wasn't keen to get involved again, much to Tim's chagrin. 'I loved Ed so much – I really went way over the top about him. But he regards me as a brother, in the way that I regard Robin, so I had to cope with exactly what Robin had to, insofar as Ed met someone else and started a love affair with him. So although he wouldn't admit it, I was to take a back seat, and that was very difficult for me.'

The experience has left Tim somewhat chastened. 'I don't regret it, because it just puts Robin's feelings in focus; now I'm able to be a little bit more considerate.'

It seems also to have put Robin and Tim's relationship in focus for them; they are now, ten years on, buying a house together, something that Robin welcomes: 'I think the move will put things far more in perspective.' But at the same time he has no illusions. 'The way Tim sees it is that he strays, as it were, and that makes me want to get closer to him. In a strange way, he quite enjoys this being pulled in two directions: he liked it when it was happening with Graham, and he liked it when it was happening with Ed – sort of re-investing one relationship with a little bit more intensity by starting another.'

Gay family: Polly and Linda ♀♀

Polly and Linda live with Polly's 15-year-old son, Michael, and Linda's 2-year-old daughter by artificial insemination, Susie, in the country in Lincolnshire. Polly also has another son, Paul, who's 18 and has left home.

Polly and Linda have been together five years; they met when Polly was 38, Linda 30. Linda was the second woman that Polly became involved with after the break-up of her marriage, whereupon she went to live in a feminist house. 'They were a mixture of people with children and people who'd decided not to have children, and I suddenly saw the pressures for women who are feminists and have children, because the desire to do what you want with your life and the demands and pulls of being a parent seemed to me to be just very intense.'

Polly found this out at first hand when she went to live on her own with her two young sons, then aged 10 and 12. 'My husband was hassling me a fair bit: his bitterness was such that he was doing everything he could to turn the children against me. He would take them out every second weekend and spend an enormous amount of money on them, and I was battling in a small flat and working and not taking any money from him, and it was hellish, it really was.'

When Polly's husband, Pete, boasted that he could do a better job of bringing up the children, Polly decided to call his bluff. 'I said, "Well perhaps you'd like to try – I just want the same rights as you." I'd adopted an attitude that if I was going to hang on to the children, I was going to face Pete's bitterness for the rest of my days; if he had them, whether for three, six or twelve months, I had a feeling he would give over.'

In the event Polly was proved right. 'My sons used to come to *me* every second weekend, and it was interesting to note that within six months, the position had changed: I was the good person and my husband was the person who, when I drove them back at ten o'clock on a Sunday night, was busy ironing and sewing on buttons and saying, "Where's your bus ticket, boys – I couldn't find it in your clothes." And I felt then, as I do now, that if you put any person of either gender in the same situation of financial strain, kids, whatever, you'll get a very similar reaction.'

So Polly's sons returned to live with her, but by this time she had met Linda. 'I felt a bit nervous about Linda not having children, about going into yet another relationship with a woman who wasn't particularly interested in them. I felt that only if *she* accepted my sons, could *I* truly accept them back. But it was uncanny the way Linda accepted the boys just as if they'd been there all her life.'

At first Linda was a kind of 'big sister' to Paul and Michael, and in this capacity she was actually able to help Polly in her relationship with her elder son that had never been easy, partly because she had wanted a girl, not a boy, and partly because his birth had been a very difficult one. 'It was the most hell-rotten experience, with back labour and front labour and him bursting to be born and induction and 48 stitches, so that it was inevitable that I held him responsible on some sort of emotional level. Consequently Linda diluted the impact of my censoring on my elder son. As for my younger son – well, there was something about the day he was born; I felt he sort of said "I've been here before and I know you very well", and I said the same to him. So he and I didn't have any hiccups.'

But Linda also became a parent to Polly's sons. 'The one advantage she has over me is that she can flow into that other type of relationship. I hear the interchange between them and I've always put it down to the fact that she's nearer to their age. In fact sometimes I think, God, she's getting closer to Michael than I am – sometimes I am conscious of the fact that he shares a new experience with her first, and I feel a little – not hurt, but left out. It's like he's got two mothers and maybe a sister as well, and when you've got two mothers, one of them is obviously going to feel something when she can see the other in that upfront situation some of the time.'

For the first few years Polly and Linda experienced no real difficulties as gay women in bringing up Polly's sons. 'But I recognized that there were periods when I needed to develop the male part of myself, because it had been so stunted in me: the feminine side was something I'd so developed, I really wanted to push it aside for a time. So I wore clothing that allowed me to express that; I'd give up wearing frocks, stockings and everything like that for a while, and I think they sometimes felt it would be nice if I wore a dress. When I went to a school function recently with Michael, he said something like "Gee, you look nice", and I realized he did like relating, as his peer group does, to a feminine mother. But I don't see it as a problem on the intellectual level – more on the social level.'

Linda takes up the point. 'If you are a lesbian, then you tend to be separatist on some levels, I think, and the older your boys get, the more the potential for conflicts between your female friends and what are now young men, and vice versa. But as long as they're comfortable in their sexuality and we're comfortable in ours, then I don't think it comes up as an area of contradiction. It's more likely that if you're heterosexual and your child shows homosexual tendencies, you're not going to be comfortable with that and *that*'s going to cause all sorts of problems.'

The difficulties that Polly and Linda did experience with Paul in his teens stemmed almost entirely from outside pressures, in this case from his Catholic school which happened to find out about their relationship. 'Paul went to school one day crying – he was having some difficulty accepting that my husband and I weren't ever going to get back together again – and a teacher asked him if he'd like to talk to her about what was wrong. And as part of laying the background to the story, he mentioned my lifestyle; consequently she told him he could talk to her in confidence, but she spoke about it afterwards in the staff room. Now for just on three years they kept that secret, the whole group of them, and when a new principal came in the second year, he was kept out of it for twelve months. But at some point he got the information, because it coincided with Paul's desire to be alternative: he took to graffiting, he took to smoking, he was seen with his arm round a girl on the bus. I found none of this wrong; I couldn't say "Don't do it"; I could only say "Don't do it to get caught", or "Recognize the difficulties." But this principal obviously held me responsible and so flattened the kid that no matter what he did, it was wrong, until finally, the year before his O-levels, Paul was so unhappy I went up to see the principal. He gave me no inkling that he knew about my relationship with Linda, and I asked him to make Paul responsible for something, so that he might develop a sense of involvement in the school, and he gave me to understand that this was fine. But then he called Paul in and asked him if he'd ever been with a boy, if he'd ever been with a girl; he said that the Church didn't approve of my relationship; and the last thing was that Paul wasn't to tell me about the conversation, he was to tell nobody. And the boy came home half an hour later to Linda and me, trembling with rage, just trembling, and we agreed that he wasn't going back.'

The next year both boys started at another school, but then their father remarried and said in their presence, 'Well I've done enough for them – I now want to get on with *my* life." This rejection further unsettled Paul. 'He started a sexual relationship with a girl he'd met on holiday who came to stay, and when Linda picked up what was happening, I knew I'd over-react, so we cleared the house for a day to talk about it. We decided we'd defuse the situation by not coming in on a moral level, but saying, "Look, it *is* a bit embarrassing when it happens in our house, but let's just get some care for you in terms of contraception." Linda took them over to the doctor's and Paul asked her to go to the chemist's and get the gear, because he was too embarrassed. But he left the dirty things in drawers – he was still the boy who wasn't taking responsibility – and consequently things got worse and worse, until he just said he wasn't going back to school. It built up to a situation where I told him, "Well listen, you're either going to do what I say, or you can walk out that bloody door." And he chose to walk out that bloody door. A week's hell of where was he, but I suspected he had friends he was staying with. He came back one night and said he wanted to stay for good, but in fact he didn't.

At this stage Polly and Linda were about to move; the plan had been for both boys to come with them. 'I felt uneasy about whether it was a good idea or not, and Paul said to me one day, "I want you to go, because I don't want to feel guilty if you don't go, but I don't want to come." What's interesting is that we recently got a phone call from him to say that he wants to come and visit, so he's coming to stay for a few months. I've got the jitters about him coming, I worry about the dependency: he's thrown school in, which I think for him was a wise decision, because it had nothing to offer him, but obviously when a boy's unwaged, it's a hand-out. But I don't think he's a bum: I think he's a very creative boy; he's taught himself to play the guitar, he wants to write a rock opera, and clearly he needs experience.'

While the situation with Paul was being resolved, Linda had become pregnant with Susie by artificial insemination. It was a decision it took her some time to reach. Like Polly, Linda had been married, but had chosen not to have children. 'As much as anything else, I was in my early twenties, I had a good job, I wanted to travel and life was more important; I always had this idea that it was the sort of thing you could do later.'

By her late twenties Linda had realized that she was gay. 'And having become a lesbian, I shelved the whole problem of children: I thought, well it's not something that's going to happen accidentally. It just never came up as an option, I never really thought about it.'

And so Linda continued until she was 30 and had met Polly. A chance remark got her thinking. 'A friend of mine said one day, "How do you feel about having a child?" I think I said something very flippant. But when we got home, Polly said, "Well I never even thought of you as someone who'd consider having a child – what *do* you think about it?" My immediate reaction was to say, "Goodness me, we've virtually got two children – surely you don't want to go back to the whole business of dirty nappies and sleep-less nights," and she said it wasn't her decision, it had to be my decision, and she would fall in with whatever I wanted to do. I respected that, because it did enable me to make the decision without her feeling that I would later turn round and say, "You stopped me having a child."'

So Linda, who had always liked children, began to think seriously about it, but she reached her decision fully aware that the only option open to her was artificial insemination. 'I felt quite strongly about that: we both have a number of friends who are men, and I wouldn't think of using them insofar as to have sex with them would, for me, be using them – it wouldn't be some-thing I could do, in any case. So that doesn't leave you with very many options: maternity clinics aren't really interested in people like me – they're much more interested in the heterosexual couple who can't have children. So that meant artificial insemination.'

Accordingly Linda went off to her doctor, only to discover that there was a shortage of donors. So she and Polly drew up their own list of eligible men from among their friends. 'They had to have children, because that has some sort of health guarantee; also the thing about someone already having children was that they would feel secure about doing it. I was so frightened that they'd come along and say "This is our child", that it seemed important at that stage that there be an anonymity about it. On the other hand, it also seemed important to me – increasingly so – that I should know who the donors were, so that if at some later stage Susie herself should want to find out, I could provide her with that infor-mation.'

In the end, for one reason or another, it came down to two men. 'As it turned out, we knew the women in each case better than we knew the men, so we actually approached them; we asked them how they felt about it. Then it was up to them, if it was OK, to talk to their men. We thought it important that it be a decision of the relationship, because it is something that can be very threatening.'

But both parties were agreeable, and so twice Linda went through a particular sequence of events. 'We would turn up at their place; the man would disappear and come back with a jam jar or suitably sterilised container. Then I would disappear and using a hypodermic syringe, I would just inject the sperm up. Each time it was a late afternoon/early evening, and I would use a diaphragm in the way it's not meant to be used – to keep the sperm in, not out – and just leave it there until the following morning.'

The clinical proceedings had their human moments. 'One thing that staggered us both', recalls Polly, 'was the amount of sperm that's produced each time – here was this great big jam jar and this tiny weeny little half-a-teaspoon of sperm. The man would invariably walk in saying, "Er – I'm sorry, this is the best I could do."' As Linda points out, 'One can talk about the strain it is for a woman, but to ask people to masturbate on demand is also a strain. It was really awful for one of them; he came back once or twice not even able to articulate that he wasn't doing very well. The other fella said to his wife, "I think you'd better come in and help me with this . . ."'

Linda eventually became pregnant; by which of the two men, as planned, she didn't then know. 'My period of ovulation was between the tenth and sixteenth day of my cycle; I did it on the tenth and twelfth day, so that at no stage early on would I have known which it was. But because Susie looks as she does, it's quite clear whose child she is – there's no way she can be the other man's.'

Linda is, after all, pleased to know the identity of the father of her child. 'We live in a society where every time you fill out a form, to get a passport, whatever, they ask you who your father is, and it's all very well for me to make the choice, but it's important that Susie is somehow protected.'

Linda has actually taken Susie to visit her donor father. 'We went and stayed for about a week when Susie was two. And he was lovely towards her without being possessive; on the other hand, he had a rather special feeling about her. I now think it is a positive thing, in a sense, because Susie obviously won't have any siblings and neither will her half-sister, and in fact the two will know that they are half-sisters at some future stage. And maybe it's important for Susie to have a sense of normality, a place in the world – other people to relate to outside us. I would always maintain contact with anyone else that I know who had a child in a similar way, so that again she's not different. In the event of me or Polly dying before she's 16, we've actually written a letter to her setting it all out – the list of donors is in there, and the sort of people she could talk to about it, so that she could resolve it were we not there to do that.'

In the meantime Susie is a happy enough child in a happy enough family. 'Both of us, as far as it's possible, parent the other person's child; I do think children benefit from having more than one parent. We've conceived this idea that yes, Susie's got a mother, but she's also got "another", which is Polly. It seems to me that it's important to have that balance, but that it doesn't necessarily have to come from a male, but from somebody else who counteracts what you do, otherwise I think it's just too much strain on one person.'

Susie is being brought up no differently from any other child with aware parents. 'She has a range of toys; she likes dolls, but we've also bought her construction toys and things like that. Again, I think it's the balance which is important: people can go too far the other way and think, with girls, they've got to get them all construction toys and no dolls, but I think you need all of it.'

Looking back on her decision to have a child by artificial insemination, Linda says her main concern was to create the circumstances whereby it could cope with life. 'It seems to me that your primary responsibility as a parent, whether heterosexual or homosexual, is to create security for your child – emotional security in particular. A lot of the children I know come from conventional families where the relationship isn't necessarily working out very well, and the problems are reflecting back on the kids; they aren't getting all the attention they need, so that they are carrying the sorts of problems that are going to come out in later life. If we can make Susie feel OK about herself and other people, then I'm sure she can cope with anything at all.'

8 The eighties and beyond – the gay scene

♂ 'The current climate is easing up, it's liberalizing . . . And there are now so many gay businesses and commercial undertakings of all sorts, and people are coming out at work . . . It isn't something that, for example, the police could put out with water cannon; it's too broad for it to be politically controlled now – it's in society. It would take a Nazi government to stop gay liberation now.'

♀ 'It's strange that gay men are becoming more acceptable in that you can expect all kinds of men to be gay, because it seems that they can come out at their workplace – especially when they're in the professional executive bracket – more easily than women; there's still some protection there for them. But I think those women who are further up in their careers are at risk anyway, and feel at risk; to come out as a lesbian is often to lose what little male support they already have and feel they need.'

In Britain nearly twenty years after the decriminalization of sex between adult male homosexuals in private, there undoubtedly exists a greater tolerance and awareness of homosexuality: it is to be seen in the increased coverage of gay matters and gay life in the media, in the now common use of the very word 'gay', as opposed to more clinical or derogatory terms, in the granting of public funds to gay organizations, in the growing interest of the straight world in doing business with the gay world and so on.

This gradual change of climate has taken place in parallel with the greater visibility of gay people, and their pubs, clubs, groups and literature, but it is, in the main, of a private and individual nature. Thus the assertively pro-gay policies of certain local authorities, for example, are due to the enlightened and tolerant views of *individual* politicians, and the increasing acceptance of gay people by straight society is due to the growing number of *individual* straight people who count among their colleagues or close friends, gay men and women.

But it is still sadly, anachronistically and wastefully the case that a public figure, who may have made a distinguished and useful contribution to society, may be forced to resign office literally overnight as a result of police activity sanctioned by laws that have not yet been erased from the statute books; it is still the case that gay men in particular are prohibited from interacting with each other in public in ways that heterosexuals take for granted; and it is still the case that the gay community is subject to arbitrary raids on its bookshops, publishing firms and meeting places by the police or customs and excise. Jeffrey Price, a former convenor of GLAD, the gay legal advice organization, and a law lecturer at King's College, London, puts the recent series of raids on gay venues into a wider political perspective.

⚦ 'In the case of the raid on the Gay's the Word bookshop, I think the police reacted very much over the top. And that overreaction, along with two or three other raids not connected but coming close together, fuels the fires of the conspiracy theorists. I don't think there is a conspiracy: it's just pure incompetence and ignorance on the part of the police. What is being attacked at Gay's the Word is not just gay rights, but everybody's rights. If you think about it, it's not just whether gay literature should be imported or not – the issue that really should confront us all squarely is whether the government should *ever* be able to prevent literature being imported into this country, or exported from it, or sold here. In my view the government should have no authority (with the possible exception of residual authority to take action against racist or defamatory material, for example) to control what people read and think. And that's what the Gay's the Word raid is about – it's an attack on the freedom of speech of gay people and therefore, of course, an attack on the freedom of speech of everybody.'

The Law

The law in Britain concerns itself primarily with male homosexuality, lesbianism having been dismissed as, like female sexuality in general, non-assertive and therefore non-threatening:

however, lesbianism is illegal in the armed forces, and lesbians may be discriminated against at work or in other areas on account of their sexual orientation.

Although the eighties has seen the liberalization of the law in both Scotland and Northern Ireland, making the age of consent for gay men now 21 throughout the UK, Britain still lags well behind other West European countries, where the age of consent is, in most cases, 15 or 16, and in the rest, 17 or 18 – despite a recent European Parliament Resolution in favour of the same age of consent for gays as for heterosexuals. The Criminal Law Revision Committee has recommended lowering the age of consent to 18 for gay men – still two years older than for heterosexuals, to which reaction in the gay community, as Jeffrey Price describes, is mixed.

'On the one hand, it's inadequate and ought to be opposed on moral grounds; on the other, maybe we ought to go for a political compromise and try and work it down to 16 five years from now, when perhaps the climate will be even more liberal than it has suddenly become.'

The law not only lays down at what age people can and cannot have sex, it also concerns itself with the whole matter of consensual sex, particularly in the case of gay men. One of the demands expressly put forward in the Campaign for Homosexual Equality's Charter for Gay Rights is that consensual sex should be removed altogether from the province of the criminal law.

As it stands, the law with regard to gays is, in the words of Jeffrey Price, 'morally indefensible and inadequate. Virtually everything two gay men do, except actually go to bed in a room with a locked door and have sex, is illegal. Every time a gay man goes into a pub and looks twice at another gay man, technically he commits an offence – the offence of soliciting. If you go up and say "Would you like to come back with me", it's an offence; you pat some guy's bum outside a pub and kiss him goodbye, it's an offence.'

As Jeffrey Price points out, a double standard is in operation which gives the lie to the whole situation. 'I've no doubt that running a gay disco is illegal technically, where the management know that people are going to have sex on the premises and that they come only to cruise, dance, pick each other up, go home and have sex – all that is solicitation, aiding and abetting solicitation, conspiracy to corrupt public morality and so on. It's ridiculous that all that should be illegal, while at the same time magistrates are granting licences to let it all go on. That is indefensible, illogical, stupid; at the end of the day it gives the police the opportunity to harass people by invoking old-fashioned laws, even though they are not enforced most of the time.'

One of the most notorious forms of police harassment is the use of agents provocateurs which, in common with many others, Jeffrey Price thinks 'wholly wrong' and 'absolutely scandalous'. 'Nobody propositions cops in uniform, so they go to a public lavatory or hang around outside a gay pub in mufti; it's preposterous that public money presumably pays for their motorcycle jackets, even maybe the nicely torn jeans, and then they're probably on double time or something . . . And of course they're there to be propositioned, they go there in the specific hope that someone is going to ask them to have sex, so that they can arrest them.'

In this country this frequently leads to prosecution and conviction. 'In America the use of an entrapping officer – they call the offence "entrapment" there – will lead to any prosecution where the offence is established, being thrown out; every time you can prove entrapment in the States, bang goes the conviction. That's not the rule in England – here, judges convict despite agents provocateurs. That is absolutely immoral, especially in relation to sexual offences, because there's no victim – the only victim is the police officer who went there in the hope that he'd be a victim of a crime.'

In general Jeffrey Price, along with other leading members of the British gay community, thinks that the law should be reformed on the principle that 'what people consent to do is their business, whether there are forty of them in a nightclub or two of them in a semi-detached house.'

The inequality that gay people suffer before the law reflects the public prejudice against them that to a large extent, still prevails; this in turn is supported by a body of myths and misconceptions about them that have taken root in the public mind and not been examined and discarded for the superstitions that they are. One of the most common of these is that gay men and women, one and all, fit certain stereotypes that do not, in fact, exist to anything like the degree they are thought to.

The myth of the stereotype

Heterosexuals tend to make a distinction between gays that they know and gays that they don't: the former are acceptable as people who may go to work and come home, have cats or dogs, like a drink now or then – in short, as people who, in many respects, are just like themselves; the latter, on the other hand, are very often assumed to conform to a variety of popular images, ranging from child-molesting ogre to pipe-smoking lesbian. Among the most enduring of these are the poof, or effeminate gay male, and the butch dyke, or gay woman who looks, dresses and behaves like a man.

⚢ 'I'm always optimistic, thinking that not everybody imagines that lesbians wear dungarees and boots and are man-haters or whatever. But whenever I meet somebody straight and I tell them I'm gay, because of the surprise they register and the inevitable comment, "Oh, you don't look like a lesbian", I wonder how much the average person's ideas are changing.'

⚣ 'The limpwristed, archetypal poof is still a common ignorant stereotype – a convenient one too, because it's non-threatening. You don't see a lot of the archetypal pansy or fairy, but you do come across them and when you do, they're all the more striking because you think, oh, I didn't think we were like that any more. But it's certainly not the common thing and we do take the piss out of that among ourselves; when gay people camp it up, they do so in a sort of self-mockery.'

They can afford to now, but there was a time when gay people took these classic stereotypes in deadly earnest.

⚢ 'When gay people were very vulnerable – gay men, for example, in pre-Wolfenden days, when it was all illegal – of course it was much more likely that they would fall into strict role-playing patterns. I think it is very important to remember that homosexuals were much less easily identified before the gay movement, the availability of clubs, etc. So an effeminate man was very identifiable; it was almost an essential for him to be able to meet another gay man. And the same with women – that's why they wore cropped hair.'

Although gay people are able to meet and interact with each other much more freely nowadays, they still need to identify with, and make themselves known to each other; hence the emergence of modern stereotypes.

♂ 'The stereotyped poof that we talked about earlier actually works in our favour sometimes: straight people don't realize that gay men are actually into macho things. There's the macho image, the clone look – short hair, moustache, checked shirt, jeans, boots or heavy shoes of some description. Then you've got the leather and denim fraternity, but they're a stereotype with a purpose; you're saying, "This is the sort of gay man I am." At the extreme end of the scale, there are very explicit sexual images and signs saying, "I like doing this", or, "I like having this done to me." But you really are now talking about a minority of gay people; the majority don't think of themselves and express themselves in terms of what they do in bed.'

This is borne out by the first impressions of the gay scene and gay people in general, of gay men and women who are just beginning to come out.

♂ 'The most important thing to me was that they were ordinary people, they weren't the stereotype. I was amazed to find out how many people I already knew were gay, once I started being a bit more open about it; talking to people, I suddenly discovered I'd got about half-a-dozen gay friends, including one guy who'd worked for me for two years.'

♀ 'The first time I went to a gay women's club, it wasn't what I expected at all; I thought it would all be quite seedy and awful, but it was all really quite healthy. There was a big butch-looking woman at the door, and I don't blame her for being there, she had a job to do. But the rest of the girls were all into their fashion and their clothes and looked very much like me. I thought, "Well, what am I worried about? They're all having a wonderful time. Nobody's getting hurt. What's the problem?" So then I thought, "Well, it's all in your head."'

The gay scene and the 'pink economy'

Perhaps the single most significant development in the British gay scene – the collective term for gay pubs, clubs, discos, etc. – in the last decade or so, has been its expansion into the pink economy, whereby many other kinds of gay businesses, from travel companies and specialist shops to publishing houses, have appeared and prospered. They are now beginning to be taken seriously by the straight business world, which is not only opening up its distribution outlets and trade associations to them, but is also, conversely, beginning to target its own goods and services at gay people.

The pink economy is almost exclusively male, reflecting the greater earning and spending power of the male; Alex McKenna, who has been in gay publishing since the early seventies and is one of the most successful gay businessmen in the country, points to the evidence for the upsurge in gay business.

'We didn't have any advertising at all for years; *Gay News* had a very, very little advertising, but it was very amateur. You looked at the ad and you knew that whoever was advertising, it was a very amateur set-up. But slowly things have changed. Now you look at the ads and you know they're professional ads, from companies that are obviously gay-owned or gay-run, or at least aimed at a gay market; the whole thing's totally different. A few years ago you wouldn't have had a hope of getting an advertisement from a film or record company, or a publisher or something, but now you occasionally do.'

But Alex McKenna is cautious about the potential for growth of the pink economy. 'I think it's all down to statistics; if you say there are, say five million gays in the country, then the pink economy is potentially very large. But we have to be fairly realistic about it and not over-inflate the whole thing, and although it's obvious, even from what I've just said, that the visible pink economy has grown enormously in ten or twelve years, I can't see that the actual number of gay or gay-oriented businesses is going to change terribly, apart from perhaps the acceptance of mainstream businesses of the gay angle. In America that does happen; you get advertising directed at the gay community for products – drink and cigarettes obviously, and even jeans by major companies.'

In the United States, particularly in cities with large gay communities, totally alternative gay societies have developed, with not only gay restaurants, bars and hotels, but even gay banks, insurance companies, real estate businesses and so on. Alex McKenna explains why that has not happened here.

'British people – not just gays – just don't seem to have the same business sense that Americans do; they seem to be born and bred on business. They all know what profit is, what selling is about – they're much more commercial in the way they think. Whereas the British tend to think that selling is not quite nice and profit is something bad. It's just this British conservatism that's got to be worn away slowly, but we are doing it.'

One of the most noticeable manifestations of the progress being made is the increase in the number of mixed venues, of which there are two kinds: clubs that are mainly single sex, but which admit guests of the opposite sex, and clubs that are straight, but that open their doors to gay people on certain nights of the week.

Although there has always been a demand for exclusively single sex bars and clubs, the growth of mixed venues has widened the choice of social amenities for both gay men and women.

⚀ 'There is a corps of women who are going to the mixed places simply because they want better facilities and better treatment from the staff there. There's also a sexual ambience that you don't get in women's bars where, in the main, women go in groups or with friends and stay that way. Because most of the men are there to cruise, the women find themselves sucked into that different sexual flavour and they do seem to enjoy it; they feel freer to go and talk to other women.'

⚁ 'The first thing I noticed when I went to some gay clubs was that it was very difficult to be accepted; you had rather a feeling of it's them and me. Everyone seemed to know each other, because I think generally on the scene a lot of people do; you can go round to different clubs and meet the same faces. I find guys who are prepared to go to a club with women will generally be much more friendly, much more open. I enjoy mixed venues because I find the facilities offered are much wider – the music is much wider, because you have to embrace a much wider range of tastes.'

A gay man who runs a club catering for both gays and straights highlights some of the differences – and some of the responsibilities.

♂ 'On the straight nights it's working class boys going down the club to have a good time, blowing their wages, drinking – rather too much – picking up a bird, that sort of thing. That intention and that atmosphere come over very strongly. On the gay nights the atmosphere is much more friendly, much more relaxed – everybody has a good time. The bar takes more money than on the straight nights, which is interesting, but I believe the club should have some gay involvement, like having a benefit for a gay organization, for example – I don't particularly like the idea of a club having a gay night just to say, right, let's fill our club with gays and make a lot of money out of them.'

Gay people tend to be sensitive about the money charged for admission and drinks, because for them, their pubs and clubs are not only places where they go to have a good time, but also often the only places, apart from their own homes, where they can relax with their friends and meet other gay people, in an environment free from heterosexual curiosity and hostility; to pay for the privilege is to add insult to injury.

Thus in a society where they are publicly tolerated only up to a point, gay people will always need their own places, whether mixed, single sex or catering for specific tastes in music, fashion or partners. Many gay men and women would like to see in Britain a more integrated gay scene, such as exists in Amsterdam for instance, one of the most progressive and liberated 'gay' cities in the world.

♀ 'I think Amsterdam's probably the best place for gay men or women, when it just comes to facilities. There are lots of little cafés, women's centres – nice places where you can play board games or meet people or whatever, and that stay open from nine a.m. to eleven p.m. and serve cheap coffee and cheap food. There is a greater mixing, a greater cheerfulness in these places; it means women aren't always forced out into nightclubs or bars if they want to be with other women. So you have something in the middle, a sort of café scene, that we just don't have. You can be a dyke all day.'

Some gay men and women go even further and in so doing, perhaps express an unconscious wish on the part of many gay people.

⚣ 'I would love to see a proper gay ghetto, a part of town where it's unusual to be straight – maybe a little backwater somewhere, where there are lots of gay coffee bars, pubs, shops – not just the usual gay clothing, leather or bookshops. Wouldn't it be fun to go somewhere and you knew the grocer was gay, and the bakery was run by a nice lady and her partner of twelve years. It would be a change, it would be refreshing to go into a gay atmosphere now and again, just to catch your breath before you go back into the straight world. If you've got a very straight life, straight family, straight job, it would give you somewhere to go, where you know it's safe. It would be comforting to have, I think.'

When gay people are equal with heterosexuals before the law, when they are protected from discrimination in their jobs, when their love for each other is deemed as valid as that between men and women, then perhaps they will not need that reassurance. But for the moment, with a considerable way still to go, they do.

Postscript –
The AIDS scare

As this book goes to print, the level of public hysteria about AIDS – fanned by the banner headlines of the popular press – is running dangerously high. Gay people have been banned from pubs and clubs; cab drivers have refused to pick passengers up from gay clubs; and most alarming of all, the panic has even spread to the prison service, hospital ancillary staff and the fire service, on whose expertise and help gay people, in common with the rest of the community, depend.

The number of AIDS cases in this country is now well over 100, the number of deaths just under half that, and the figures are rising. Meanwhile the emergence of AIDS as a lethal disease with, as yet, no known cure is bringing to a head all the latent fears and prejudices about homosexuals, one of the groups most at risk, and their way of life.

It is important that AIDS be seen in the context of the killer diseases that from time to time ravage the human race and for which human ingenuity has, with time, invariably found a cure; at the end of the day it may even come to be seen as a catalyst for a general clearing of the air by forcing out in the open much of the latent homophobia of heterosexual society.

Appendix

Advice and support groups

Action For Lesbian Parents 01 251 6577; c/o Rights of Women, 52–4 Featherstone St., London EC1.

AIDS Helpline 01 278 8745; Mon–Fri 8–10 p.m. confidential advice and information from Terence Higgins Trust volunteers.

Brothers and Sisters Group – for deaf or hard of hearing gays. Write BM B & S, London WC1N 3XX.

Galop Write 38 Mount Pleasant, London WC1X OAP; 01 278 6215. Monitors police treatment of gay people, records problems, advises on rights, and assists in complaints against the police.

Gay Bereavement Project 01 837 7324 (contact through London Gay Switchboard); or write c/o Unitarian Rooms, Hoop Lane, London NW11. Support and counselling for bereaved gay people.

Gay Black Group 01 278 7654; c/o Gay's the Word Bookshop, 66 Marchmont Street, London WC1N 1AB. Meet Fri 7.30 p.m.

Gay Christian Movement 01 283 5165; or write BM Box 6914, London WC1N 3XX.

Gay Men's Disabled Group c/o Gay's the Word Bookshop, 66 Marchmont St., London WC1N 1AB. Support and social group for all disabled gay men.

Gay Rights At Work c/o Pickwick Court, London SE9 4SA. Advises on gay trade union groups, a support group for gay rights at work.

Gay Youth Movement Write BM GYM, London WC1N 3XX. A campaigning and coordinating body nationwide; can put you in touch with local gay youth groups, or help you start a new one (for those under 26 years old).

Gemma BM Box 5700, London WC1N 3XX. National friendship and information group for lesbians with or without disabilities, all ages; socials and penfriends.

Icebreakers 01 274 9590; Mon, Wed, Thur, Fri 7.30–10.30 p.m. For gays who want to come out, make friends and change the world.

Identity 01 289 6175. Counselling and advice.

Jewish Gay Group 01 903 2381; or write BM JGG, London WC1N 3XX.

Kenric Write to the Secretary, Kenric, BM Kenric, London WC1N 3XX. International non-political organization for gay women, social activities.

Glad (Gay Legal Advice) 01 821 7672; every evening 7–10 p.m.

Lesbian Line 01 251 6911; Mon and Fri 2–10 p.m., Tues–Thurs 7–10 p.m.; help and advice for women only.

London Bisexual Group 01 274 7970; or write BM/BI, London WC1N 3XX. For information enclose s.a.e.

London Friend 01 359 7371; every evening 7.30–10 p.m. Youth group Friday evenings (under 25s). Counselling for those who feel they have problems.

London Friend Women's Line 01 354 1846 Thurs 7.30–10 p.m. Counselling and advice for gay women.

London Gay Teenage Group 01 272 5741 Weds 7–10 p.m., Sun 3–7 p.m. Youth club and helpline in North London for 16–21 year olds.

Parents Enquiry 01 698 1815 or write to Mrs Rose Robertson, 10 Honley Rd., Catford, London SE6 2HZ. Counselling for parents of young gays and advice for gay teenagers.

Rose Rimpel 01 789 9134. Social groups for older gay men and women.

Quest (for gay Roman Catholics) 01 995 9474 Fri–Sun 7–11pm or write BM Box 2585, London WC1N 3XX. Weekends, evenings. Meeting and counselling service.

Sigma 01 837 7324 or write BM Sigma, London WC1N 3XX. Support group for heterosexual people in mixed relationships.

South London Gay People's Group 01 697 7435 Mon 7–10 p.m. Youth club and phone line in the Lewisham area.

Universal Fellowship of Metropolitan Community Churches (UFMCC) (for gay Christians) 01 670 9755 or write 2A Sistova Road, Balham, London SW12.

Young Lesbian Group 01 263 5932 Mondays 7.30–10.30. p.m. Youth club and phone line for young lesbians (16–21 years).

Organizations

National gay organizations campaigning for gay rights:

England & Wales: Campaign for Homosexual Equality (CHE), 274 Upper St., London N1 2UA 01 359 3973: Tues–Fri 10 a.m.–6 p.m.

Scotland: Scottish Homosexual Rights Group (SHRG), 60 Broughton St., Edinburgh EH1 3SA 031 556 4049

N. Ireland: Northern Ireland Gay Rights Association (NIGRA), P.O. Box 44, Belfast BT1 1SH

N.C.C.L. (National Council for Civil Liberties) 01 403 3888; 21 Tabard St, London SE1.

Gay switchboards

Gay switchboards are now all over the country and can be phoned for a guide to pubs and clubs, gay groups, advice and legal referrals.

London Gay Switchboard: 01 837 7324: 24 hours a day. A phone service offering all kinds of help, advice, information, counselling, entertainments guide, accommodation or just general advice and a chat if you're confused or lonely. Write to: BM Switchboard, London WC1N 3XX

Note: The London Gay Switchboard recommends calling them if you are unable to get in touch with any of the regional switchboards listed in this appendix as they are the central point for the latest information on new groups etc.

Avon
Bristol Switchboard: 0272 425927: nightly 8–10 p.m.

Berkshire
Reading Switchboard: 0734 597269: Tues & Fri 8–10 p.m.
Windsor Switchboard: 95 56521: Wed only 8–10 p.m.

Bucks
High Wycombe Switchboard: 0494 33655: Mon & Thur 8–10 p.m.
Milton-Keynes Switchboard: 0908 312196: Mon only 7–9 p.m.

Cambridgeshire
Cambridge Lesbian Switchboard: 0223 246113: Fri 6–10 p.m.

Derbyshire
Derby Friend: 0332 371725: Wed 7–10 p.m.

Devonshire
Plymouth Switchboard: 0752 266041: Thur 8–10 p.m.

Dorset
Solent Switchboard: 0703 37363: Tues & Thur 7.30–10.30 p.m.

Essex
Colchester Switchboard: 0206 864233: Wed 6–10 p.m.

Humberside
Hull Friend: 0482 443333: Mon only 8–10 p.m.

Kent
Medway and Maidstone Switchboard: 0634 826925: Thur & Fri
    8–9.30 p.m.
East Kent Befrienders: 0227 276945: Tues 7–10 p.m.
West Kent Friend: 0892 40443: Mon & Wed 8–10 p.m.

Lancashire
Lancaster Gay Information: 0524 63021: Thur & Fri 7–9 p.m.
Preston Gay Information Service: 0772 51122: Tue & Thur 8–9.30 p.m.,
    Sat 2–4 p.m.
Preston Lesbian Line: 0772 51122: Mon & Wed 8–9.30 p.m.

Leicestershire
Leicester Gayline Friend: 0533 826299: Mon–Fri 7.30–10.30 p.m.

Greater Manchester
Manchester Gay Information Service: 061 236 5986: nightly 4–10 p.m.
Manchester Lesbian Link: 061 236 6205: Mon–Thur 4–10 p.m.
Manchester Friend: 061 236 6283: Mon–Fri 7–10 p.m.

Merseyside
Merseyside Friend: 051 708 9552: 7–10 nightly; men only
Merseyside Friend: 051 709 0234: Tues & Thur; women only

West Midlands
West Midlands Switchboard: 021 622 6589: nightly 7–10 p.m.
West Midlands Lesbian Line: 021 359 3192: Mon, Wed & Fri 7–10 p.m.
Birmingham Friend: 021 622 7351: Mon, Tues & Thur 7.30–9.30 p.m.
Coventry Friend: 0203 25991: Tues, Wed & Fri 7–10 p.m.

Norfolk
Norwich Friend: 0603 28055: Sun 7–9 p.m.

Nottinghamshire
Nottingham Switchboard: 0602 411454: Mon, Wed & Thur 7–10 p.m.
Nottingham Lesbian Line: 0602 410652: Mon 7.30–9.30 p.m.

Oxfordshire
Oxford Friend: 0865 726893: Sun, Mon, Thur & Sat 7–9 p.m.
Oxford Lesbian Line: 0865 242333: Wed 7–10 p.m.

Staffordshire
North Staffs Switchboard: 0782 266998: Mon 8–10 p.m.
North Staffs Lesbian Support: 07832 266998: Fri 8–10 p.m.

Surrey
Surrey Switchboard: 0252 330366: Mon–Thur 8–10 p.m.
Croydon Friend: 01 656 0122: Mon and Fri 7.30–9.30 p.m.

Sussex
Brighton Switchboard: 0273 690825: nightly 8–10, Sat 6–10 p.m.

Tyne & Wear
Newcastle Friend: 0632 618555: Mon–Fri 7–10 p.m. Newcastle Lesbian
   Line: 0632 612277: Thur & Fri 7–10 p.m.

Yorkshire
Bradford Switchboard: 0274 42895: Tues, Thur & Sun 7–9 p.m.
Bradford Friend: 0274 723802: Mon & Wed 6.30–8.45 p.m
Bradford Lesbian Line: 0274 305525: Thur 7–9 p.m.
Hull Friend: 0482 443333: Mon only 8–10 p.m.
Leeds Switchboard: 0532 453588: Tues 7.30–9.30 p.m.
Sheffield Gayphone: 0742 584489: Mon & Wed 8–10 p.m.
Sheffield CHE Information Service: Sheffield 584489: Mon & Wed
   8–10 p.m.
Sheffield Lesbian Line: 0742 584489: Thur 7–10 p.m.
York Switchboard: 0904 411399: Thur 7–9 p.m.

Scottish Gay Switchboards
Aberdeen Switchboard: 0224 26869: Wed only 7–10 p.m.
Dundee Tay Gayline: 0382 24591: Tues only 7.30–9.30 p.m.
Edinburgh Switchboard: 031 556 4049: Mon & Fri 8–10 p.m., Sat–Sun
   3–5 p.m.
Fife Switchboard: 0592 759384: Tues & Thur 7–10 p.m.
Glasgow Switchboard: 041 221 8372: Nightly 7–10 p.m.
Glasgow Lesbian Line: 041 248 4596: Mon only 7–10 p.m.
Paisley & Renfrew Switchboard: 041 889 4114: Tues 7.30–9.30 p.m.

Northern Ireland
Belfast Cara Friend: 0232 222023: Mon & Wed 7.30–10 p.m.

UK publications

Capital Gay: 38 Mount Pleasant, London WC1X 0AP. Tel: 01 278 3766. London's free local gay newspaper published weekly by gay men.

City Limits: 313 Upper St., London N1 2XQ Tel: 01 226 0080 A London listings magazine covering gay events and places to go.

Gay News: Lamb House, Church St., Chiswick, London W4 2PH. Tel: 01 995 3335. Fortnightly news magazine for gay men and women. News, features, reviews, contact ads, diary of gay events and gay guide.

Gay Scotland: 58a Broughton St., Edinburgh EH1 3SA. Tel: 031 557 2625/1662. Scotland's national gay general interest magazine incorporating Lesbian Scotland. Published every two months.

Gay Star: P.O. Box 44, Belfast BT1 1SH. Belfast's magazine for homosexual women and men and the official publication of the Northern Ireland Gay Rights Association.

Gay Times/Him: 283 Camden High St., London NW1 7BX. Tel: 01 482 2576. Britain's biggest gay magazine. News, features, interviews, reviews, fashion, advice, Round Britain Gay Guide, small ads. Published monthly.

Mancunian Gay: Gay Centre, 61a Bloom St., Manchester M1 3LY. Manchester's gay newspaper.

Out: The Metro Store, 231 The Vale, Acton, London W3. A fortnightly free sheet for gay men, available from pubs and clubs.

Spare Rib: 27 Clerkenwell Close, London EC1. Tel: 01 253 9792. A women's liberation magazine with articles of interest to lesbians. Published monthly.

Time Out: Tower House, Southampton St., London WC2. Tel: 01 836 4411. A London listings magazine covering gay events and places to go.

Eire

Advice and support groups

Irish Gay Rights Movement Gay Switchboard: (01) 78 65 93. Mon–Fri 7.30–9 p.m., Sat 3–6 p.m. Confidential information and befriending service for gay men and women.

LGS Befriending Group: 18 North Lotts, Dublin 1. Tues 8–10 p.m., Sat 3–6 p.m. For people new on the scene and visitors.

Tel-A-Friend: (01) 71 06 08 Mon–Fri, Sun 8–10 p.m., Sat 3–6 p.m.; Thurs women only. Confidential independently operated telephone counselling service.

Organizations

Campaign for Homosexual Law Reform: P.O. Box 931, Dublin 4.

International Coordination & Information Centre on Religion: P.O. Box 1, Cork.

Irish Gay Rights Movement – Munster Regional Council: HQ: Phoenix Gay Centre, 4a Mac Curtain Street, Cork City. (021) 50 53 94. Postal: P.O. Box 1, Cork. Coordinates activities for Co. Clare, Co. Limerick, Co. Kerry, Co. Cork, Co. Waterford and Co. Tipperary.

National Gay Federation: 10 Fownes Street Upper, Dublin 2. (01) 71 09 39.

Cork
Cork Gay Collective: c/o P.O. Box 39, Cork. Independent political action group.

GaySoc: The Secretary, Students Union, 4 Carrigside, Cork.

Munster Gay Switchboard: (021) 50 53 94 Mon–Fri 8–10 p.m. Information, advice, legal, medical and religious referrals.

Outreach: The Secretary, P.O. Box 1, Cork. Non-denominational independent gay organization for Christians in Ireland.

Phoenix Gay Centre: 4a Mac Curtain Street, Cork City. (021) 50 53 94.

Dublin
Hirschfeld Gay Centre: 10 Fownes Street, Dublin 2. (01) 71 09 39.

Irish publications

NGF News: 10 Fownes Street, Dublin 2. National Gay Federation Newsletter. Ten issues a year.

International Gay Religious Directory and News Bulletin: IGA/ICIC/REL, P.O. Box 1, Cork. Publication of the International Coordination and Information Centre on Religion.

Munster Gaze: The Secretary, Munster Regional Council IGRM , P.O. Box 1, Cork.

Australia

Gay publications

Campaign: 3rd floor, 259 Clarence St., Sydney (02) 267 85 66; Postal: Box A228, Sydney South, N.S.W. 2000. Tabloid format. Very well established monthly gay paper.

Outrage: Gay publication cooperative. P.O. Box 21, Carlton South, 3053 (03) 417 17 66. Published eleven times a year. News, reviews, events of interest to the gay community.

Australian Capital Territory

Gay Contact: (062) 47 2726 Fri & Sat 6–8 p.m.: Provides friendly, confidential information and support. Recorded message other times.

Metropolitan Community Church: (062) 51 2753 for details of services.

New South Wales

Acceptance-Gay Switchboard: (02) 212 5247 Weekday evenings from 7–10 p.m. Counselling and information service for the gay community.

Gay Business Association (GBA): (02) 33 0925; P.O. Box 41, 2021. Objectives: to promote, develop, protect and assist the business, professional and civic interests in the community of this state.

Gay-Care Counselling Service: Wayside Chapel, Kings Cross; (02) 358 6577 (24 hrs).

Gays Counselling Service: CAMP N.S.W., 51–52 Holt St., Surry Hills (02) 211–1436 24hr recorded message. Counselling and Phone Service (02) 211 1177 6–10 p.m. every night. Weds Women only.

Lesbian Line: (02) 810 5630 Fri 6–10 p.m. A service offering support and information for gay women.

Newgamma: P.O. Box 57, Islington, NSW 2296. A counselling group for married gays.

Young Gays: Sydney Gay Centre, 51 Holt St., Surry Hills (02) 51 3463 Sat 3–6 p.m. Social and support group for young gays.

Twenty-Ten: Sydney Gay Centre, 51 Holt St., Surry Hills (02) 33 3218/3285. A project for gay youth; accommodation and legal problems etc.

Metropolitan Community Church: (02) 358 2635 for details of services.

Queensland

Young Gays: 379 George St., Brisbane. Mons 7.30 p.m. Social/support group for under 25s.

Women's House: 54 Browning St., West End (07) 44 4008. Information and support on women's issues (run by feminists).

Metropolitan Community Church: (07) 52 1414 for details of services.

South Australia

Gay Community Centre: 238A Rundle St., Adelaide 5000.

Gay Counselling Service Inc.: P.O. Box 459, North Adelaide 5006 (08) 268 5577.

Gayline: (08) 268 5577 Information and help from 7–10 p.m. every night.

Womens Information Switchboard: (08) 223 1244 9.30 a.m. to 9.30 p.m. daily.

Young Gays: (08) 268 5577. Young lesbians and gay men.

Metropolitan Community Church: (08) 332 0815 for details of services.

Victoria

Gamma: Contact Gamma through P.O. Box 41, Richmond, Victoria 3121. Gay married group.

Gay Advisory Service: (03) 489 2059 Information and advice.

Gayline: (03) 329 5555 7.30–11 p.m. daily and from 6 p.m. Fri and Sat. Information, advice and referral.

Lesbian Line: (03) 329 8515 Thur 12.30–2.30 p.m. and 6–10 p.m. Information, support and referral for women.

Metropolitan Community Church: (03) 529 7487 for details of services.

Western Australia

Camp WA: (09) 328 9044 Mon and Sat 8–11 p.m. and Sun 2–5 p.m. Counselling service.

Perth Guide for Gay Men and Women: P.O. Box 1031, Perth 6001 (09) 328 9044.

Canada

Gay publications

The Body Politic: P.O. Box 7289, Station A, Toronto, Ontario M5W 1X9 (416/977 63 20) The most important gay newspaper in Canada.

British Columbia

(Kelowna): Okanagan: (604) 763 8008. Mutual support for gays.

(Vancouver): Search: (604) 689 1039. Information and counselling.

(Vancouver): Lesbian Information Line: (604) 734 1016 Thurs & Sun 7–10 p.m.

(Vancouver): Gay Community Centre: 1244 Seymour Street, Box 2259, MPO, V6B 3W2 (604) 684 6869.

(Vancouver): Metropolitan Community Church: (604) 681–8525 for details of services.

Alberta

(Provincial): Alberta Lesbian and Gay Rights Association (ALGRA): Box 1852, Edmonton T5J 2P2.

(Calgary): Camp 181 Association: Box 965, Stn T, T2H 2H4. Leisure and sports activities for lesbians and gay men.

(Calgary): Lesbian Information Link: (403) 265 9488 Tues and Fri 8–10 p.m. with 24hr answering service of details

(Calgary): Metropolitan Community Church: (403) 277 4004 for details of services.

(Edmonton): Gay Alliance Toward Equality: (403) 8361 Mon to Sat 7–10 p.m. Sun 2–5 p.m. Information and counselling.

(Edmonton): Metropolitan Community Church: (403) 438 5168 for details of services.

Saskatchewan

(Prince Albert): Prince Albert Gay Community Centre: (306) 922 4650. Phone for details of events.

(Saskatoon) Gayline: (306) 665 9129 Mon to Thurs 7.30–10.30 p.m.

(Saskatoon) Gay/Lesbian Community Centre: P.O. Box 1662 S7K 3R8; Phone Gayline for details.

Manitoba

(Winnipeg): Gays For Equality: (204) 786 3976. Counselling and information.

(Winnipeg): Lesbian Line: (204) 786 3976 Tuesdays only.

(Winnipeg): Mutual Friendship Inc: (204) 774 3576. Social and educational programmes.

Ontario

(Provincial): Coalition For Gay Rights In Ontario: (416) 533 6824

(Hamilton): Gayline: (416) 523 7055 Wed to Sun 7–11 p.m. Information and counselling.

(Mississauga/Brampton): Gayline West: (416) 453 GGCO. Counselling service.

(Niagara Region): Gayline: (416) 354 3173

(North Bay): Gay Fellowship of North Bay: Box 665, Callendar, ON POH 1HO. Discussion meetings every Sunday for gay people.

(Ottawa): Gayline: (613) 238 1717 Mon to Thur 7.30–10.30 p.m. Recording other times.

(Windsor): Lesbian/Gay Youth Group: (519) 973 4951.

Quebec

(Montreal): Gay Information: (514) 933 2395 Thur to Sat 7.30–10.30 p.m. Recorded message other times. Counselling and information.

(Montreal): Gay and Lesbian Social Services: (514) 937 9581.

New Brunswick
(Fredericton): Lesbian and Gays: (506) 457 2156 Meets second Wed of
month.
(Saint John): Lesbian and Gay Organization (Lago St): Box 6494, Stn A, St.
John E2L 4RG

Nova Scotia
Gay Alliance For Equality Inc: (902) 429 4294
Gayline: (902) 423 1389 Thurs to Sat 7–10 p.m. Referrals and counselling.

Newfoundland
(Provisional): Gay Association of Newfoundland: Box 1364, Stn C, St.
John's A1C 5N5

In Picador

Germaine Greer
Sex and Destiny £2.95

'*Sex and Destiny* is one of the more important books to be written this century . . . Ms Greer's thesis is this: our Western societies are sterile and corrupt. More, we are busy infecting the underdeveloped East with our disastrous notions of what the good life is: more contraception, more abortion, more family planning, more population control, more death, in fact, less life. The power and importance of Ms Greer's book is that perhaps now, if we pay it attention we will know *why* we want these terrible things and what is happening to us' FAY WELDON

'No reader will be left unaffected by this book. Miss Greer's passionate and intentionally provocative style either entertains or enrages. This is a feast of strongly expressed opinions, delivered as a stern lesson from the podium' NEW YORK TIMES BOOK REVIEW

'A great book' SUNDAY TELEGRAPH

Edmund White
A Boy's Own Story £2.75

'This is not exclusively a homosexual boy's story. It is any boy's story, to the marvellous degree that it evokes the inchoate longing of late childhood and adolescence, the sense that somehow, someday, somewhere life will provide a focus for these longings, and the agonizing length of time that life seems to take in getting around to this particular piece of business. For all I know it may be any girl's story as well . . . we are in the hands of a superior craftsman. I can say with conviction that it is one of the two or three best novels I've read all this season' THE NEW YORK TIMES

'A whole young life, abstracted and vulnerable as a Picasso acrobat, on its highwire between invention and total recall. The style can take your breath away' JAMES MERRILL